$11 BILLION

THE
$11 BILLION
YEAR

From Sundance to the Oscars,® an Inside Look at the Changing Hollywood System

ANNE THOMPSON

newmarket press
for itbooks
AN IMPRINT OF HARPERCOLLINS PUBLISHERS

THE $11 BILLION YEAR. Copyright © 2014 by Anne Thompson. All rights reserved. Printed in the United States of America. No part of this book may be used or reproduced in any manner whatsoever without written permission except in the case of brief quotations embodied in critical articles and reviews. For information address HarperCollins Publishers, 10 East 53rd Street, New York, NY 10022.

HarperCollins books may be purchased for educational, business, or sales promotional use. For information, please e-mail the Special Markets Department at SPsales@harpercollins.com.

FIRST EDITION

Designed by Shannon Plunkett

Library of Congress Cataloging-in-Publication Data has been applied for.

ISBN 978-0-06-221801-8

14 15 16 17 18   OV/RRD   10 9 8 7 6 5 4 3 2 1

For David and Nora

CONTENTS

INTRODUCTION

It looks good on paper: at final count, the 2012 domestic movie box office delivered a record-breaking $11 billion ($10,954,921,197, according to one source,* up 8.4 percent from the previous year). If record foreign dollars were added to the total, this book would be *The $35 Billion Year.* But despite appearances, the movie business isn't thriving. For one thing, much of that growth was from premium 3-D ticket sales, which are already in steady decline, a victim of overexuberance. Many consumers are watching their content on smaller screens, either in their homes or in their hands. And yet, against all odds, Hollywood studios and theater chains are still keeping the romance of moviegoing alive. But for how long? Netflix accuses theaters of "killing the movies." Amazon Studios debuts new television series. Blockbuster closes all of its brick-and-mortar stores. Hollywood is like Harold Lloyd in *Safety Last,* hanging desperately to the hands of that old (silent) clock, which is moving inevitably toward future time.

Global audiences flocked to the top ten highest-grossing movies at the 2012 box office, all but two (*Brave, Ted*) based on some well-known intellectual property—or IP, as they say in the trade—such as Marvel's *The Avengers,* DC's *The Dark Knight Rises,* and the young adult franchise *The Hunger Games.*

But the seeds of the industry's destruction were present in 2012. The major studios with billion-dollar annual production budgets plunked their money on wowing audiences with easy-sell pre-branded event movies. Costs burgeoned and studios needed to score in foreign markets, especially China, which grew 36 percent in 2012 and outstripped Japan in box-office sales to become the world's number two market. The studios and thriving independents, from Harvey Weinstein to Disney, were willing to curry favor with the mighty Chinese censors to gain access to that market, going so far as to reedit such films as *Django Unchained* and *Iron Man 3.*

With remarkable prescience, in June 2013, at a University of Southern California event with George Lucas, Steven Spielberg predicted an "implosion" in the industry: the failure at the box office of up to a half dozen megabudget movies, or "tentpoles," "that are going to go crashing to the ground, and that's going to change the paradigm." Lucas concurred. Within six weeks Spielberg's prediction came true. Five would-be blockbusters tanked during the summer of 2013, all too expensive to make and market to earn their money back, even with foreign dollars added in: *White House Down, After Earth, The Lone Ranger, Turbo,* and the biggest flop of the lot, *R.I.P.D.*

Spielberg and Lucas were basically calling attention to the end of the movie business in which they grew up, one that didn't rely so heavily on tentpoles, that nurtured movies as varied as *American Graffiti* and *Star Wars, E.T.* and *Schindler's List.* Supposedly at the top of the Hollywood pyramid, Spielberg was horrified two years earlier when he had to hustle to get the backing to make *Lincoln* as a motion picture; he considered turning to HBO. Steven Soderbergh took the latter route with his entertaining Emmy-winning Liberace biopic *Behind the Candelabra,* which starred Michael Douglas and Matt Damon in top form. That movie would have cost a studio $70 million to make and market as a theatrical feature, Soderbergh estimated. As an HBO film, it cost $23 million. Something is wrong when Soderbergh elects to retire from studio moviemaking and take his best ideas to television.

In its desperate quest for audiences eager to show up on opening weekends, the film industry seemed bent on chasing young males around the globe with simple-minded, visually dense, formula action fare, and doing so at the expense of driving many other groups who love movies to television and other alternative screens. This was how the major studios, under increasing pressure from their corporate parents, were coping with the multiple threats that were challenging their entrenched ways of doing business. At the same time, innovative funding, distribution, and marketing strategies were bubbling up from the independents, free from the restraints tethering the established studio behemoths. Now what?

As a film journalist and critic who has been watching this industry evolve over decades, I have always been fascinated by the ways in which the Hollywood system works. For many years I wrote hundreds of columns and features about the industry for various publications, including *Film Comment, Premiere,* the *New York Times,* the *Washington Post, LA Weekly, Entertainment Weekly,* the *Hollywood Reporter,* and *Variety.* Today, I continue to track the business full-time, only now it's not for a print bimonthly, monthly, weekly, or daily; it's online 24/7. My berth at my daily blog, *Thompson on Hollywood (TOH!),* which I founded in 2007, gives me a unique window from which to observe and report on moviemakers, marketers, and the different kinds of movies produced and released, from micro-budget do-it-yourself (DIY) films to global blockbusters.

Though online reporting has a currency and excitement all its own, it doesn't pause well for reflection and portraiture. So I figured that a book would give me room to share my experience as an insider reporting on an industry in the throes of radical change. Inspired by William Goldman's classic *The Season: A Candid Look at*

Broadway, about the plays and musicals presented during one theatrical season, I thought, what if I focused on one calendar year of the film business? What would such a chronicle tell us about the way the system was working—or not?

Each chapter could cover a different facet of the movie business: I would follow key films through their discovery and release—and when they're very good, very lucky, or very well-marketed, I would follow their trajectory through the award season. I would look at which movies work and don't work at the indies and the studios, from script development, financing, production, and marketing to getting a movie in front of eyeballs—and not necessarily into theaters. And so this book was born. And the year 2012 turned out to be a stunning year to track.

Along with radical structural movement and box-office disasters, it brought sublime moviemaking. Even with all the changes and worries and anxieties about the future, 2012 broke the box-office record, and the nine 2012 Best Picture Oscar contenders marked a high point in quality—while also scoring big at the box office. But those movies were all, in one way or another, exceptions to the rule. Like *Lincoln,* they were passion projects of filmmakers who had to struggle to get them made.

As it turned out, a lot else happened in 2012 to make it a truly transformative year. Lucas retired, and Spielberg, like many of his generation who find themselves too narrowly defined by the studios—see, for example, Martin Scorsese, Oliver Stone, Michael Mann, and Neil Jordan—headed for television with *Falling Skies, Under the Dome,* and *Extant.* There are manifold reasons why the studios are willfully allowing their creative brain trust to nurture what critics are calling a Third Golden Age of Television, and why gifted talents from Lena Dunham (*Girls*) and Claire Danes (*Homeland*) to Soderbergh, Jane Campion (*Top of the Lake*), Robert Towne (*Mad Men*), and producer Cathy Konrad (*Vegas*) have detoured from pursuing film careers.

Look at the fortunes of three of the top producers in Hollywood. Jerry Bruckheimer, Brian Grazer, and Scott Rudin once commanded the richest production deals, the best projects, and the most resources at their respective studios. Even these successful producers have been cut back. New York class act Rudin, now based at Sony, is producing for Broadway (*Book of Mormon, Fences*) as well as Hollywood, making such films as David Fincher's *The Social Network,* the Coens' *Inside Llewyn Davis,* and Paul Greengrass's *Captain Phillips* that are aimed at the fall Oscar corridor—the only way to make quality films of any scope these days.

Once Disney's star producer, Jerry Bruckheimer luckily has a booming television career (*The Amazing Race*). For even though he scored big with the $3.7 billion *Pirates of the Caribbean* series, in September 2013 the studio did not renew his deal after a string of failures: *Prince of Persia, The Sorcerer's Apprentice,* and most notably the $250 million Johnny Depp western *The Lone Ranger,* which cost Disney a $190 million write-off in 2013.

And Universal trimmed back Grazer and partner Ron Howard's Imagine Entertainment deal, after such duds as *Cinderella Man,* succès d'estime *Frost/Nixon,* and dumb male comedy *The Dilemma.* Tellingly, Grazer and Howard had to raise money for movies like Formula 1 racing film *Rush* from global investors, just like everyone else.

Major stars who once commanded $20 million upfront guarantees are no longer carrying their weight, except for the few who still command overseas followings in established sequels: Tom Cruise, Bruce Willis, and Will Smith. These action stars are replaceable because they're squandering their talent in green-screen high-concept action pictures packed with digital visual effects. Which is not helping them to win their first Oscar, either.

Look at onetime superstar Tom Hanks. He collected a royal payday for Imagine's *Da Vinci Code* franchise, but his $20 million salaries are no more. He's developing web series and starring on Broadway. He didn't get paid much for *Cloud Atlas,* which Andy and Lana Wachowski (best known for *The Matrix* series) funded independently overseas and finished with their own money. Despite the presence of several other once-surefire stars, it flopped. Hanks marked a return in Paul Greengrass's awards-quality drama *Captain Phillips*. Another onetime A-lister, Richard Gere, now stars in low-budget indie movies like *Arbitrage* for peanuts.

Hollywood is struggling to protect its profit margins while supporting an incredibly expensive infrastructure. Why are pricey movies like Hasbro's *Battleship* made? When they hit, such tentpoles pay for the studios' overhead. And the studios believe costly event movies and franchises are the only way to compete with the glut of content available as consumers gain near-instant access to films and TV shows via an eight-dollar monthly subscription to Netflix, as well as through mobile apps and extraordinary cable offerings. They would rather spend heavily on playing it safe than spend less on something innovative.

As music, books, television, journalism, and radio adapt to digital platforms, so must the movies.

Also in 2012, substantial paradigm shifts finally came to fruition: the rise of video on demand (VOD) began to compensate for diminishing revenues from sales of DVDs and other ancillary products, and a continuing shortened window of time between first theatrical release and video home entertainment. Theaters and studios struggled to find a new status quo as pressure increased to give audiences what they want, when they want.

The relatively unencumbered indies are able to push innovation while the studios know they have to stay ahead of competitors and not miss the new road to riches—or even survival. Nipping at the heels of the six major studios is the newly anointed seventh major Lionsgate-Summit, which is pushing full steam ahead and enjoyed a billion-dollar 2012, beating Twentieth Century Fox and Paramount in market share. Those two majors, along with Disney, Sony, Universal, and Warner Bros., all risk becoming dinosaurs. (It's notable that throughout 2012 and 2013 management shifts rocked Disney, Universal, Fox, and Warners.)

2012 was the first year that 35-millimeter celluloid was no longer the primary exhibition medium projected in theaters. It was also the year that the industry completed the circle of digital production and exhibition as theater owners, dependent on their studio suppliers, struggled to keep their doors open. Meanwhile, television became more exciting, and many moviemakers headed where the creativity and money was. As women and ethnic minorities continued to be marginalized in an industry still hidebound by old ideas, conventions, and almost superstitious beliefs and taboos, the studios continued to chase one primary demographic—young men—with big-budget action entertainments. This is also the demographic with the most competing leisure options. Meanwhile, the audience segment most in the habit of going to the movies, adults, are being shunted to television.

WHAT THE PUBLIC KNOWS ABOUT the entertainment industry is the tip of the iceberg. It's a business controlled by the savviest PR machine in the world. Everything is geared toward putting the best possible face on the players, the stars, and the movies. In this book, my aim is not to promote the industry, but to take you with me through one year in the movie business in order to reveal how the system works.

It was impossible to mention all of the 670-plus movies released in 2012, but I touch on many of them along the way. I talk to many sources—from studio execs, distributors, moguls, and producers to screenwriters, filmmakers, creative visionaries, and actors—who risk it all to rope us into their dreams and make a killing. They talk about scripts, casting, production, editing, marketing, distribution, release publicity, and reviews. All these things lead to the most important moment in any film's life: opening weekend, when a movie lives or dies.

And it looked like 2012 was the year of the ultimate killing . . . on the surface at least. I start at January's Sundance Film Festival, which functions as an independent showcase for developing talent, a marketplace for making deals, and an early bellwether for awards. I track several rising filmmakers lucky enough to land studio distributors, including Benh Zeitlin of *Beasts of the Southern Wild,* as well as documentaries and features headed toward a variety of alternative distribution options.

March reveals the studios' mad rush to establish franchises, as two studios gambled hundreds of millions: on *John Carter,* which cost Disney $200 million in losses, and on *The Hunger Games,* which succeeded far beyond Lionsgate's wildest dreams.

In April, I attend South by Southwest (SXSW) in Austin, Texas, where the worlds of Silicon Valley, Hollywood, and music collide with mutually beneficial results. I also visit the annual theatrical exhibitors convention, CinemaCon, in Las Vegas as the industry faces myriad threats and challenges, trying to hang onto audiences as production costs and premium ticket prices soar. As always, Hollywood is embracing new technology: the shift to digital, whether it's 3-D, IMAX, or VOD. I report on the increasingly fraught partnership between the studios and the theater owners—who battle to hang onto the experience of moviegoing in theaters and their share of the shrinking box-office pie—and cover the industry's move away from analog formats, examining how that affects the way audiences will consume content in the future.

May's Cannes Film Festival introduces more key players in the awards race, from Harvey Weinstein to Sony's Michael Barker and Tom Bernard, as well as a number of films heading toward Oscar contention, including *Moonrise Kingdom* and *Amour.*

July's Comic-Con in San Diego is a massive showcase for the studios' summer comic-book juggernauts, aimed mostly at fanboys. These movies include *The Avengers* and *Man of Steel,* from rival comics empires Marvel and DC, respectively.

Summer's end brings Venice and Telluride and the start of the fall film festival circuit, including Toronto, New York, and AFI Fest, which filters and launches the award season players, from Ben Affleck (*Argo*) and David O. Russell (*Silver Linings Playbook*) to Ang Lee (*Life of Pi*) and Steven Spielberg (*Lincoln*).

While looking at the making of December's *Zero Dark Thirty*, Kathryn Bigelow's brilliant follow-up to *The Hurt Locker,* I address the challenges for women in Hollywood. Bigelow proves that even a woman director taken seriously by the male-skewed studio establishment can be dive-bombed at Oscar time.

Late-breaking Christmas movies often have the Oscar advantage, and in 2012 they included Tom Hooper's *Les Misérables* and Quentin Tarantino's *Django Unchained*. In the final chapter, I track the key decisive moments in the race to the Oscars, and I cover the big night, from following Adele and Anne Hathaway down the red carpet to congratulating the winners at the Governor's Ball.

This chronicle of 2012 is a slice of what happened during a watershed year for the Hollywood movie industry. It's not the whole story, but it's a mosaic of what went on, and why, and of where things are heading. It's just what one workaholic cinephile was able to capture about one year. Welcome to my world. Enjoy.

THE
$11 BILLION
YEAR

CHAPTER 1

JANUARY: THE SUNDANCE FILM FESTIVAL

SEARCHING FOR SUGAR MAN, THE SESSIONS, BEASTS OF THE SOUTHERN WILD, SAFETY NOT GUARANTEED, BLACK ROCK, YOUR SISTER'S SISTER, ARBITRAGE, DETROPIA, THE INVISIBLE WAR

It's Saturday morning at the Sundance Film Festival, January 21, 2012, the third day of the ten-day festival. I'm having eggs and coffee with *Indiewire* editor-in-chief Dana Harris at the Yarrow Hotel when I get an e-mail from a mutual friend in New York telling me that Bingham Ray, fifty-seven, has suffered a massive stroke during the Art House Convergence conference in nearby Midway, Utah. We're stunned. It's as if the heart of the American independent film movement has broken.

I first started going to Park City back in 1987. Over the years I made a set of friends in the independent community, from fellow film writers to distributors and filmmakers, who tracked the key world film festivals throughout each year: Sundance in January, Berlin in February, SXSW in March, Cannes in May, Seattle and Los Angeles in June, Venice in August, Telluride over Labor Day weekend, Toronto in September, New York in October, AFI Fest and the American Film Market in November. One of my favorite festival buddies was Bingham Ray. When we started going to Sundance, we'd hang all day in the back of one of the tiny screens at Park City's Holiday Cinema to watch obscure movies that had never been screened before in public. That was the joy: the discovery.

We were born the same year, 1954, him in Bronxville, New York, and me in Manhattan. He was another ardent movie lover who had grown up watching the *Million Dollar Movie* and *Chiller Theatre* on TV. He was on a mission to share the films he cared about, ones with depth, style, integrity, and nuance. Working at various indie distributors, from Goldwyn and October Films to United Artists, he had released key films by Mike Leigh, David Lynch, Lars von Trier, and Michael Moore.

I make some calls and find out that Ray is at a Provo hospital; Dana Harris drives us through a nasty snowstorm to join other friends and his family at his side. He bounced back from a near-fatal car accident years before. If anyone can tough it through this, we figure, it's him. We get a brief moment to file into his hospital room and say good-bye. He's in bad shape. The next day, he is gone.

At the impromptu January 23 memorial service at the High West Distillery in Park City and at later, more formally organized events in New York and Los Angeles, we wonder why Ray's death has hit us so hard. The premature loss of a dear friend pierces our hearts, of course, but it is more than that.

As a journalist I loved talking to Ray because he gave great quote. He was more candid and analytical than most—he could see the overview, the bigger picture. He was a student of the industry, and generous in a non-self-serving way. He liked sharing what he knew. And filmmakers adored him for always being ready to push for that rare, risky, less-than-commercial movie that aimed artistically high. He was always the life of the party, a rebel and a rapscallion who chafed within any corporate environment. Often to his own detriment, he was willing to piss off bosses and power brokers, as recounted in the pages of Peter Biskind's 2004 *Down and Dirty Pictures: Miramax, Sundance and the Rise of Independent Film.*

In fact, Biskind gave Ray the final word in his book's postscript:

> I still believe that there are decisions that you make that aren't motivated by financial gain. The independent world isn't like the Hollywood world. The motives are different, the goals are different, people aren't necessarily trying to get rich and powerful, they're trying to push art first while thinking everything else will take care of itself. That's the naive part of it, it doesn't happen that way. You can't even talk about that with a straight face or people will laugh you off the planet. But there's a big part of me that really does believe that. And will always believe that.

No question that Ray fought hard, with guile and wits and strength, for the better movie. He figured he was going to make you like what he liked. Ray wasn't in the game of predicting and numbers-crunching. He believed in challenging the specialty film crowd. He saw his job as making them want to sample his discoveries. Sometimes he succeeded and sometimes he didn't.

On February 9, the Bingham Ray memorial at New York's premiere East Side art house, the Paris Movie Theatre, was filled to bursting with more than one generation of people in the indie world who looked up to Ray. As several speakers noted, it was never about money for him (although he did more than okay); it was about sharing great movies with the culture at large. At the same time he also embodied what they were most afraid of: the career in autumn decline, along with the sagging fortunes of limited-release specialty films.

Ray knew the art of picking, marketing, and distributing smart films, but as distributors balk at the punitive costs of releasing movies in theaters, the market is shifting toward the microbudget DIY digital self-released model, if not in multiplexes then via online streaming and cable VOD. After decades of pushing movies into the marketplace, Ray was moving west to run the San Francisco International Film Festival, where he had intended to continue to push his avocation for great cinema. It seemed like the perfect fit, but it was not to be.

The New York memorial was a who's who of the indie world. Sony Pictures Classics copresident Michael Barker took part in the moving tribute, comparing Ray to Jimmy Stewart and even showing a clip of *It's a Wonderful Life*. Filmmaker Jim Jarmusch recalled being too broke to buy tickets at the Bleecker Street Cinema in Greenwich Village; Ray, who managed the theater at the time, helped him to sneak in.

Actors Oliver Platt and Patricia Clarkson told of Ray's role in *Pieces of April,* one of many commercially risky films championed by Ray. After the ceremony, writer-director Peter Hedges reminded me that Ray had also backed Clarkson as the lead when no one else wanted her. Ray's loss means one less person pushing for movies that often don't get made without that extra boost from a passionate advocate.

Robert Redford said it straight out at Sundance: "We lost a true warrior."

The film industry has changed dramatically since 1979, when Redford founded the Sundance Institute in Utah. The activist, actor, Oscar-winning director-producer, and avid downhill racer has told the story of Sundance's founding many times in the succeeding decades. He saw the need to counteract the prevailing studio trends with a support system for indies, starting with mentor workshops that eventually led to a place to showcase the work—the Sundance Film Festival. (The name comes from the character he played opposite Paul Newman in William Goldman and George Roy Hill's Oscar-winning 1969 buddy western *Butch Cassidy and the Sundance Kid.*)

At a 2013 Sundance Institute fund-raiser in Los Angeles, Redford again told the story of the first 1980 meetings at his Provo Canyon ski resort in the Wasatch Mountains, and how he and the film program's founding director Michelle Satter (who became a nurturing angel to countless films that might never have come to life without her) sat on the lawn imagining how to organize workshops with mentors: "There were no buildings. A ski lift and a restaurant, that was it. We were gathered together to sort out how this process might work, this mechanism to create opportunity for new artists to have a voice and focus on a category that was DOA at that time, independent film."

The Sundance Institute wouldn't officially take over the Utah/ U.S. Film Festival, which Redford had helped to launch in 1978 as chairman, for another six years. It was director Sydney Pollack's idea to lure Hollywood players by moving the festival from Salt Lake City in September to Park City for the 1981 January ski season. The early festival morphed from a classics and good-for-you granola film showcase—at a time when foreign films were thriving but the American independents barely existed—to a vital hub in indie distribution, serving as a gatekeeper and exhibition platform for filmmakers, and a farm system for emerging talent heading for Hollywood. "We didn't know if it would create enough interest to increase audiences for independent filmmakers," Redford told the crowd.

Sundance has done far more than that. The festival has grown with the burgeoning indie film movement, evolving over the years into one of the most influential forces in American cinema. And through all the changes in the world around it, Sundance's mission stays the same. "It's about the filmmakers," Redford repeats like a mantra, every year.

The first big Sundance breakout came in 1989, the year that twenty-six-year-old writer-director Steven Soderbergh introduced *sex, lies, and videotape.* Harvey and Bob Weinstein's Miramax Films scooped it up and entered it in competition at the Cannes Film

Festival, where it won the top prize, the Palme d'Or—and started the indie new wave. I was among the first to interview the Louisiana filmmaker that year, for my *LA Weekly* column "Risky Business." I watched him grow from brainy indie (*King of the Hill*) to Hollywood player (the Oscar-winning *Traffic* and *Erin Brockovich, Ocean's Eleven* and its sequels) and back to maverick again (*Haywire, Magic Mike, Side Effects*). Many of the filmmakers who are invited to Sundance lead the rest of their lives in quiet obscurity. But people remember that Soderbergh showed what a zero-to-sixty festival rocket launch looked like. That fantasy lures more and more filmmakers every year to apply to the festival.

Ever since, Sundance has been a magnet for the movie industry, a place to mark a fresh new year with marathon sessions of networking and talent-scouting at movies, at parties, or on the slopes. Sundance has proved so effective a venue to view and discover new films and talent that agents, producers, managers, lawyers, distributors, casting agents, exhibitors, and media all attend—along with the lucky few whose movies are selected each year from the thousands submitted.

Sundance audiences were the first to see not only *sex, lies, and videotape,* but also Quentin Tarantino's *Reservoir Dogs,* Richard Linklater's *Slacker,* Kevin Smith's *Clerks,* and Tilda Swinton as Sally Potter's androgynous *Orlando.* That moment of recognition of major new talent is what Sundance is about.

Year after year in Park City, I scoop up and interview rising directors and actors just as their careers are taking off: Edward Burns (*The Brothers McMullen*), Sam Rockwell (*Moon*), Ashley Judd (*Ruby in Paradise*), Kerry Washington (*Lift*), and Brit Marling (*Another Earth* and *Sound of My Voice*). After I pulled actor-turned-director Todd Field off Main Street into a local bar to grill him on his first feature, *In the Bedroom,* he got so intense about what it took for him to make the film that we ended up in tears. Miramax Films pushed *In the Bedroom* to an unexpected Best Picture nomination. I like to talk to emerging talent before their heads get turned by sweet-talking Hollywood agents, managers, producers, and executives who tell them how brilliant they are. All too soon they get used to the sycophantic attention and, as part of their job, begin to conduct themselves as smoothly as PR professionals. It's never the same.

Every year a few Sundance grads go on to participate in the Oscar dance later in the year. In 2006, I interviewed former vice president Al Gore and filmmaker Davis Guggenheim in a small Yarrow Hotel suite for eventual Documentary Feature Oscar winner *An Inconvenient Truth,* and Original Screenplay winner Michael Arndt for *Little Miss Sunshine;* in 2009, I talked to Best Actress nominee Carey Mulligan for *An Education* and Best Actress nominee Gabourey Sidibe for *Precious.* In the watershed year of 2010, nine films first introduced at Sundance scored fifteen Oscar nominations, including *Blue Valentine* (Best Actress), *The Kids Are All Right* (Best Picture, Original Screenplay, Best Actress, Best Supporting Actor), and Debra Granik's *Winter's Bone,* which earned nominations for Best Picture and Adapted Screenplay as well as landing Jennifer Lawrence and John Hawkes their first Oscar nominations.

Going into the festival, I try to check out films with awards potential. The trick at Sundance is staying flexible and keeping your ear to the ground so that you make the right choices about what movies to see in which section—not just the snazzy star-studded films featured as "Premieres" at the big Eccles Theatre, but the unexpected gems in the dramatic, documentary, and world cinema selections. It's torture to be missing the hot movie as your Twitter feed lights up with raves. But catching everything is just impossible. Everyone wants to cover the big stories: the talent breakouts, the hot acquisition titles, and the possible Oscar contenders. 2012 had all of the above.

Even though a pall had been cast by Ray's death, his friends soon rejoined the festival's common cause: finding the players who would nourish the community for years to come.

SUPPLYING SUNDANCE

The independent film community has thrived in myriad ways. It's on the one hand more corporate and more risk averse than it used to be, and on the other more DIY and cooperative. And it has never been more vital. As Hollywood seeks to bank on risk-free brands and eye-popping epic entertainment, the studios are letting go of more and more of their modest-scale ventures. As those budgets evaporate, the indies are the only way to get these movies made, either via foreign sales companies who sell advance guarantees to films, based on what the cast can command territory by territory, or through an always replenishing list of equity investors who look to get into Hollywood by plowing their cash into a movie.

The Hollywood talent agencies are more than eager to help. As the studios have stepped back, the agents have stepped forward to find more work for their clients. William Morris Endeavor (WME), Creative Artists (CAA), and United Talent (UTA) are among the agencies who advise leading investors such as former eBay president Jeff Skoll's Participant Media (*Lincoln, An Inconvenient Truth*); Oracle scion Megan Ellison's Annapurna Pictures (*Zero Dark Thirty, The Master, Foxcatcher, American Hustle*), which also owns foreign sales arm Panorama; production and foreign sales company Red Granite (*Out of the Furnace, Friends with Kids*); Tom Rice of Sycamore Pictures (*The Presence, The Way, Way Back*); Chicago-based Hyatt Hotel heiress Gigi Pritzker's OddLot Entertainment (*Rabbit Hole, Drive, The Way, Way Back, Ender's Game*), which has acquired stakes in foreign sales company Sierra/Affinity; and New York lawyer John Sloss's independent distributor and sales company Cinetic Media (*Exit Through the Gift Shop*).

The increase in independent production means that Sundance Film Festival director John Cooper and his programmers must sift through a burgeoning number of annual submissions. To their credit, the programmers are rigorous about quality, even though they're under pressure to help provide a launchpad for films without North American distribution. For 2012, they logged more than 4,000 feature submissions for the 114 narrative, documentary, midnight, and international sections. Cooper believes there are more movies getting made partly because over the years a vital independent film community has materialized. The quality of submissions has gone up, he says, not only because "well-known actors are willing to be in indie films," but also because of "the creation of better film teams, creative producers, art directors, and the surge of talent that is both creating and staying with indie films as a career."

By staying true to Redford's help-the-filmmakers mission, Sundance has continued to thrive, even as attendees (46,731 in 2012) and Main Street swag suites have spread like kudzu. Redford and the festival staffers say they try to distance themselves from the hordes of marketers who descend on the resort city to trade on the cachet of the young and hip, handing out free designer jeans, complimentary facials, and snow boots to young celebs like Kate Bosworth and Andy Samberg at the Vevo PowerStation and Sorel Suite, or at the Puma Social Lounge in the T-Mobile Village at the Lift. But there's not much they can do about the lack of parking or the tow-away fees or the many other ways that Park City gouges festival interlopers. If Sundance wants to be perceived as successful, legitimate sponsors, swag, and freeloaders go with the territory. Redford's attitude is to challenge festival visitors by not making the experience too easy: if they really believe in the indie mission, they'll come.

The fest lures agents and producers looking for new talent; a ballooning number of global distributors trawling for product for TV and theaters; festival programmers and scouts from Austin, Cannes, Seattle, Telluride, and Toronto; and more than 950 members of the press from twenty countries hungry for access to movie stars and new films to review.

Starting Friday evening, the opening weekend in Park City is always party central, from Park Avenue hotels to the condos in Deer Valley. At Tuesday night's traditional Cinetic Media party, hosted by John Sloss at the restaurant Zoom, buyers and sellers and media converge in the upstairs room to find out the gory details of the latest nightlong condo negotiation or hallway shoving match, and which neophyte distributor hoping to make a splash has overpaid some outrageous minimum guarantee (MG, a cash advance payable to the producer upon delivery of the completed film in exchange for exclusive rights to distribute a film in a sales territory).

Such deals, though, are increasingly a thing of the past, as MGs are often replaced by hefty spending commitments for theatrical print and advertising buys in multiple markets—which create later value. Looking back, the advances offered in the heat of that first Sundance weekend often seem absurd in the harsh light of what the films take in at the box office.

The buyers calculate dollars advanced against a movie's likely returns from theaters, DVD, VOD, and global ancillary markets—and they crunch numbers on what they're willing to spend to wrest the title away from their rivals. It's often the new distributor on the block, inexperienced in the vagaries of the market, who will overspend.

While more pictures are produced in this microbudget era—wherein anyone can pick up a digital camera and shoot—getting movies in front of audiences is still an issue. Long gone are the halcyon days when a movie like *Happy, Texas* or *Spitfire Grill* sold for some $10 million. In prerecession 2008, Focus Features spent $10 million to buy *Hamlet 2* worldwide and Fox Searchlight advanced $5 million domestically for *Choke,* while Overture put up $3.5 million for *Henry Poole Is Here* and $2 million for *Sunshine Cleaning.* And Paramount Vantage plunked down more than $1 million for high school documentary *American Teen.* You've never heard of those films? None of them made back those advances. Tellingly, Vantage and Overture no longer exist. "I've lost money on movies I've loved and acquired, and made money on movies I've loved and acquired," Focus Features founder James Schamus once told me. "I'll overpay this year if I feel like it."

By 2011, the business had adjusted to a new reality. While Sundance sales were healthy that year, they were by no means spectacular. Distributors spread the wealth on a wide swath of cautious, modest buys. Out of 117 films screened for the first time at Sundance in 2011, 60 percent were released theatrically in the United States—a higher percentage than at other major festivals. Even so, several high-profile acquisitions underperformed at the box office, including Fox Searchlight's *Martha Marcy May Marlene* and Sony Pictures Classics' *Take Shelter*. According to Sundance Institute executive director Keri Putnam, who put in her time at both Miramax and HBO Films, "there's been an independent distribution tipping point. Only a small percentage of independently released films make their money back."

By independently released films, she is referring to those not handled by traditional theatrical distributors. Many films have to take the route of self-distribution, which requires that a filmmaker hire and supervise professional marketers, bookers, and publicists. One problem with this approach is that digital and independent revenue streams, whether theatrical or nontheatrical, need to be reliable and transparent enough to make investors confident (like ancillary markets such as foreign and broadcast and cable television), which is not the case so far. "We're sitting on the cusp," Putnam says. "But no model has been developed to take revenue streams to the bank."

This is the rub. The independent community is waiting for self-distribution or VOD or social media or crowdsourcing to reach some kind of critical mass. At this point, while it's never been easier to make a film and it's possible to raise funds from the public using platforms like Kickstarter, which allows the public to pledge money against an achievable benchmark goal during a prescribed time frame, distribution is still a challenge. Only microbudget films can come out ahead. Under Putnam's assertive leadership, the Institute created Sundance Artists Services to aid filmmakers—only those affiliated with the workshops or festivals—by bringing them together with marketers as well as digital aggregators such as Hulu (owned by three major studios) and Amazon.

As someone with a healthy respect for marketing, publicity, and distribution professionals, I worry that so many young filmmakers whose films present marketing challenges face an even more daunting prospect: teaching themselves to market and release their own movies. Film schools have tended to teach students how to make features, not how to market and distribute them. (Though the University of California, Los Angeles, for one, started a festival strategies workshop in 2011.) For every voraciously curious filmmaker like Ava DuVernay (*Middle of Nowhere*) or Joe Swanberg (*V/H/S*) who is gifted with self-promotional social media moxie, there are many more who are less comfortable with hawking their wares on Facebook, Twitter, and Tumblr. At what point do you turn people off by sharing too much information?

At Sundance 2012, the ongoing tension between theatrical release and digital VOD on multiple platforms—cable, iTunes, Netflix, Hulu, and Amazon—is intensifying. For many of the filmmakers, just getting booked at one festival after another is the most distribution they'll get. But going into Sundance, each is praying they will not need Artists Services. They want their movie to be one of the lucky, lucky few to land a theatrical distribution deal.

Over ten days at Sundance, acquisitions and marketing execs and their bosses are like heat-seeking missiles tracking that rare find: the breakout. Many sales agents hold off on showing a film until the festival—usually the filmmakers are rushing to finish against the deadline anyway—because they want the crucible of a theater full of enthusiastic fans and want the press to witness their reaction. It's often the first time filmmakers have shown the movie to the public.

Arbitrage producer Laura Bickford (*Traffic*) was an anxious wreck carrying her two 35-millimeter reels, still "wet" from the film print lab, onto the plane from LAX to Salt Lake City. Stakes are high.

At the high-profile red-carpet Eccles Theatre premieres, each buying team assembles at the movies for sale with at least one top decision-maker on hand—Harvey Weinstein or his COO David Glasser, Nancy Utley or Steve Gilula of Fox Searchlight, Rob Friedman or Patrick Wachsberger from Lionsgate, Howard Cohen or Eric d'Arbeloff from Roadside Attractions, James Schamus or Andrew Karpen of Universal's Focus Features, Jonathan Sehring or Arianna Bocco of IFC Films, Eamonn Bowles or Dori Begley of Magnolia Pictures, Michael Barker or Tom Bernard of Sony Pictures Classics. These leading distributors huddle with their teams afterward to read the audience and press reaction and decide whether or not to make a bid. They need to be able to move quickly and decisively.

As they try to gauge which movie the media and filmgoers will consider a must-see, they have to calibrate how much they are willing to wager before losing the project to a higher bidder. Most of the time, they've already selected the movies they are ready to buy; in some cases they've been following them for years, giving notes to the filmmakers and trying to be helpful. Why not prebuy before the film is finished and take them off the table? Sometimes they do, when they are confident in a relationship with a filmmaker or producer. But most of the time, the distributors' caution is based on waiting to make sure that the film actually plays with an audience.

Occasionally, a company like Fox Searchlight will fall in love with a little film out of nowhere like John Carney's 2007 Irish musical *Once,* starring musicians Glen Hansard and Markéta Irglová, and be willing to plow in the time and energy to bring it to audiences. They'll figure out a game plan to sell the movie, even if it's relying on good old-fashioned audience word of mouth by keeping it in theaters for weeks or even months. They also need to get a sense of how a few key critics will react.

At Sundance, after each screening, writers from the likes of *Hit-Fix*, *The Playlist*, and *Vulture* tweet immediate 140-character feedback, followed within hours by more thoughtful reviews from the trades. The *Hollywood Reporter*'s Todd McCarthy, *Variety*'s Scott Foundas, and *Indiewire*'s Eric Kohn post online, as do countless movie sites such as *Twitch*, Movies.com, *Film School Rejects*, *Badass Digest*, *Collider*, and *Slashfilm*, which interact directly with rabid movie fans who may buy tickets or stream later on. Review aggregators Criticwire, Rotten Tomatoes, and Metacritic also collect festival reviews and post their rankings. Major newspapers will also post roundups during Sundance, but most top critics save their good stuff for the day the movie hits theaters.

For filmmakers at Sundance, the fantasy is that an established distributor will plunk down money to release their film. The reality is that only a handful will make the big score, landing an MG from a studio subsidiary, complete with marketing commitment. The rest may land VOD distribution or self-release their film, which allows them to keep more of the proceeds. But even so, most will never make back their production and marketing costs.

THE BRASS RING: THE STUDIO PICKUP

On opening night of Sundance 2012, Tom Bernard of Sony Pictures Classics swoops down on the documentary *Searching for Sugar Man*, convinced that it will prove to be one of the best films at the festival. The next day, his warm breath trailing in the cold air as we talk in front of the Eccles, Bernard is still grinning at how well the movie played; he closed the deal right after the screening. Like the hockey player he is, he knows he has scored a goal.

Sundance has played a vital role in the global documentary film movement that is now in full bloom. As costs for digital filmmakers have come down, rules of storytelling have become less rigid. Point is, crowd-pleasers like *Searching for Sugar Man* remind us that docs no longer have to be dull, expository explorations of world issues (as worthy as some of those films may be). They can be crazy fun. Of the 114 films selected for Sundance in 2012, an astounding 39 are documentaries.

Searching for Sugar Man plays like a narrative feature. Swedish director Malik Bendjelloul cannily manipulates the story so that audiences eagerly follow clues, seeking the answer to various mysteries that unfold in delightful and surprising ways. The film reveals an expert filmmaker who knows what tidbits to unspool and when to withhold information. It's worked since the dawn of storytelling.

The Sony art-house film division was founded in December 1991 by copresidents Tom Bernard and Michael Barker, one of the movie business's most durable partnerships. They met in 1979, when both were working with Films Incorporated, which rented movies to colleges and prisons. The friendship was formed when they pulled each other's names for that year's Secret Santa gift exchange.

Barker and Bernard went on to create and run United Artists Classics, followed by Orion Classics. When Orion's parent company went bankrupt in December 1991, they needed to find a place to continue releasing the specialty films from around the world they loved. Sony gave them a home—and allowed them to continue running their unit autonomously.

Over the past twenty-one years, SPC has established an enviable track record as one of the most successful boutique distributors in the history of the industry: some 371 releases thus far, which as of 2013 had earned 135 Oscar nominations and 31 wins. Meanwhile, it has forged invaluable bonds with such global auteurs as Woody Allen, Akira Kurosawa, Pedro Almodóvar, and Michael Haneke.

Searching for Sugar Man, about a seventies Mexican American folk-rocker known as Rodriguez, was only supposed to show on Swedish TV. It took thirty-four-year-old Bendjelloul five years to make. It's his first feature. After shooting short biodocs on Björk, Sting, Rod Stewart, and Elton John; a Prince concert film; and docs that provided the source material for features *The Men Who Stare at Goats* and *The Terminal,* Bendjelloul traveled around Africa for six months looking for a great story to film. Out of six possibilities, the one he finally pursued was "the best story I ever heard," he says at screening Q&As.

Bendjelloul discovered that Rodriguez was a huge star in South Africa, as big as Dylan or Hendrix; he was the South African Elvis. Somehow his soft ballads had hit the anti-Apartheid zeitgeist without his ever stepping foot there. He was the spokesman for a generation, a household name who sold countless records. But no one had seen the man in three decades; his Sussex record label had gone bankrupt thirty-five years before. So Bendjelloul went in search of him. The movie reveals what he found, and audiences at Sundance told Bernard what he needed to know: the movie moved people.

Two of the best-reviewed Sundance 2012 feature film entries landed coveted slots at Fox Searchlight—*The Sessions* and *Beasts of the Southern Wild.* Searchlight is one of three thriving studio subsidiaries (Paramount Vantage, Disney's Miramax Films, and Warner Independent Pictures did not survive) and tends to spend more on marketing budgets than Universal's Focus Features or Sony Pictures Classics. In fact, Searchlight is willing to invest substantial money, time, and energy into making their handpicked slate work every year. It's as if they can take a movie like Terrence Malick's Cannes Palme d'Or winner *The Tree of Life* and will it into becoming an art-house Oscar contender.

Run by gifted marketer Nancy Utley and exhibition veteran Steve Gilula, the company still operates on the successful economic model burnished by Rupert Murdoch protégé Peter Rice, who moved on to run Fox TV. Searchlight rarely spends more than $15 million on producing a film, and for every project it finances, or gives the "green light," and every finished film that it acquires as a "pickup," the executive team has to agree. Production executive Claudia Lewis works closely with writers and filmmakers, while acquisition chief Tony Safford once programmed the early Sundance Film Festival. This impressive brain trust still make mistakes—for every Hilary Swank Oscar-winning hit *Boys Don't Cry*, there's also an *Amelia* or *Conviction*—but they know how to reach their target smart audience (a broader demo than the conventional adult art-house crowd) whether old or young, male or female, via sophisticated social media marketing and substantial spending against the playing out of a movie in theaters over weeks, even months.

Searchlight is no slouch at cherry-picking Oscar contenders (see *Slumdog Millionaire, The Descendants, The Wrestler,* and Sundance hit *Little Miss Sunshine*). At Sundance 2012 they land the biggest buy of the festival, paying $6 million for world rights to *The Surrogate* (which they quickly retitle *The Sessions*), an intimate relationship movie that rests on two main performances (*Variety* slang: two-hander) and is written and directed by Australian Ben Lewin, who has not made a feature film in eighteen years. They take the risk with this almost painfully raw film about the sexual challenges of a paraplegic because it has a ring of authenticity, much like 2011 Oscar winner *The King's Speech,* which touched people partly because screenwriter David Seidler brought his own struggle with stuttering to his portrait of the tongue-tied King George VI. Similarly, Lewin, writer of *The Sessions,* suffered polio as a youth. When he climbs the stairs to the stage at the Eccles Theatre, he limps with a cane.

Oscar veterans Helen Hunt (Best Actress winner for *As Good As It Gets*) and John Hawkes (nominated for *Winter's Bone*) are nothing if not fussy when they pick roles. They both vetted the script and director and saw rich material in this eighties story about the late intellectual Mark O'Brien (Hawkes), who wanted more from life than lying immobile in an iron lung. He hires a sex surrogate (Hunt) to help him find intimacy. The film is not a romance. While the surrogate comes to care deeply for O'Brien—within the confines of a professional relationship—she is able to teach him how to make another woman happy. He goes on to find the love of his life.

"I've never seen a story where both of them meet with the intention to give him a future," Hunt tells me during a Los Angeles Screen Actors Guild Q&A. "Anyone who could write like that, he knew how to tell a story. That's what I clung to before we started."

This sexual soufflé is so delicate and sensitive that it could easily have gone flat. Audiences are often uncomfortable with sex in cinema, and *The Sessions* embraces moments that are awkward and embarrassing, even humiliating. Both actors are literally naked. "I was vulnerable," admits Hunt. "By the end of the day I needed my clothes on."

Yet Lewin and his cast stayed on course; they filmed in chronological order, building trust as they went. This movie demanded subtle, careful handling from everyone involved. For his part, Hawkes was in considerable discomfort as he lay on a soccer-ball-sized piece of foam that twisted his spine, he tells me. "It was a small amount of pain, but it was the most physically challenging thing I've ever done."

THE BREAKOUT

Searchlight also nabs the hit of the festival, Benh Zeitlin's four-hankie dystopian family drama *Beasts of the Southern Wild*, starring newcomer Quvenzhané Wallis as six-year-old Hushpuppy and, as her father, baker Dwight Henry, who agreed to accept the role so long as he could continue to run his bakery shop. Finished two days before the festival, the microbudget $1.5 million picture was filmed with Zeitlin's Court 13 film collective, a nonhierarchical gang of artist friends, on a constantly flooding abandoned delta island below the New Orleans levees.

The group started to coalesce around a squash court in 2002, when Zeitlin was working on his Wesleyan University animated thesis film *Egg*, and it grew from there. He believes in everyone on the project having creative input into the final film. "The people making the film are sculptors, architects, boat builders," he told the *Huffington Post.* "The location person is a musician. The casting person is a surfer. They're not there to advance their careers. They're all artists in their own right. And the idea is that we let the material and the script be flexible enough that artists are able to express themselves in whatever they're doing."

They didn't do it alone. They had some help going into the project (which was loosely inspired by Lucy Alibar's one-act play *Juicy and Delicious*) from the Sundance Institute screenwriters and directors labs, as well as a grant from the San Francisco Film Society. "I came with the messy, craziest ideas on paper," the director tells me during a flip-cam interview on a sunny roof overlooking snowy Park City. At the Labs, "they made me justify my choices and boil it down to the specific core of the film, which I discovered through the process."

Flexible and free form, Zeitlin's filmmaking process yielded extraordinary results. Inspired by the eroding coastal geography of southern Louisiana, Zeitlin and Alibar started with a full conventional screenplay. A group of fifteen went on an eight-parish casting search to find the girl to play young Hushpuppy. When Wallis walked in, Zeitlin knew he had found her, and that she would transform his movie: "She had this quiet moral compass, a fierce sense of right and wrong that I knew deep down had to be there. But it took her walking into the room to bring that out. She saved us; we would have crashed without her."

According to producer Dan Janvey, in preproduction they workshopped the script with the performers; Wallis and the other characters opened up the language. Zeitlin was open to changing the script to accommodate them.

They shot the storm-tossed movie from the limited perspective of a six-year-old girl and her imagination, without computer graphic (CG) effects. "The flooding that was already there made me realize we could make a film about the end of the world without any money at all," says Zeitlin. "We felt combining the real end of the world with the more mythological end of the world made perfect sense."

Shot in a chaotic run-and-gun cinema verité style with handheld digital cameras floating at the eye level of the diminutive leading lady to capture her point of view, Zeitlin says, "it's really about a giant group of us going somewhere, living the story, and creating the movie. The mentality toward production is more collaborative and free. It's not a hierarchical machine like most movies."

The filmmakers got the most out of their locations and nonprofessional actors. "It's about a feeling that your place may be taken away and learning how to survive that," says Zeitlin. "People from the region all understood that better than me. In their eyes and mentality they are already survivors, living that fight, sticking by their place."

The filmmakers took their time finding their movie in the editing room: *Beasts* spent a year and a half in postproduction. Thirty-year-old Zeitlin, the eldest son of folklorists who once worked for the Smithsonian, never imagined that his little movie would gross $12.8 million domestically and travel so far and wide. He says, "I'm grateful that people all over the world will see this story that felt so small and rooted, but the emotions are universal."

COLLABORATORS AND MULTITASKERS

The new indie model, based on scarce resources, relies on collaborator-friends often encountered at festivals who roam the country helping each other out by playing different roles: editing, writing, photographing, producing, acting. Mumblecore is one name that has been applied to both a generation of young independent filmmakers and the microbudget relationship films they shoot with a low-key naturalistic aesthetic.

At Sundance 2012, three popular hits are collaborations with writer-director Mark Duplass (*Cyrus,* TV's *The League*), who executive-produced and starred in Colin Trevorrow's offbeat sci-fi romance *Safety Not Guaranteed;* wrote and produced his wife Katie Aselton's second feature, horror thriller *Black Rock;* and costarred with Emily Blunt and Rosemarie DeWitt in Lynn Shelton's *Your Sister's Sister.* Duplass is the consummate collaborator-multitasker, producing, writing, and acting for friends as well as directing films with his brother Jay, from indie-financed Paramount release *Jeff, Who Lives at Home* to Scott Rudin's planned remake *Same Time, Next Year.*

The roots of *Safety Not Guaranteed* are bizarre, to say the least. The story of a reporter and two interns who track down the source of a strange newspaper ad about time travel was inspired by a 1997 classified ad that appeared in a backwoods survivalist magazine in northern Oregon, later becoming an Internet meme.

Director Trevorrow's writing partner, Derek Connolly, saw a glimmer of an idea for a larger story, and the two worked up a draft for an emotional time-travel comedy. They brought in as exec producers Mark and Jay Duplass. Mark, especially, helped to develop the character that he eventually played. "Mark made awesome choices that helped to ground that character," says Trevorrow. "It was a tonal tightrope walk."

A child of the eighties, of Richard Donner and Robert Zemeckis and Steven Spielberg, Trevorrow wanted to infuse his movie with "the same kind of naturalism that Mark and Jay are so good at. Where I come from is where they come from: hybrid, honest, real, and intimate, but you also have cinematic moments."

The role of the girlish newspaper intern who pulls a jaded reporter into the plot was written for *Parks and Recreation* star Aubrey Plaza, with whom Trevorrow and Connolly share a manager. They lined up Plaza and the director's friend of ten years, actor Jake M. Johnson, and "hit a lot of resistance at a lot places," admits Trevorrow. "They were not close to being movie stars. I said, 'We can't do this,' and Mark said, 'You can do this but for a certain amount of money.' We figured out we could make it for under $1 million. We didn't want an audience to feel they were watching something cheap or chintzy."

They sent the script to *Little Miss Sunshine* backer Big Beach because their films have a "consistent tone," says Trevorrow. "They make films that are interesting and dark and in the end uplifting. The first one they read is the one we shot. No changes. We were given complete freedom."

Eventually Duplass came around to playing Kenneth, the time traveler, says Trevorrow. "He was the missing piece of the whole project. I didn't want him to be a broad silly character, but a grounded real person who our heroine is falling in love with. We buy Mark as a real man. He has a naturalistic presence on screen. We asked if he would do it, and he said yes."

Duplass wasn't doing it for the paycheck. "This is a tiny little movie," says Trevorrow. "Mark was very eager to take on the challenge of a real character, not just playing another version of himself."

In fact, several actors on the film had something to prove. Plaza "wanted to show that she could go beyond the eye-rolling intern in the corner," says Trevorrow. "Mark wanted to show he could act, not just emote, as himself. Jake Johnson wanted to make clear that he was the great American actor, not just the funny guy on *New Girl*."

When they cast Johnson, *New Girl* hadn't actually aired yet. "It was me knowing him," says Trevorrow, "wanting to show the world. Coincidentally other people figured that out at the same time. Now we have a big TV star in the movie."

While Connolly's first draft was more of a "comedy mystery road trip movie, the same characters and scenes," Trevorrow pushed the movie in a more romantic, heartfelt direction.

The movie was a balancing act between comedy and drama. "All we did in every scene was to find the truth in the moment and make it honest," says Trevorrow. "This was tightly scripted, but we took advantage of having Mark there and have everyone be willing to take time to open the scenes and have intimate moments. The difficult line to walk tonally: we felt it in the editing room, and followed our instincts all the way to keep people engaged and be romantic and funny." But the R-rated movie has sharp edges; Duplass's character may well be crazy. And Johnson says mean things about women.

The biggest anxiety came after Sundance accepted the film in the dramatic competition and Trevorrow agonized over changing the ending, moving away from the script. "I knew something was wrong, that people weren't feeling the way I had hoped. So I did the opposite of [the ending] we had, and turned the movie upside down." His instincts turn out to be correct. After a bidding war erupts following the movie's rousing Sunday, January 22, premiere at the Library Center, FilmDistrict beats out the Weinstein Company, Fox Searchlight, Focus Features, and LD Distribution, paying more than seven figures for U.S. rights.

As a writer who has been working within the studio system for a while, Trevorrow hopes that production executives will now feel comfortable selling him to their bosses. "I like to believe that intimate moments between characters don't need to be relegated to independent films," he says. "They can coexist with big exciting things happening; they are not mutually exclusive. Big movies could use a little mumblecore and humanity."

Mark Duplass has also enjoyed a close collaboration with writer-director Lynn Shelton, who broke out in 2009 with her Sundance-jury-prize-winning *Humpday*, costarring Joshua Leonard (*The Blair Witch Project*) and Duplass, who shares her improvisational acting aesthetic. In fact, they did so well together with *Humpday* that Duplass came back to her with a new idea for a movie, one she ran with—and totally changed. Her fourth feature, *Your Sister's Sister*, debuted at Toronto, where it was acquired by VOD distributor IFC Films, and went on to play Sundance, Tribeca, San Francisco, and Seattle.

Trained as an actress and photographer, the lanky, strikingly beautiful Shelton shot documentaries and music videos, building her base out of her native Seattle as well as at Sundance, Toronto, and SXSW. With *Your Sister's Sister,* the director focuses her roving camera on a complex love triangle that twists through past relationships and issues of sexual identity and sibling rivalry. Duplass plays a man lost and depressed after the death of his brother. His best friend (Emily Blunt) sends him to a remote island to recuperate. He huffs and puffs on his bike out to her family cabin in the woods, where he is surprised to find her half sister (Rosemarie DeWitt). After much alcohol, the two sleep together. And then the next day her sister (Blunt) shows up. Much hilarity ensues, and all is not as it seems. It's not your ordinary relationship comedy.

Shelton changed gears on *Your Sister's Sister* to accommodate a pair of actresses who were not as fearlessly confident as Duplass with improvising in front of close-up digital cameras. They adjusted. "It's about intimacy and the ability to create an emotionally safe environment," Shelton tells me later. "That's a huge component of how I like to work: to feel totally safe. Collaboration is at its best when everybody is bringing the best out of each other. You have to have an incredible amount of trust. I carefully consider who I'm going to ask onto that set. It has to be the right number of bodies, a baker's dozen of crew members, and that's it. There's no toxicity on the set. The actors know I'm never going to let any of their misfires show up on screen. They know I'm only going to show them at their best."

Shelton supports her independent movie habit by directing such television shows as *Mad Men* and *New Girl.* This allows her to tune in to her own drummer, living far away from the big studios, in Seattle. "It's an intimate, mutually supportive community of film collaborators there," she says. "My gaffer and assistant director are directing right now. Every time somebody starts up (a film), we all go and help. It's a beautiful, very satisfying community to be part of. We're hoping for the best for each other. My acting teacher in New York years ago told us never to feel competitive or jealous when other people have success. Success comes in bunches. If people around you are succeeding, it means you are next: only wish well for the people around you."

Likewise, Duplass is free to pursue indie directing projects with his brother Jay (such as microbudget *The Do-Deca-Pentathlon*) with his earnings from the ongoing hit FX comedy series *The League*, which costars his wife, Katie Aselton. Duplass wrote 2012 Sundance Midnight chiller *Black Rock* as a directing and starring vehicle for her. It's Aselton's second feature after *The Freebie*, a marital relationship comedy costarring improv whiz Dax Shepard. The R-rated isolated island thriller starring three women (Aselton, Kate Bosworth, and Lake Bell) who fight off male attackers sold to Mickey Liddell and David Dinerstein's LD Distribution.

Aselton is yet another indie actress-writer-director who has taken matters into her own hands, figuring there was no point in waiting for her career to come to her. "Mark was my ass-kicker," she admits. "I was convinced my phone was never going to ring again. 'Just make something on your own,' he told me. 'You can't say it's too hard.' He really was my champion in taking control. I drummed up the idea for *The Freebie*. It felt simple and easy enough to attack on my own. It was less intimidating than a large story; it was really small, with a couple people."

The actress wrote a high-concept six-page outline about a long-married couple who decide to take one night off with someone else. "I had an amazing time doing it," she says. "It was the biggest confidence booster. It's not rocket science to make a movie." Phase 4 picked up *The Freebie* out of Sundance. "It was so cheap to make," she says, "that it was one of those rare things where everyone who worked on it made money."

On *Black Rock*, a believable action thriller, Aselton dug deeper with a larger-scale cast and crew and more shooting days: "It was a larger adventure on all fronts." She came up with the basic idea of three women friends on their own in Maine, but Duplass wrote the first draft of the script during a twelve-hour layover in L.A., complete with a juicy role that would allow his wife to show off her action chops.

Aselton's character takes her two girlfriends—played by Kate Bosworth (*Superman Returns*) and Lake Bell (*What Happens in Vegas*)—on a bonding vacation to a deserted island off the coast of Maine, where their isolated camping trip is interrupted by an encounter with three hunting ex-servicemen. Unfortunately, the women become their prey and must defend themselves in order to survive. "It's *Deliverance* meets *Thelma & Louise*," Aselton says. "The story was so compelling to me. Once I had my girls I was ready to go. It happened so fast."

She raised $33,000 on Kickstarter toward the cost of a $40,000 Arri Alexa camera package and shot the film in June in her hometown of Milbridge, Maine, up the coast from Bar Harbor. "It was freezing, truly uncomfortable, 43 degrees." She enjoyed picking camera angles, following all the character arcs from start to finish, and learning to put more trust in her collaborators, she says. "It was like a creative collective jumping off the cliff together."

While *The Freebie* was improvised and shaped in the editing room during postproduction, *Black Rock* was already fully scripted, prepped, and shaped, she says, "so post was easier, it was clearer to see what the final film was. Look, if the opportunities are not being presented to me, I'm going to take the reins and do it," she says. "Brit Marling was not waiting for the phone to ring. The great roles are not there to be had. If you have an idea, do it." *Black Rock* opened in limited theaters on the same day as a solid VOD release, followed by a strong DVD release through Lionsgate.

THE VIDEO-ON-DEMAND (VOD) RELEASE

All the distributors flocked to the first screening of one of the most anticipated offerings at Sundance 2012: Nicholas Jarecki's Wall

Street thriller *Arbitrage,* starring Richard Gere as a hedge fund tycoon in both money and family trouble.

As much of a marquee draw as Gere remains overseas, these days it is challenging to sell a wide theatrical stateside release on the power of a movie star. "Gere is a draw for women and men," insists producer Laura Bickford at Sundance. "This is the kind of film the studios used to make. It's an emotional family story, a suspense thriller, and a *policier.*"

First-time director Jarecki, thirty-two, is the youngest of three filmmaker brothers. Brother Eugene is also at the festival with the war-on-drugs documentary *The House I Live In,* and brother Andrew had his own Sundance hit in 2003 with *Capturing the Friedmans.* Nicholas started out as a computer analyst who consulted on the film *Hackers* and later caught the directing bug. He made music videos and wrote a book in which he interviewed directors about breaking into Hollywood.

Jarecki executive-produced the James Toback documentary *The Outsider* and cowrote the Bret Easton Ellis adaptation *The Informers,* which he and Ellis were pushed out of before the movie flopped at Sundance 2008. Ellis introduced Bickford and the filmmaker in 2009, when Jarecki was developing an early *Arbitrage* draft with writer Kevin Turen.

Bickford helped Jarecki to land his ensemble cast, led by Gere, who made it possible for sales company Parlay to raise enough presales to get bank loans for a $15 million budget. Gere happened to be getting on a plane when he got the script, read it, and immediately wanted to meet Jarecki, who with Bickford joined Gere at the restaurant at his Bedford Post Inn in upstate New York. It didn't hurt when Bickford's *Traffic* stars Michael Douglas and Catherine Zeta-Jones came over to their table in the restaurant to urge Gere to do the movie.

Gere's presence in a project helps to get it made—not that he still commands the serious studio millions he once did. Those days are over, as they have been for most movie actors for some time. In a way, that's a good thing, if not for them, then for the movies. If actors aren't tempted to star in studio formula fare they're more apt to consider the quality of a given role.

"I'm glad I was there when we could make movies like this and get paid really well—that was great," Gere tells me before the release. "You can make movies like this now and not get paid so well. It's good for younger filmmaker-writers. They're like the guys in the sixties and seventies, inventing new ways of making movies."

The studios "don't make the kind of movies I make anymore," the sixty-three-year-old actor admits. "So it's not even relevant at the studio level. The drama was part of what the studio did. They made five or six intelligent movies with Oscars in mind . . . No more."

Bickford and Jarecki let go of a financier who wanted the Wall Street movie to be shot in New Orleans, but Bickford took to the phone and found five more equity investors. In the end, Yorick Le Saux, director of photography of French TV series *Carlos* and Italian drama *I Am Love,* shot the film in New York City, where Jarecki grew up with his commodity trader father. "Nick knows that world," says Bickford.

Susan Sarandon joined the cast for her second film with Gere, playing his wife, while the filmmakers cast former investment banker Brit Marling as his daughter just after her 2011 Sundance success in *Another Earth*. "You could believe she was running her father's company," says Bickford, "not the bimbo playing the brain surgeon." Up-and-comer Nate Parker, thirty-two (who also starred in another film at the festival, Spike Lee's *Red Hook Summer*), came aboard as a young family friend of the titan-in-trouble. After *Arbitrage* was accepted in rough form for Sundance, Jarecki went back into the editing room to make it better.

Sundance reviews for the film are largely positive. From the start, as leverage to land domestic rights for *Arbitrage,* Roadside Attractions hypes its success with its 2011 Sundance pickup, the Wall

Street drama *Margin Call,* which worked in both VOD ($6 million) and theaters ($5.4 million) without one format stealing viewers from the other. (It also scored an Original Screenplay Oscar nomination for rookie filmmaker J.C. Chandor.) The boutique distributor acquired *Margin Call* for $2.1 million and went on to spend about $2.5 million in marketing.

One of the strongest independent distributors, Roadside was co-founded in 2003 by ex-agent Howard Cohen and his life partner, Eric d'Arbeloff. After breaking out with such specialty pictures as *Ladies in Lavender, Amazing Grace,* and *Super Size Me,* Roadside sold a 43 percent minority stake in 2007 to Lionsgate, which handles their films on home video. Ivy League–educated, experienced, and possessing excellent taste, Cohen and d'Arbeloff are clever at picking films they can market, often with awards in mind (*Winter's Bone, Biutiful, Albert Nobbs*), but they don't always have the deep pockets to compete with their well-financed studio rivals unless Lionsgate or another partner comes in with them.

With *Arbitrage,* Roadside wanted to follow the *Margin Call* template—a simultaneous, or "day-and-date," release on VOD and in theaters—which was closely watched as a successful paradigm by the film industry. It tends to work best for films with name actors. Because the major theater chains still disapprove of theater bookings concurrent with VOD availability, Roadside had to "four-wall" several hundred theaters—buying them out at a fixed rate—which was slightly higher for *Arbitrage* than it had been for *Margin Call.* But the percentage of four-walled theaters for *Arbitrage* was less, 25 percent, accounting for about $1.5 million of the gross, according to Cohen, who says the movie still came out well ahead.

Jarecki was impressed with *Margin Call*'s numbers and thought that his film could exceed them. "I thought, 'We can do maybe double the business, if not more, with this film,'" he says. "We can expand this model, we got to three or four hundred theaters on this one, we believed that there's a whole group of people missing indie films because they are not going to go to the theater—for whatever reasons. Facebook individuals write me that they're in a wheelchair with cancer and don't like to go to the cinema. They'd love to be able to watch this movie at home and still be part of the first cycle of the conversation. I love this inclusive model, where everyone is invited. It appeared to me humane on a business level. Why leave anyone out? Anybody who wants to give us money, let's take it. If they're having a party, you're invited. Not even counting the VOD, it's groundbreaking what they did. A lot of filmmakers will try this. They sent people to the theater to ask, 'Did you know that you could watch this at home?' Ninety percent didn't know that. They're a theatrical audience, they're going to go. They're not aware of media platforms. And a whole home audience is not going to go to the theater."

The point is, backing a wide release in theaters demands serious coin. It can cost $20 million to release a movie on three thousand screens, but it takes a fraction of that to open VOD. The cable companies run plenty of advertising. (It also helps to have a title that starts with the letter *A*.) And where stardom can be hit or miss when it comes to pulling audiences into theaters, it works like a charm on VOD. By that measure, Gere is a major draw.

Arbitrage was the number one movie on iTunes its opening weekend, September 14, 2012—and still opened to over $2 million on 197 screens en route to an $8 million domestic total. Roadside was so pleased with how the movie performed via Internet, cable, and satellite television that it removed the veil of secrecy on VOD numbers and boasted about how well it did—well north of $11 million. Not bad.

Close to a quarter of the 2012 Sundance releases were made available concurrent with or before their theatrical openings on VOD outlets—cable, iTunes, Hulu, or filmmakers' own websites. Boasting better-known stars and aimed at a broader audience, eight of the sixteen films in the high-profile Premieres section took the VOD route. Thus 2012 marked a huge sea change in delivery that yielded more profits for the Sundance slate.

The Weinstein Company launched its RADiUS VOD division in 2012 with a $2 million Sundance acquisition, the angry-girl comedy *Bachelorette*. More of a crowd-pleaser than critics' picture, the film was given a minimal inexpensive theatrical launch (mainly to build awareness) that grossed under $500,000. But the VOD take was $5.5 million, which more than covered the film's costs—and produced a nice profit.

VOD pioneers Magnolia and IFC together accounted for a dozen Sundance 2012 films released on VOD. None grossed more than $1 million in theaters. Distributor Magnolia, which is owned by Mark Cuban and Todd Wagner's 2929 Entertainment, can book its films day-and-date with VOD at their own independent Landmark Theatre chain, as can AMC Networks' IFC Films, which specializes in VOD releases, thanks to a deal between cash princes Cuban and AMC Networks owner, Cablevision CEO Chuck Dolan.

Early in 2005, Magnolia and Landmark experimented by opening Steven Soderbergh's $1.6 million movie *Bubble* simultaneously in theaters and on VOD. It was a dud, grossing only $145,626. The 'day-and-date' model has come a long way since then.

Just because he has to go along with IFC and Magnolia bookings doesn't mean that Landmark head Ted Mundorff has to like the practices: like most theater owners, he believes strongly that day-and-date VOD could be the death of the exhibition business. Therefore, he won't allow any other day-and-date bookings.

And the business is evolving. Now that so many movies are heading toward VOD, a pecking order is starting to emerge. It's better to be branded with an identity and reviews before you hit VOD, so the day-and-date model—or the "premium," even more expensive VOD release some weeks before a movie hits theaters—is not the preferred way to go for the smaller films with no stars, which are struggling now to land theatrical openings at all. Movie stars like Richard Gere can carry advance VOD, which also demands strong positioning by cable companies and iTunes. The trend now is toward establishing a movie with reviews and one week of word-of-mouth before going to VOD. The VOD model is maturing and evolving but has yet to supplant the successful theatrical studio subsidiary release, which is buttressed by international TV output deals.

THE AGITPROP DOCUMENTARY

Also grabbing attention at Sundance is Kirby Dick's gripping activist doc *The Invisible War,* which exposes the epidemic of rape in the U.S. military. Remarkably, perhaps more than any documentary released to date, the film will go on to have a huge impact on redressing the injustice it reveals.

The L.A. filmmaker has made a name for himself by writing and directing documentaries that challenge powerful institutions, from the Catholic Church (the Oscar-nominated *Twist of Faith*) to the Motion Picture Association of America ratings board (*This Film Is Not Yet Rated*).

Most filmmakers hope that their movies will be seen, talked about, make money, earn awards, and maybe have some influence on the culture at large. With *The Invisible War,* Dick and producer Amy Ziering set their sights on the U.S. military establishment. They were determined to shake things up and push for change, because to allow what was happening to continue was intolerable, unthinkable.

Dick tells me at Sundance that he was astonished that nobody had made a movie about the shocking number of male and female rapes in the military—a consistent, unchanging 19,000 a year, about 80 percent not reported. Twenty percent of all servicewomen have been assaulted while serving, often by serial predators; estimates are that 500,000 people total have been sexually assaulted in the U.S. military. Prosecution rates are low: less than 21 percent of reported cases went to trial in 2010. Of 529 alleged perpetrators, only 53 percent were convicted. Plus, there is no sex offender registry in the military.

Dick soon realized that no one seemed to know what was going on due to the gulf between America's military culture and all-volunteer army and the filmmaking community: never the twain shall meet. That was why the liberal intelligentsia—the sort of people who make documentaries—didn't know what was happening. The Canadian Broadcasting Corporation, PBS-owned Independent Television Service (ITVS), and France's Canal Plus came in to back the film, along with homeless advocate Maria Cuomo Cole (sister of New York's governor) and other nonprofit donors. But not as many as Dick had expected.

"I had hoped that the movie would bring veterans and feminists together, two constituencies that are not seen as aligned," Dick says. He did not marshal support from either group until long after he had spent a year crisscrossing the country shooting interviews, most conducted by Ziering. Many of the victims were talking about their rapes for the first time. "You just decide you are going to make this film," says Dick, "and somehow it's going to work out in the end. It's harder to find a really good subject for a film than it is to find money."

The question was whether the film could light a fire under the Obama administration. "Would they step up and make substantial changes?" Dick asked. *The Invisible War* shows how many upstanding, idealistic young women patriotically choose to serve their country only to be rewarded with humiliating and traumatic violence that ruins their lives. Isolated in Alaska, Trina McDonald, a U.S. Navy seaman, was horrifyingly trapped in a life-threatening situation with no support. U.S. Coast Guard seaman Kori Cioca was beaten up, suffering an injury to her jaw that has yet to stop producing pain, and the long years she spent fighting for medical support strained her marriage.

But reform is coming. After Sundance, the filmmakers undertook a massive screening campaign for influencers around the country, targeting especially the Washington, D.C., media, major nonprofits, retired generals, the Department of Defense, and the Obama administration. Eventually a screener of the film got to Defense Secretary Leon Panetta, although the filmmakers are not sure how.

In a follow-up telephone interview, Dick says that it was soon after Panetta saw the film that he held an April press conference laying out planned changes in the rules governing sexual assault in the military: commanders would pass investigations to an outside, higher-ranked colonel or captain, moving the prosecution up the level of command; each armed forces branch would have a special victims unit, and more prosecutions would be pursued. At the 2012 White House Correspondents' Dinner, Panetta thanked executive producer Jennifer Siebel Newsom (wife of California lieutenant governor Gavin Newsom) for making the film and told her it moved him.

Dick is "cautiously optimistic" that these first steps will lead to improvements. But having investigations stay within the chain of command still leaves open the potential for conflicts of interest, he says. Two parallel pieces of legislation are moving slowly through the Senate and the House. "It's a start. We advocate that people have to be moved outside chain of command so an arbiter makes the decision to investigate or prosecute, as is done in all civilian systems."

U.S. Representative Niki Tsongas of Massachusetts brought up *The Invisible War* to Veterans Affairs Secretary Eric Shinseki at a July 25 joint hearing of the House Armed Services and House Veterans Affairs Committees. She had heard that Shinseki had seen the doc the day before. In the hearing she told Shinseki she was "heartened" by his interest in the film, and remarked how the film "painfully highlights" the bureaucratic hurdles that survivors of sexual assault have to endure to get their proper benefits.

Showing the film seems to have an effect. To keep applying pressure on the government, the filmmakers pulled together several groups—victims of sexual assault, veterans, human rights activists, and the nonprofit group Protect Our Defenders—into an umbrella coalition called Invisible No More. A May screening of the film at an armed forces Sexual Harassment/Assault Prevention Summit had a significant impact, says Dick. "We heard immediately that people wanted to order the film. The Army itself seems very proactive on using this film, ordered it for a number of bases, scheduled dozens of screenings at military establishments."

While Dick was prepared for some real resistance or counterattack from the military establishment, "in fact that has not happened," he says. "They've been receptive in using the film in training." That's because the film helps to put a human face on the suffering these attacks cause and reveals the limited tools available to people dealing with sexual assault. "People on the ground know it's a problem and are doing everything they can to address the problem with tools that are ineffectual," says Dick. "They're glad to get hold of the film, to show exactly what happens." Seeing the film, in other words, hits you in the gut in a way that reading clinical reports could not.

THE SELF-RELEASING MODEL

Another topical Sundance documentary, *Detropia,* shows that as popular as the DIY distribution model may be, it's not easy as it looks. Filmmakers are figuring out that while they can do better for themselves much of the time, there's a steep learning curve.

Shot around the ruins of contemporary Detroit, *Detropia* marks Heidi Ewing and Rachel Grady's most cinematic film to date. The filmmaking team zero in on the economic disintegration, the literal downsizing of Detroit—which has shrunk to 700,000 souls from its peak population of 2,000,000—and the city's ballooning gap between rich and poor. The cautionary tale uses the Motor City as a bellwether for the entire country. But this moving doc is no death knell. The filmmakers find heroes in many walks of Detroit life, ordinary and extraordinary folks fostering new possibilities and surprising hope amid crushing hardships. (In July 2013, the city of Detroit declared bankruptcy.)

As established producer-directors, the duo was able to raise $950,000 in six months for their documentary, including support from the Sundance documentary fund, the Ford Foundation, and other investors. "We've earned our luck over the years," says Ewing, who knew the money they nabbed for TV rights from ITVS would make it tougher to sell later to a theatrical distributor. It's always easier to sell a movie with all rights available than it is to sell one with only "split" rights. But it was worth it to get the advance fees, she says: "We knew the offers were going to be paltry. But we love ITVS." Otherwise, Ewing explains, filmmakers have to borrow money and take out loans to make the movie, which often means not paying their support staff.

So they took the movie to Sundance, hired a publicist, and courted the usual suspects on the distribution side. They wanted to show the film in theaters—before the automotive bailout was no longer a hot election topic. (The film wouldn't air on ITVS until May 2013.)

After Sundance, the *Detropia* filmmakers were so unhappy with the onerous deal terms available that they decided to jump into self-distribution. They set up their own IFC Center opening in New York, hired industry vet Michael Tuckman to book theaters for them, and paid for some marketing and publicity by raising a $70,000 budget for prints and ads on Kickstarter.

As EWING AND GRADY FOUND out the hard way, self-releasing demands learning the intricacies of marketing and distribution, skills that take professionals years to acquire. And the landscape is constantly changing. These days, however, distributors often have less time and fewer resources to devote to selling the movies they release. And the deals they offer are skimpy at best. So more filmmakers are doing the math and doing it for themselves. But while some people are natural self-promoters who have an instinct for hawking their wares on social media, others haven't a clue.

After Sundance, Ewing and Grady's conversations with distributors yielded offers from three well-known legitimate companies, as well as two smaller outfits. Most of the deals committed to release the movie in two to five cities at most, with some proposing just a one-week minimal New York and Los Angeles run to qualify for the Academy Awards. The problem with the offers, besides the "shitty money," Ewing tells me during an interview at a Starbucks in Los Angeles, was that they weren't accompanied by any passion for pushing the movie to audiences. "There wasn't a lot of vision around it. They'd take it, not try at their end, offer a nice DVD package."

Ewing's dissatisfaction may be partly due to her entrepreneurial bent. Her father ran a family business outside Detroit. "I am from a family of manufacturing entrepreneurs who kept reinventing the company," she says. "All my father's colleagues went under when everything changed to being made elsewhere, but he made specialty parts that were difficult to produce. He keeps innovating. I took something from that: to stay current and reinvent. Just making films, you think someone else will do the release for you. But it's a business. Now you have to do it as well. I see a lot of deer in headlights. If everyone doesn't up their game they will be taken advantage of. You have to know when to shift gears. Filmmakers need to be better businesspeople."

Figuring that they owed it to the movie not to let it "just drop off a cliff after we do Sundance," says Ewing, they decided they "needed to consider independent releasing." One investor, Impact Partners' Dan Cogan, was their cheerleader through the process. "He said, 'All the deals suck,'" she recalls. "They weren't inspiring at all." They decided to research their options. In eleven days they put up a trailer and of the donors who gave a total $71,000 for publicity, prints, and ads on Kickstarter, 866 were friends, 500 were strangers.

Did they know how much they needed? No. They guessed. "We were afraid to ask for more," admits Ewing. "We asked for sixty thousand dollars and needed ninety thousand. An angel came in with twenty thousand. You get what you ask for."

Out of their New York Loki Films office, Ewing and Grady organized six interns, who sent out a *Detropia* newsletter and e-mail blast to the lists the filmmakers have been building ever since their 2006 Oscar-nominated Pentecostal documentary *Jesus Camp*. "We kept track of every item of press," says Ewing. "You've got to be smart and organized or forget about it. We're trying new stuff. Even if Sony Pictures Classics was with us we'd be working our ass off. The nature of independent cinema is that distributors have limited budgets for P&A [prints and advertising]. It's hard to get butts in seats. There's a lot of stuff in the ether fighting for attention, people wanting to get home to watch *True Blood*."

Tellingly, absolutely no 35-millimeter prints were involved. With theater booker Tuckman they slowly rolled out the movie on Digital Cinema Packages (DCPs)—a collection of digital files used to store and convey digital audio, image, and data streams—to thirty-five cities, landing an opening on September 7 at New York's IFC Center, on September 14 for the hometown premiere in Detroit, on September 28 in the Bay Area, and on October 5 in Los Angeles. Some bookings were limited runs, some open, from two to five days. Boston's Coolidge Corner booked the film for five days; the Goodrich Theater Chain took the films to little towns in the Midwest for one or two nights only, offering a Skype Q&A with the directors. "How great that people in little towns can see this," Ewing thought.

With the self-release model, Ewing and Grady own their own VOD and DVD rights. For the first time they collaborated on those releases (January 2013) with New Video through the Sundance Artist Services program.

Ewing still doesn't know if they did the right thing. "It was not about the money," she says. "We made an artistic movie close to my heart. We took more ownership. It continues to be creative. I'll never know if the others would have done better." The film grossed a robust $400,000 (for a documentary) at the theatrical box office. Other filmmakers are so impressed that they plan to follow this model, including established documentarian A. J. Schnack, who considered taking out his Branson, Missouri, documentary, *We Always Lie to Strangers,* this way. Imitation is the sincerest form of flattery.

SUNDANCE SALES 2012

In the end, Sundance 2012 sales declined for the top buys. About 100 of the fest's 114 films landed some sort of theatrical, VOD, cable, PBS, and/or DVD release—or were self-distributed. The theatrical gross for the 2011 Sundance films totaled $90 million; the 2012 films topped out at $75 million, with only two films grossing $11 million or more, and only thirteen grossing $1.5 million or more, which is at the low end for a specialized film.

One of two top grossers was the badly reviewed Bradley Cooper vehicle *The Words,* which sold to CBS Films for $2.1 million on the basis of a $1.5 million fifteen-city 2,800-screen theatrical commitment for prints and ads. It grossed $11 million at the box office and bettered that take on home video.

The other top earner was *Beasts of the Southern Wild,* which Searchlight was able to nurture on a smaller scale (but for a longer time) with a $2 million minimum marketing guarantee and far fewer ads. But it achieved a similar gross. That's because it could rely on word-of-mouth to sell a movie that played like gangbusters, and instead of a large upfront payment, made a back-end deal to share the box-office gross with the filmmakers.

Safety Not Guaranteed won the Waldo Salt Screenwriting Award for Derek Connolly and grossed $4 million in theaters, a modest hit for FilmDistrict, a distributor then allied with Sony Pictures Worldwide Acquisitions that tends to focus on wide-release genre fare.

At Sundance awards night, the Sundance NEXT section audience award goes to standup comedian Mike Birbiglia's comedy *Sleepwalk with Me*, which, before its August 24 opening, is heavily promoted by producer Ira Glass to smart audiences of his well-branded *This American Life* radio show. It becomes a breakout hit, playing to packed houses (where it grosses $2.3 million) and scoring on VOD as well.

By the end of Sundance 2012, everyone knows which films have the right stuff to go all the way to the Oscars: features *The Sessions* and *Beasts of the Southern Wild*, and docs *Searching for Sugar Man, Detropia*, and *The Invisible War*.

At the Sundance closing-night awards ceremony, *Searching for Sugar Man* wins both the World Cinema Documentary Audience Award and a special jury prize. Sony Pictures Classics later puts Rodriguez on the fest circuit with his retuned guitar, and he even winds up on *60 Minutes* as the film heads toward a $3.7 million gross and Oscar frontrunner status.

The Invisible War wins the U.S. Documentary Audience Award; digital distributor Cinedigm picks up the film after the festival and in summer 2012 releases it in a limited number of theaters, allowing it to qualify for the Oscars. It grosses $72,000. Releases follow on iTunes and cable VOD in October. On its road to an Oscar nod, *The Invisible War* also receives a coveted International Documentary Association nomination for Best Feature. ITVS shows the film as part of its Independent Lens series over Memorial Day 2013.

The Sessions wins two Sundance prizes, the Dramatic Audience Award and a special jury prize for its extraordinary ensemble acting. The battle for Searchlight is to coax audiences to go out to see a drama about a paraplegic's sex life. So they play *The Sessions* at fall festivals to build awareness. When it opens October 19, critics praise it for being moving and uplifting without an ounce of sentiment or string-pulling, because it is less about settling for less than it is about striving for more. Searchlight keeps the film in limited release for months, waiting to make a strong pitch for award attention. For all their labors and substantial marketing costs, they squeeze out $6 million in North America for a total of $9.1 million worldwide—half of which is shared with theaters. That's less than they paid for the film.

Beasts of the Southern Wild takes home Sundance's highest honor, the Grand Jury Prize, along with a cinematography award for Ben Richardson. Zeitlin tells the awards night crowd, "We had more freedom to make this film than any filmmakers in America—ever." He exhorts producers to take note of this and let other filmmakers run just as wild.

After Sundance, Searchlight takes the movie and the creative team on a global promo tour to build an identity in advance of playing New Directors/New Films in New York and Un Certain Regard at Cannes, where it wins the FIPRESCI Prize and Golden Camera. Accompanied by rave reviews, the film lands in theaters June 27, 2012, and totals $12.8 million at the box office, plus another $8 million abroad. Unusually, for all his public appearances and exposure to Hollywood, Zeitlin is never tempted by any of the many offers coming his way. He sticks to his original plan of returning home to find and develop another story that would come out of a particular Louisiana community and culture.

While no single organization can remove all the impediments facing filmmakers who want to find audiences for their films, Redford's Sundance Institute and annual film festival continue to be vital in shaping cinema's future.

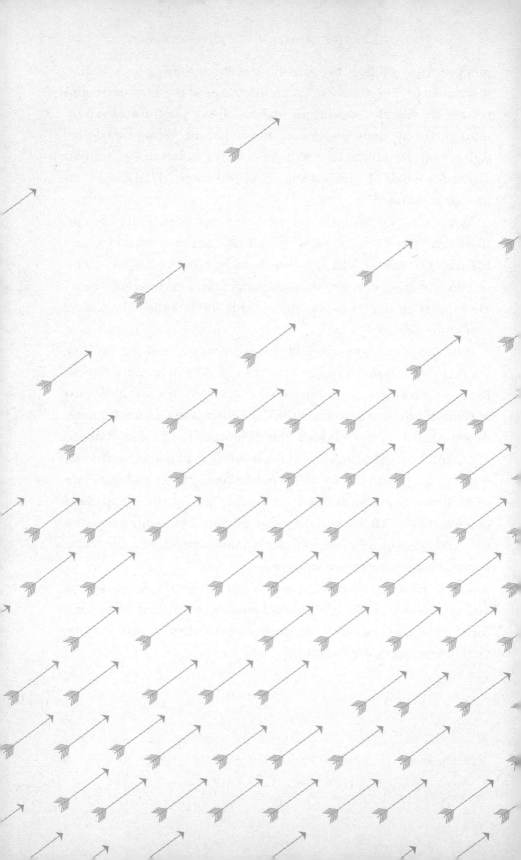

CHAPTER 2

MARCH: CHASING THE FRANCHISE

JOHN CARTER VS. *THE HUNGER GAMES*

If Robert Redford didn't like what he saw back in the seventies and eighties, he could never have imagined the Hollywood of today, chasing frantically after easy-to-sell titles based on already established brands, whether remakes, sequels, or anything else already proven popular with audiences. It's up to the independents now to support modestly budgeted dramas or anything original—unless it's a comedy or an animated feature.

The studios' thirst for sequels is nothing new. From the start it was rooted in extreme risk aversion. In a now famous story, when Coca-Cola acquired Columbia Pictures, it researched the safest possible movie to produce and release. Answer: the sequel. Hollywood already knew that. Studio hits have spawned sequels from the early days of the Ma and Pa Kettle comedies, Depression-era Gold Digger musicals, and Andy Hardy movies to multiple iterations of "Me Tarzan, you Jane." But back in the Golden Age of Hollywood, which ended in the late fifties, sequels were a small part of the annual output from the studio factories. They churned out a wide range of movies—from slapstick and romantic comedies to melodramas, actioners, westerns, war films, musicals, biopics, and serious dramas—aimed at audience niches from adult men and women to families.

The major studios released their pictures in small numbers of theaters, city by city, responding to local demand. Those were the days when word-of-mouth carried the day. Even as recently as 1982, Steven Spielberg's sci-fi smash *E.T.: The Extra-Terrestrial* played on screens for more than a year, and as late as 1997, James Cameron's blockbuster *Titanic* enjoyed a rare ten-month domestic run. Perhaps the only disappointment to the mega-billion dollar hit for partners Twentieth Century Fox and Paramount was that there could be no sequel.

But with the rise of the wide-release movie in the eighties, when movies opened in the top-twenty markets in the country all at once, the studios began to reverse themselves. It all started with indie Tom Laughlin's successful thousand-theater release of *The Trial of Billy Jack* in 1974, which Universal imitated the next year with Steven Spielberg's summer scare-fest *Jaws*. Instead of high-class A-movies slowly building support city by city via highly publicized talent promo tours, or road shows—with low-brow B-movies playing shorter runs around the country—distributors saw that they could sell commercial fare by targeting different wide audience swatches with blanket buys of TV spots.

Many have blamed *Jaws*, the quickest movie to pass the $100 million mark at the box office, for introducing a widely emulated new business model. "*Jaws* whetted corporate appetites for big profits quickly, which is to say studios wanted every film to be *Jaws*," Peter Biskind wrote in 1998's *Easy Riders, Raging Bulls*. Added John Podhoretz in 2010 in the *Weekly Standard:* "Hollywood had been happy to hit for average. After 'Jaws,' it began swinging for grand slams."

Over the decades the movie studios—which had become smaller parts of corporations run by business executives with an eye on

Wall Street who were skittish about narrow profit margins—steadily moved away from risky, execution-dependent quality films for adults. That's because these films demanded painstakingly slow campaigns in order to build title awareness and "want to see" excitement, as opposed to presold titles. "Why should we rely on molasses-speed word-of-mouth creation for an unknown product that could die in one weekend?" asked more and more executives, under pressure from bosses who had to answer to the bottom line.

That old-fashioned review-driven limited "platform" release— starting out in a few cities and slowly broadening out as buzz builds on a title—survives today mainly as the operative model for quality adult fare, publicized and branded via reviews by critics at fall film festivals, and aiming at the extra promotional boost provided by award season attention.

For the studios, "give the people what they already want" was the new mantra.

Through the nineties and into the twenty-first century, Hollywood marketers decided that they were better off selling a beloved James Bond or Harry Callahan or Indiana Jones than a seven-figure-per-movie star like Tom Cruise in something no one ever heard of. Better still, they could make films based on established plays (*Mamma Mia!, Les Misérables*), movies (*The Wizard of Oz, Planet of the Apes*), comics (*Superman, Batman, Thor, X-Men, Fantastic Four, Iron Man, Captain America, The Avengers*), video games (*Resident Evil, Mortal Kombat*), toys and games (*Transformers, Battleship*), TV series (*Mission: Impossible, Star Trek*) and bestselling books and classics (*The Three Musketeers, Twilight, Robin Hood, Alice in Wonderland, The Lord of the Rings,* the Harry Potter series).

It comes down to this: an executive who lives in fear of losing his job won't take unnecessary risks. Only the most confident studio head with solid performers behind and ahead can gamble on failure. Which is why they need the security that multiple vital franchises provide.

Even the venerable James Bond series, which in 2012 celebrated its fiftieth birthday and twenty-third and possibly best-ever installment, Sam Mendes's *Skyfall*, originally sprang to life on the screen in 1962 with *Dr. No*, based on the popular Bond novels by British writer Ian Fleming. Bond is the model—a film franchise oft-imitated, from parody *Our Man Flint* to *xXx* to the Bourne series—developed and sustained first by producer Cubby Broccoli and then by his daughter Barbara Broccoli and stepson Michael Wilson. The family protected, nurtured, and modernized their sexy but deadly secret agent through six incarnations, from the most popular, Sean Connery, through the least, Timothy Dalton, to current 007 Daniel Craig. *Skyfall*, released November 9, 2012, became the highest-grossing film in the series, with $1.1 billion in the till worldwide.

Audiences today have an appetite for immersing themselves in exotic worlds like Middle-earth, Tatooine, and Pandora. Characters, not movie stars, are pulling them into theaters. That said, many of the most successful Hollywood franchises started as originals, including George Lucas's *Star Wars*, the *Die Hard* series, the Wachowskis' cyberpunk series *The Matrix*, and Dick Donner's *Lethal Weapon* to James Cameron's 2009 3-D film *Avatar*, which beat only his 1997 *Titanic* as the biggest global blockbuster of all time—thanks to 3-D premium ticket sales. That's what Hollywood often forgets in its never-ending search for the sure, sure thing.

Both *Titanic* and *Avatar* were seen as terrifying gambles. But each time, Twentieth Century Fox execs hung tough as Cameron's production budgets mounted, because he had a track record as a writer, director, and technological explorer able to deliver characters moviegoers could care about and eye-popping effects they had never seen before. That's the secret sauce.

For every Harry Potter, which eventually came to an end in 2011 after eight films and set an all-time franchise record with $7.7 billion in worldwide receipts, there are many others— *Eragon*, *The Last Airbender*, *R.I.P.D.*, *Max Payne*—that go nowhere.

In March 2012, two make-or-break franchises for their studios,

Disney's *John Carter* and Lionsgate's *The Hunger Games*, reached theaters. Both were based on preestablished bestsellers, but the *Hunger Games* trilogy was launched in 2008 by novelist Suzanne Collins and still flying off the shelves, whereas *John Carter* was based on *A Princess of Mars*, the first in a series of eleven pulp novels written by Tarzan creator Edgar Rice Burroughs, and launched in 1912. Remarkably, Burroughs's Mars novels are still in print and have inspired generations of writers and filmmakers since: their DNA is in both *Star Wars* and *Avatar*.

But it's one thing to believe that a book can launch a movie franchise and another to deliver it. Compare and contrast the respective fates of these two would-be blockbusters. Disney produced *John Carter* under inexperienced new studio chairman Rich Ross, who placed his trust in Pixar star director Andrew Stanton (*Finding Nemo, Wall-E*), who had never before directed a live-action movie. Neither of them knew what they were doing, and their lack of expertise combined to yield a disastrous $200 million write-off for Disney, the largest in Hollywood history.

On the other hand, fans of Collins's dystopian trilogy *The Hunger Games* were delighted with Lionsgate's faithful movie adaptation of the first installment in the still-bestselling young adult series, whose appeal spread over the years from high school girls and boys to their parents, both women and men. Reviewers raved about how well *Winter's Bone* star Jennifer Lawrence fit the similar role of tomboyish sixteen-year-old adult child Katniss Everdeen, who is athletic, resourceful, honest, and strong-minded. The movie, adapted and directed by Gary Ross (*Seabiscuit*), managed to walk a careful line, neither diluting nor sugarcoating the book, nor making the violence sensational or glamorized. Released March 23, *The Hunger Games* easily broke *Alice in Wonderland*'s $116 million March opening box-office record with $152.5 million and soared to $684 million worldwide.

And so one franchise was born, while the other met a different fate.

JOHN CARTER

John Carter had been in development for decades. Director John McTiernan (*Die Hard, The Hunt for Red October*) tried to mount it first at Disney in 1990. Then Paramount producer James Jacks (*The Mummy*) gave it a whirl with a series of directors: Guillermo del Toro, digital techno-whizzes Robert Rodriguez (*Spy Kids*) and Kerry Conran (*Sky Captain and the World of Tomorrow*), and, finally, Jon Favreau, who had shown off his directing chops in *Elf* and the space adventure *Zathura*.

But the project languished as Paramount went through a management shift; TV import Gail Berman came in to run the studio in 2005, and shortly before she left in 2007, she dumped the ambitious project, which carried a high cost and degree of difficulty. When Paramount did not renew their option on the rights with the Burroughs estate, Favreau moved on to direct Marvel blockbuster *Iron Man*.

Watching like a hawk the entire time was writer-director Andrew Stanton, forty, who had grown up on the Martian novels and had waited decades to grab the movie rights. Disney's then-chairman Dick Cook agreed to scoop them up in 2006 and green-lit a $250 million feature to be adapted and directed by Stanton. Disney eventually brought in writer Michael Chabon, the Pulitzer Prize–winning author, and Mark Andrews, Pixar's story supervisor for *The Incredibles*, who would later take Pixar's animated *Brave* to the Oscar finish line. But Stanton was in charge.

"When you're ten or eleven years old, and you've discovered girls, but they haven't discovered you yet," Stanton told the *Los Angeles Times,* "and you're reading about this ordinary guy that's suddenly extraordinary on another planet, he's got the coolest best friend, the coolest pet, and he's winning the heart of the most beautiful girl in the universe, that's like a checklist of everything you've ever wanted." Along the way, rather than confuse moviegoers with the girl-friendly title *A Princess of Mars,* and in order to boost its male appeal, the studio changed the title to *John Carter of Mars*. In this planetary romance, our hero is a Confederate soldier who is magically teleported from a Civil War battlefield to the surface of the desert planet Barsoom (Mars), where his superhuman strength turns him into a mighty warrior; he must vanquish many formidable foes so that he can win the heart of the magnificent Princess Dejah Thoris.

As it turned out, Disney, like Paramount, was also undergoing a change in stewardship. Three years after he acquired the property, marketing and distribution exec turned studio chief Cook, a thirty-year Disney veteran, made way for the new boss, Rich Ross, who was promoted from the Disney Channel by Walt Disney Company CEO Robert Iger.

As Disney movie studio chief, Ross never felt right to Hollywood. He had made his reputation in television molding teen stars like Miley Cyrus and Zac Efron into household names. Now Iger had tasked him with updating the Disney movie brand with the right mix of family-oriented fare. "The film business is changing before our very eyes," Ross wrote in an e-mail to his staff, "and we must all rise to the occasion to meet our consumers' changing needs." Six months later, in April 2010, the new Disney chairman put on a show-and-tell at Team Disney, the studio headquarters on the Burbank lot, to introduce himself to a group of about two dozen entertainment business beat reporters, including me; he wanted to alert Wall Street to a strong studio lineup in advance of an upcoming Disney earnings call.

Ramrod stiff and geekily awkward, Ross apologized for having been inaccessible, admitting that he had a lot to learn. He paced in front of a Disney screening room as he delivered a well-rehearsed sales pitch for a series of trailers, several clips, and a timeline of the studio's upcoming slate, and he let loose a lot of corporate-speak about brands and market quadrants and giving consumers what they want, which clearly was the new company line as the studio sought to narrow the gap between theatrical and DVD and VOD release windows and cross-pollinate a consistent marketing message across multiple platforms.

Ross showed us footage from Pixar's upcoming 2010 summer release *Toy Story 3,* which was adding Barbie and Ken to the familiar gang, and announced two more Pixar movies to come: Disney was scheduling Pixar's thirteenth film, *Brave,* for June 15, 2012, and a *Monsters, Inc.* sequel for November 15, 2012. Also, as the studio had just acquired Marvel, *The Avengers* would be coming on May 4, 2012.

In addition, the studio had just closed a deal to distribute the output from Steven Spielberg and Stacey Snider's DreamWorks, which, with financing from Indian company Reliance, had extricated itself from Paramount and was rapidly ramping up its slate to be released through Disney's Touchstone label. (Family actioner *Real Steel* starring Hugh Jackman was already under way.) Altogether, Ross was expecting to release fourteen to sixteen pictures a year, he told the group.

Jerry Bruckheimer (*Bad Boys, Top Gun*) was another key Disney tentpole supplier, whose costly vid-game-based visual-effects (VFX) action-adventure *Prince of Persia* and *Fantasia*-inspired live-action *The Sorcerer's Apprentice* starring Nicholas Cage would be coming that summer (and turn into major disappointments for Bruckheimer and the studio). Ross announced that his first green light was Bruckheimer's fourth installment in the lucrative *Pirates of the Caribbean* franchise, which was starting to film in London and Hawaii with Johnny Depp and an international cast including Penelope Cruz. (That $250 million movie, released in 2011, yielded $1 billion worldwide, most of it overseas, for a series total of $3.7 billion to date. Needless to say, a fifth is in the works.)

Occasionally some genuine enthusiasm slipped through Ross's corporate-speak, including for Sean Bailey's visually spectacular December 3-D sequel *Tron: Legacy* and for *Prom,* a coming-of-age high school story told in a John Hughes/Cameron Crowe vein that Ross called an authentic, honest look at teen life. He was also clearly impressed not only with the revenue stream from Tim Burton's *Alice in Wonderland,* but with its filmmaker's stop-motion black-and-white coming-of-age horror flick *Frankenweenie,* arriving in 2012. (The movie played better for the Academy and critics than it did for audiences.) Ross was upbeat as well about Jason Segel's upcoming live-action Muppet movie, which would prove a modest success.

Disney's 2011 slate was mainly composed of films from known labels and franchises that Ross had inherited from his predecessor. Ross had also inherited *John Carter,* which was projected for a 2012 release. The neophyte executive was in a tricky position, trying to put the best possible face on a project that had millions spent against it and Disney animation/Pixar powerhouse John Lasseter protecting his star director's flank.

Despite Andrew Stanton's crucial participation in such Pixar animated blockbusters as *Wall-E* and *Finding Nemo,* which combined had made $1.3 billion worldwide, giving the writer-director-animator a live-action movie like *John Carter* to supervise was a huge gamble. Pixar, a brilliant, slow-moving collective overseen by benevolent dictator Lasseter, who is considered by Hollywood to be the contemporary Walt Disney, was at the top of the animation heap with an enviable and unprecedented run of eleven blockbusters (*Toy Story 3* and *Brave* would become twelve and thirteen). The reason Pixar could deliver such consistent winners was threefold: they had top in-house animators who could always return to the drawing board, Lasseter could replace directors at will, and Pixar could rewrite and redo sections of a movie until they fired on all cylinders. Stanton was a vital part of a team that relied on rewrites, rough animation assemblages (animatics), and the constant changing of storylines until each film played perfectly.

Live action is altogether a different sort of beast. It relies on a single captain to make creative decisions, approving scripts, casting, designs, and visual effects—hopefully backed by experience, in the form of problem-solving producers. The director sits at the helm of a sprawling and expensive enterprise. Marshaling all these resources on location with sets, props, camera equipment, teamsters, actors, and extras—not to mention the ongoing painstaking visual effects pipeline—can cost millions of dollars per day. As soon as a movie gets a green light, the clock is ticking.

And *John Carter* was huge. The budget was $250 million, because Burroughs's exotic Mars landscape was crammed not only with palaces, warriors, weapons, and spacecraft, but with exotic alien creatures that needed to be designed. Not since *Star Wars* or *Avatar* had such a rich world been created from scratch.

It was always going to be a challenge to pull audiences into Burroughs's Martian fantasy world on the red planet Barsoom. Many readers of a certain age loved escaping into this exotic universe of warriors, princesses, and six-limbed Tharks, including Lucas and Cameron, who had already mined that territory themselves, bringing to the screen a new level of live action mixed with digital environments and multiple performance-capture characters.

As crucial as Stanton had been at Pixar, he had not established himself as a quality brand like Spielberg who pulls audiences into movie theaters. And *X-Men Origins: Wolverine* costars Taylor Kitsch and Lynn Collins, along with *Rome* costars Ciarán Hinds and James Purefoy, were hardly marquee names able to put butts in seats like Johnny Depp or Angelina Jolie.

Inexperienced Disney chief Ross was supervising a behemoth that was well under way, with millions already spent. And at the same time, under Iger's directives, he let go of many of Disney's experienced production, distribution, and marketing professionals. He had hired young producer Sean Bailey (*Tron: Legacy, Gone Baby Gone, The Core*) to run motion picture production, and advertising outsider M. T. Carney to run studio marketing. When the studio tested the movie's "materials" months before release—characters, title, designs—they did not play well with audiences. Burroughs's Martian novels are not as well known as his Tarzan series, which have fueled countless film and TV iterations over the decades. No one knew these books or characters beyond hardcore fans like Stanton who had grown up with comics based on the series. Younger generations were no longer familiar with the titles. Disney would have to reintroduce them, and build excitement about a new exotic world, Barsoom, as Cameron did for Pandora.

Ross was relying on a new marketing team run by Carney, who chose not to place the movie inside the proper obvious genre context, the male sci-fi fantasy universe, but instead, with so much investment on the line, took the mass-audience appeal-to-everyone approach. Disastrously, the marketers got rid of the most commercial element of the project by trimming the title *John Carter of Mars*—in order to avoid any association with the Bob Zemeckis–produced flop *Mars Loves Moms*—to *John Carter.* And fearful of the period dud *Cowboys & Aliens,* Disney stayed away from the film's western elements as well.

Whatever the strengths and weaknesses of outgoing studio chief Cook, he was an ace marketer who would never have so mishandled this campaign. *John Carter* was now generic: its stand-alone JC logo meant nothing, and even conjured up squirmy religious connotations. Disney then made another crucial error, opting not to promote the movie in advance to its prime demographic at the July 2011 Comic-Con, San Diego's gargantuan convention for sci-fi/fantasy and comic-book fans. Instead, Disney chose to give fans a first look at *John Carter* at their own family-friendly D23 Expo in August in Anaheim, where Stanton's show-and-tell on the movie bombed. It just didn't belong.

Clearly, Disney marketing didn't know how to brand *John Carter* and build fans for an elaborate new universe. While Stanton stayed true to Burroughs's century-old *Princess of Mars* novel, the fantasy adventure no longer carried mass recognition or appeal for contemporary audiences, and Disney failed to find a way to connect with them.

By the time *John Carter* finally opened on March 9, 2012, after three years in production, industry insiders and pundits had already called out the epic as a misfire. No studio picture had trumpeted "disaster" so loudly since Sony's misbegotten remake of *Godzilla* (1998) or Warner Bros.'s box-office bombs *Poseidon* (2006) and *Green Lantern* (2011). Stanton's deep passion for the material and reliance on thousands of VFX shots didn't preclude the movie from requiring eighteen days of reshoots. That telegraphed a problem film. And for a $250 million movie to open at $30 million for its first three days—with full-bore studio marketing salvos behind it—was shocking. And as a *New Yorker* profile on Stanton pointed out ahead of the release, *John Carter* would have to take in $700 million worldwide to make any money. That's a gross at the level of *Pirates of the Caribbean, Transformers,* or *Spider-Man.*

So Rich Ross did what every beleaguered studio boss has to do when under duress. In November 2011, four months before the movie's launch, he scapegoated his marketing head M. T. Carney and replaced her with Hollywood insider Ricky Strauss. He came into a tough situation and started to right the ship by admitting that, yes, the core target audience was male—young males, the ones who tune into the fanboy demo and should have been targeted at Comic-Con the previous summer. That was a start, and sure enough, Austin, Texas's webmaster to the fanboys, Harry Knowles, who had been a producer when James Jacks's *John Carter of Mars* was in development at Paramount, gave the film a rave on his *Ain't It Cool News* website.

When I saw *John Carter* at its LA Live premiere, I thought so many things might have been fixed by a more experienced studio production team. For the most part, Disney had let headstrong Stanton do his thing until he showed them a rough cut. The main story elements—gravity-enhanced jaded ex-soldier Carter (Kitsch), who can leap across the barren Barsoom landscape (Utah); his romance with spoiled Martian princess Dejah Thoris (Collins); his alliance with honorable Thark chief Tars Tarkas (voiced by Willem Dafoe); and various battles with Martian creatures and armies—played fairly well. Tellingly, the best thing in the movie was Carter's toothy pet Woola, who was animated.

But so much also went wrong. For starters, the film (which gained nothing from badly retrofitted 3-D) opened right in the middle of a confusing Martian air battle and took too long to bring Civil War vet Carter to red planet Barsoom. The crucial design of the green, nine-foot-tall, tusked, and four-armed Tharks was misguided (too much like Lucas's infamous digital misfire Jar Jar Binks), many of the large-scale air battles were murky and overpixelated, and Collins as the princess of Mars boasted an inexact Brit accent. These were fixable mistakes among myriad others, like exactly who among this motley crew you were supposed to root for. Finally, Stanton was so close to the material that he didn't know how to make this live-action film coherent and engaging.

The reviews did not help.

The *Hollywood Reporter*: "If 'Avatar' had never existed, it's possible that 'John Carter' would have seemed like more of a genre breakthrough. Although the result is quite a mishmash, dramatic coherence prevails over visual flair."

The Playlist: "'John Carter' is a mess. Strangely uninvolving and needlessly convoluted, 'John Carter' spends over two hours making the case for being a franchise, without ever really becoming a movie."

The damage had been done. Iger might have wanted to break his studio away from its hidebound traditions and practices. He had long been straining to move more swiftly into the digital future, taking full advantage of the studio's legacy and brand identification with audiences all over the world. That approach worked like a charm for Ross at the Disney Channel. But bringing too many outsiders into a movie studio often courts disaster. The rules of this world are too entrenched and arcane—the egos too sensitive, the need to be on top of the latest marketing trends too great—for there to be any margin for error. Smart as he was, Ross had too much to learn.

Although former Disney chief Michael Eisner, Bob Daly of Warner Bros., Columbia/Universal's Frank Price, and Paramount/Fox's Barry Diller were able to transition from television to movies, all were sharp enough to know what they didn't know and to surround themselves with talent who did. Most of the time it's a risky move—as it was at Paramount with NBC chief Brandon Tartikoff and, decades later, with Fox TV's Gail Berman. There, too, Paramount owner Sumner Redstone of Viacom charged his then lieutenant, MTV chief Tom Freston, with making radical changes at the studio and then threw the exec and others under the bus when the pace of change proved too fast. (Freston's biggest mistake: letting Twentieth Century Fox snag MySpace!) New Paramount chief Brad Grey jettisoned the old Paramount team and brought in Berman, who had been a television success, but wasn't able to navigate the shoals of the movie business. Even though buying DreamWorks didn't work out for Grey—the two companies kept fighting for territory—he saved his job as DreamWorks decamped by importing its executives and successful creative culture to buttress Paramount's flailing one.

Disney's Iger made his changes at a cost. In the wake of the biggest write-off in Hollywood history, that $200 million dollar Hoover Dam of red ink, Ross was forced to step down, citing a lack of passion for the job.

That's because *John Carter* was a tidal wave disaster that no studio chief could survive, even if he did inherit it. Truth is, *Carter* was surrounded by too few mitigating hits that Ross could claim—no one was going to give him credit for the inherited *Pirates of the Caribbean* sequel or *The Muppets*—and too many money-losers, from the worst films of producer Jerry Bruckheimer's career to Ross's own *The Prom*. In Hollywood, you can fire the head of marketing, as Ross did, letting go of Carney as the dimensions of the *John Carter* debacle became clear, but you can't escape the ax without some claim to success.

Disney's only Oscar traction under Ross's tenure came from Pixar's long-in-the-works *Toy Story 3* and Steven Spielberg and Stacey Snider's Tiffany boutique DreamWorks, which produced *The Help*, *War Horse*, and Visual Effects Oscar nominee *Real Steel*. But DreamWorks made clear it was miserable with Carney and her marketing team, and was pushing for more change. Iger needed someone with the authority to manage these high-octane star players.

He did not make the same mistake twice. Brought in to take

over the movie studio was a valuable piece of experienced talent who had run Warner Bros. for twelve years: seventyish Alan Horn, a well-regarded éminence grise who knew how to run a company, could take credit for the Harry Potter series and Warner's franchise strategy, and handle big creative egos and labels.

Horn came in just as Disney was poised to open two enormous blockbusters from studio labels over which Ross had little oversight—Marvel's *The Avengers* and Pixar's *Brave.* And Iger had another trick up his sleeve that played brilliantly on Wall Street: Disney scooped up the rights to the biggest franchise of all time, *Star Wars,* by buying George Lucas's Bay Area Lucasfilm for $4.05 billion. This was going to feed the theme parks, stores, and TV and film studios for decades to come.

Iger made it clear during a conference call after the October 30, 2012, announcement that he'd rather pay through the nose for an established brand than risk creating anything new. He was banking on longtime Spielberg producer Kathleen Kennedy, whom Lucas had already appointed as president of Lucasfilm when he retired, to take Lucas's blueprint for new *Star Wars* episodes and reinvent the series with fresh writers and directors. Kennedy was already prepared to reboot the movie franchise with the original cast, a script by *Toy Story 3* scribe Michael Arndt, and the director behind Paramount's successful *Star Trek* relaunch, J. J. Abrams. (Paramount's Grey was not happy when he heard the news.)

Star Wars: Episode VII is due for release in 2015. Disney will stick to its plan to release each year one to two Marvel films, one Pixar animated film, one Disney animated film, and four to six live-action films; *Star Wars* would take one of the annual live-action tentpole slots—and could be exploited in TV as well. Said Iger on the announcement conference call: "*Star Wars* is one of the great entertainment brands of all time."

With those headlines blazing, *John Carter* and Rich Ross were soon forgotten.

But *John Carter* did provide a super-size cautionary tale for other studio heads, who came to recognize that in today's viral media world, audiences can suss out a must-to-avoid pretty fast. Via mobile tweets and texts, bad word can make hundreds of millions of investment dollars disappear overnight. The studios saw that they'd better deliver audiences something eye-popping, or millions could go down the drain. It had become clear that while the conventional wisdom was that big-budget tentpoles tend to yield more profits than smaller pictures, they also carry more risks at escalating levels of production and marketing.

Several studios began pushing back films for reshoots and editing-room tinkering so that they could put their best foot forward. And if *John Carter* didn't persuade them, Universal's $220 million *Battleship* did. That was a movie that no one expected to be good—not even Universal—but somehow its production kept moving forward; the movie was developed by Hasbro Films, and the studio jumped on signing Peter Berg (*Friday Night Lights, Hancock*) when he threatened to leave for another project. Studio chiefs Adam Fogelson and Donna Langley considered killing it, but they didn't because the movie filled a needed slot in the studio's global film and TV distribution pipeline.

As these giant trains gain momentum, and tens of millions of dollars are invested, it becomes difficult to maneuver them, much less apply the brakes. And when the time came to create trailers and TV spots, the studio belatedly realized that the big VFX shots they were using to sell the movie too closely resembled another entrenched franchise, *Transformers,* also from Hasbro. One risk with franchises is winding up with something too familiar that audiences feel they have seen before and can afford to skip—like too-costly *Men in Black 3, Dark Shadows, The Amazing Spider-Man,* and a second *X-Men* film with "Wolverine" in the title.

Universal and Hasbro forgot that what makes a successful franchise work is not a name or title but an immersive world and characters that people care about. *Battleship,* which finally opened on May 18, 2012, to 41 percent rotten reviews on review aggregator

Rotten Tomatoes, had none of those things. The studio tried to mitigate the weak numbers by first opening overseas. It eked out a miserable $65.4 million domestically and $238 million foreign, resulting in a $150 million loss for the studio.

With bad word swirling on *John Carter* and *Battleship,* Paramount pushed back by a year its sequel *G.I. Joe: Retaliation,* starring Dwayne "The Rock" Johnson, to put in more time on making it 3-D and to beef up rising star Channing Tatum's role (total worldwide gross: $375.7 million). It did the same with its troubled $220 million zombie epic *World War Z,* starring Brad Pitt, which required a costly page-one rewrite and reshoot of its last forty minutes. Both came out better than they might have: *World War Z* even earned good reviews (total worldwide gross: $540 million). Similarly, Universal postponed the release of its beleaguered $200 million Keanu Reeves period martial arts actioner, *47 Ronin,* until December 2013. Whether or not the studios score a franchise, at these cost levels they can't afford to lose their shirts.

THE HUNGER GAMES

Just as Disney was announcing a $200 million write-off on *John Carter,* a new movie produced by ex-Disney production president Nina Jacobson was hitting big at the box office. A brilliant and openly gay story executive with stints at Universal and DreamWorks behind her, Jacobson was pushed out of Disney by Dick Cook in 2006 (as her partner happened to be giving birth to their third child). Since then indie producer Jacobson—who opted not to ally herself with a studio, preferring to go her own way project by project, in order to retain more control—had already spawned a successful franchise on her own at Fox (*Diary of a Wimpy Kid*) and produced Lone Scherfig's *One Day,* starring Anne Hathaway, at Focus Features.

Jacobson was author Suzanne Collins's handpicked choice to shepherd her *Hunger Games* trilogy to the big screen. Lionsgate, now merged with Summit and, because of its outstanding box-office performances, ranked by theater owners as "the seventh studio," spent $45 million in marketing and opened *The Hunger Games* on March 23 in 4,137 theaters, the studio's widest opening to date. It grossed $152.5 million its first weekend, at the time the third-biggest opening in history after *The Dark Knight* and *Harry Potter and the Deathly Hallows: Part 2*. (It's now in sixth place.) It was the best opening ever for a nonsequel, and by the end of 2013 the film ranked as the fourteenth highest-grossing movie of all time.

The Hunger Games is yet another case—like the Harry Potter films, *The Twilight Saga*, or *The Lord of the Rings*—where sticking to the material that excited readers in the first place is the right course. While Suzanne Collins may not be J. K. Rowling, Collins retained control by going with independent producer Jacobson, who lobbied the author hard in early 2009, soon after the first *Hunger Games* installment came out and well before it was a phenomenon. By the time the movie opened in 2012, the book had sold twenty-six million copies and been translated into twenty-six languages. The original three books have sold fifty million copies in the United States alone, and spent two hundred consecutive weeks on the bestseller list.

Together, Collins and Jacobson chose Lionsgate as the film's proper steward, all over the world. (Warner Bros./Spyglass and New Regency/Summit, also vying for the prize, might not have yielded such strong results.) Collins wrote the script, with Billy Ray (*Shattered Glass*) providing a polish. "It was about finding the bandwidth between two places," says Jacobson. "If you failed, you were at risk of missing the point of the book, or worse, guilty of the sins committed in the book."

Crucially, the *Hunger Games* team hired skilled writer-director Gary Ross (*Dave, Pleasantville*), a genuine fan who had been introduced to the material by his kids and also chased the project, following Jacobson to London to give her his pitch and later presenting an elaborate video show-and-tell for Lionsgate. Jacobson leaned on indie producer Jon Kilik (*Babel*) to run production on this large VFX movie on a responsible scale. Jacobson's previous film, *One Day,* had a $15 million budget, and the *Wimpy Kid* series was also made for a modest amount. "I know what I don't know," Jacobson says. "There's no substitute for hands-on experience."

Shot in North Carolina with generous tax rebates, *The Hunger Games* wound up with a reasonable $80 million price tag. Lionsgate's departing chief Joe Drake, who has substantial production and distribution experience; production exec Alli Shearmur; and marketing czar Tim Palen were on board every step of the way. Jacobson felt supported but not second-guessed, she says.

Ross carried the movie to completion without losing track of the characters or going over the top with grandiose visuals, as many filmmakers would have been tempted to do. "He's a smart, thoughtful, and inspired filmmaker," Jacobson says. "Lionsgate gave him the room to succeed. So frequently things get lost in translation. With a great filmmaker with a great script you can get Chris Nolan to make *The Dark Knight.* There's often so much fear and second-guessing that there's not a chance for a real voice to emerge and engage the audience."

The filmmakers cast the roles well, choosing Liam Hemsworth (*Paranoia*) and Josh Hutcherson (*The Kids Are All Right*) for the young male leads and, for the supporting adults, selecting *Deadwood*'s Paula Malcomson, along with the eclectic cast of colorful characters from the film's uber-glamorous Games site, the Capitol: Lenny Kravitz, Woody Harrelson, Elizabeth Banks, and Stanley Tucci. Every young actress was eager to land the crucial lead role of tough but tender archer Katniss Everdeen.

During her audition, Jennifer Lawrence clinched the deal with the scene in which Katniss says good-bye to sister Prim. "It was so definite and decisive," says Jacobson. "Game over. Nobody could touch her. We were crying. She's an unusually gifted actress. There was no way we were going to cast anyone else in that part. She brings authenticity, humanity, and accessibility. The movie relies on her to an extraordinary degree."

The most dramatic changes from book to film, however, have to do with the shift from a story told strictly from the point of view of our heroine to a movie where scenes that she does not know about unfold away from her. This makes *The Hunger Games* more of a social issue movie, and its humanity-fights-fascism message more heavy-handed than the book. But it works to turn dictator Coriolanus Snow (Donald Sutherland) and his rule-changing Games henchman Seneca Crane (Wes Bentley) into movie bad guys.

The film efficiently establishes Everdeen's world in District 12, in the postapocalyptic North America now known as Panem. Her home is hardscrabble poor, like a depressed Appalachian coal-mining town. She's the main support of her widowed mom (Malcomson) and younger sister (Willow Shields). She and friend Gale (Liam Hemsworth) are chums who feed their families by hunting and trapping in the woods together using bows and arrows. At the annual tribute day, when the country's children are subject to a televised lottery in which one boy and one girl aged twelve to eighteen are selected from a dozen districts to compete in a nationally transmitted battle in which only one will survive, Katniss steps in to replace her sister. She is joined in the seventy-fourth annual Hunger Games by baker's son Peeta (Hutcherson), who was once kind to her when she was starving.

The train trip to the intoxicating Emerald City—er, Capitol—introduces their drunk "mentor" (Harrelson), a Games winner who counsels them on how to survive and win. We are invested in what Katniss is going through as we enter the decadent overscale metropolis, with its *Truman Show* audience and Olympic Games spectacle. "We wanted it to be more ominous," says Jacobson, "not magical and wonderful but intimidating and frightening, freak-show-ish."

"Happy Hunger Games, and may the odds be ever in your favor," intones President Snow. "In two weeks twenty-two of you will be dead." Katniss does what she does in the sci-fi survival adventure—killing in self-defense, playing up her budding romance with Peeta to ubiquitous TV cameras—not for civic pride or political motives but to win the Games so that she can go home to her sister. That is what is at stake. The Games transform her; over the course of the series, Katniss matures into a more evolved leader of other people.

Jacobson and Ross leaned on an experienced team, many of them indies, from Kilik and Oscar-winning music supervisor T-Bone Burnett to French editor Juliette Welfling (*The Diving Bell and the Butterfly, A Prophet*), who tag-teamed with Stephen Mirrione, a frequent collaborator with Steven Soderbergh. Ross shot the film knowing how it would be edited, with jump cuts off handheld cameras and bobbing close-ups, to intensify Katniss's POV. "We were inspired by Juliette's work," says Jacobson. It was also cheaper to run and gun in the woods and save expensive dolly and crane shots for the cityscapes.

There was never any question that the movie would be anything but PG-13. Ross depicts the film's extreme violence without showing too much or getting gratuitous with it. In the end, Jacobson is proud that she did not mess up the book: "I love it and didn't want to let people or Suzanne down. I worried a lot about that."

Lionsgate, which developed and released *The Hunger Games*, was in many ways following the model set by another rising independent studio, Summit Entertainment, which developed and released the young adult *Twilight Saga* based on the Stephenie Meyer novels—and which merged with Lionsgate just as the series was about to end with *Breaking Dawn—Part II*.

Experienced foreign sales chief Patrick Wachsberger is a genial Frenchman who expanded Summit into a full-blown studio with his partner, former Warner and Paramount exec Rob Friedman, a wily, clear-eyed administrator with a shock of white hair who understands marketing, distribution, and production. The two combine sophisticated know-how with die-hard conservatism and occasional risk-taking. They sold Summit at its peak and made a deal to take over Lionsgate's worldwide motion picture operations.

Having impeccably pushed the *Twilight* franchise through its paces—carrying Summit to profits it could never have achieved without it—the new Lionsgate team swiftly pushed forward with development and production on the next two *Hunger Games* books. With Ross opting out of a rushed follow-up, the company brought in Francis Lawrence (*Water for Elephants*) to direct three sequels; the first one, *Catching Fire,* opened November 22, 2013, to be followed by the two *Mockingjay* installments in 2014 and 2015. Jacobson, in order to protect her position with Friedman, who had thrown director Catherine Hardwicke off the second *Twilight* movie, went to her friend, Hollywood power broker Skip Paul, who has known Friedman for years. He took the initiative to help them get to know each other so that Friedman would know the movies were in good hands. (She also had author Collins in her corner.)

The Hunger Games couldn't be more vital to Lionsgate's future. But the studio doesn't rest on its laurels, proceeding apace with two franchise candidates presented at Comic-Con in July 2013: Orson Scott Card's sci-fi classic *Ender's Game,* starring Harrison Ford and Ben Kingsley as two adults training a team of young warriors who must save the world from alien attack, and *Divergent,* based on Veronica Roth's young adult bestseller set in a dystopian Chicago, starring Kate Winslet, Brit hunk Theo James, and Shailene Woodley (*The Descendants*).

Every studio is banking on its stable of franchise properties going forward. Here's what they've got:

Disney, which has become a fiend for mega-mergers, now owns all *Star Wars* characters, every Pixar creation, the Muppets, Winnie the Pooh, and many Marvel characters (like Iron Man and the Avengers), with the exception of Spider-Man and Ghost Rider (see Sony), and the X-Men and the Fantastic Four (see Fox). Disney is in a strong position, as it also has powerful creative players in place, such as Lucasfilm's Kathleen Kennedy and Marvel's Kevin Feige, to supervise the ongoing execution of the films.

Warner Bros. owns DC Comics and its stable of characters (think cash-cow Batman, and Superman) and all Looney Tunes characters. But Warner has had mixed results with DC, which has never found its equivalent to Marvel chief Feige, and animation is not its strong suit (see *Space Jam*). The gift that kept on giving, Harry Potter, is no more. Christopher Nolan is done with Batman, and so is Christian Bale. After motion picture chief Jeff Robinov entrusted Zack Snyder, Nolan, and David S. Goyer with the not entirely successful reboot *Man of Steel* ($391 million worldwide), starring Henry Cavill, Robinov left his job, having clashed with new boss Kevin Tsujihara. At Comic-Con 2013, Warner announced that Goyer and Snyder were developing a Superman-Batman movie, and cast Ben Affleck as their older and wiser Dark Knight. The fans, all too predictably, wailed in protest.

MGM rules the character shires of *The Hobbit,* James Bond, and *RoboCop,* but shares the spoils with its partners Eon and Sony (Bond and *RoboCop*) and New Line/Warner (*The Hobbit*). While *Skyfall* is the biggest Bond film ever, it remains to be seen how avid the global appetite is for not one, but three returns to Middle-earth.

Paramount lost its Marvel deal and struggled with Hasbro's postponed *G.I. Joe: Retaliation,* and there's a question about how many more *Transformers* pixels audiences can absorb. J. J. Abrams masterminded still-vital *Mission: Impossible* and *Star Trek* iterations, but for the time being has moved on to Disney's *Star Wars.* With Dream-Works Animation gone, Paramount really needs these franchises to deliver. Disney's Lucasfilm and DreamWorks' Steven Spielberg could revisit Paramount's *Indiana Jones* franchise, but it seems dormant for now.

Twentieth Century Fox rules over the *Planet of the Apes* (which came back strong with *Rise of the Planet of the Apes* and will be followed soon by *Dawn of the Planet of the Apes*); the less profitable *Alien/Prometheus* franchise; Marvel's X-Men and Fantastic Four; and James Cameron's *Avatar.* With longtime cochairman Tom Rothman gone, Fox brought original director Bryan Singer back to the X-Men series for *Days of Future Past*, which combines his older ensemble with their younger counterparts. Though many think Singer desecrated *Superman Returns,* the truth is that Warner was angrier at his out-of-control spending (budget: more than $250 million) than the respectable grosses ($391 million worldwide). We'll see if he's on his best behavior at Fox. Cameron has always worked closely with now solo studio chairman Jim Gianopulos, and three pricey VFX-bending 3-D *Avatar* sequels are in progress.

Sony has the popular Spider-Man, which they expensively remounted with director Marc Webb as *The Amazing Spider-Man* to respectable returns. His sequel is in the pipeline, with Jamie Foxx playing the villain Electro. The studio also has the less popular Ghost Rider. *Men in Black 3* was a costly sequel, and *Ghostbusters* has long proved too expensive to profitably relaunch. *The Girl with the Dragon Tattoo* franchise could pay off in the long run if the studio can keep prices down on subsequent iterations without perfectionist David Fincher.

Universal has rights to all Universal Monsters (this includes Wolf Man, Frankenstein, and the Mummy), plus the revved-up *Fast & Furious* series and Jason Bourne. Tony Gilroy delivered a solid Jeremy Renner–starring Bourne film, but the studio needs to lure back Matt Damon. They're going with Renner for the next one—to be helmed by *Fast & Furious* czar Justin Lin. They had a good run with *The Mummy* (with another sequel ramping up), but *The Wolfman* was a bust.

"The truth is, a huge hit can cover a number of mistakes," says ex–Universal cochairman Adam Fogelson. "And most, but not all, huge hits come from big bets. What's more, even mid-level performance from a tentpole film has some real value—driving international TV deals, theme park opportunities, sequels, etc. Unfortunately, mid-level performance from a tentpole is no longer a remotely reliable outcome. No matter how much you spend to make and market a film, if people don't like what they see, they won't come. And that new reality is having repercussions throughout the industry."

CHAPTER 3

SPRING: CINEMACON, SXSW, AND THE MOVE TO DIGITAL

2012 is the year that the word "film" officially becomes an anachronism.

The forces that combine to put celluloid on the endangered list come together in April at CinemaCon, the annual convention mounted at Caesars Palace in Las Vegas by the National Association of Theater Owners (NATO), which represents some 30,000 movie screens in the United States and cinemas in fifty countries worldwide. About five thousand people—NATO exhibitors, major studio chiefs and key marketing staff, independent producers and distributors, concessionaires, agents, and trade press—congregate for four days and nights to review the past and get a glimpse of the future. Longtime partners, the majors and exhibitors have historically struggled in their symbiotic relationship, but cannot thrive without cooperating. That partnership has never been more fractured than it is now, as their mutual interests are no longer the same.

The CinemaCon annual rituals are simple: the major studios display their wares via show reels and fly a few stars into Las Vegas by company jet. The stars understand that the theater owners are their bread and butter: the work that they do to sell movies locally to moviegoers helps to build actors' careers. Thus, at CinemaCon 2013, Adam Sandler comes out onstage—trumpeted by Roman soldiers in tunics and breastplates and sandals—to promote Sony's *Grownups 2*. "It's a fucking four-quadrant movie," Sandler exhorts the theater owners in the Colosseum at Caesars Palace. "Let's get it done, motherfuckers!"

Joining Sandler in Las Vegas are Brad Pitt, Harrison Ford, Ben Stiller, Melissa McCarthy, Sandra Bullock, Chris Pine, Zachary Quinto, Kevin Hart, and Vin Diesel, among others, which is one reason why more media outlets than ever want to track the goings on.

Truth is, the four-quadrant movie—that plays young, old, male, and female—is pretty hard to come by.

And the star system that defined Hollywood for most of its history is not what it once was either. Aging stars like Ford, Mel Gibson, and Arnold Schwarzenegger no longer command $25 million paydays; they're reduced to costarring with Sylvester Stallone in *The Expendables 3*. Will Smith, Tom Hanks, Bruce Willis, and Tom Cruise still mean something if they star in a familiar franchise like *Men in Black, The Da Vinci Code, Die Hard,* or *Mission: Impossible,* but outside those parameters, they no longer guarantee a huge opening. As James Bond, Jack Ryan, and Batman prove, audiences fall for characters more than the stars who play them, who are endlessly replaceable.

Like everyone else, theater owners and studios are dealing with the shift to digital, which has radically changed everything about how movies are produced and released. The Internet gives and takes away, competing for eyeballs with so much noisy content—video games, social media, streaming, downloads, video on demand—that studios and theaters need to be smart about reaching consumers and luring them to the multiplex.

THE CHANGE BEGINS

For the first time since the move to sound in 1929, Hollywood has been going through a seismic technological change. For a hundred years, 35-millimeter film was the gold standard. Movies were shot in various celluloid formats, processed with photochemicals, and projected in movie theaters by throwing powerful beams of light through film onto a giant white screen. Until the past few years, studios spent millions annually creating film negatives, striking 35-millimeter prints, and shipping them by the reel in heavy cans to theaters, where they were loaded onto reel-to-reel projectors.

Most moviegoers are unaware of the industry's slow move to digital. In the 1990s, analog magnetic sound recording and mixing—added to celluloid on magnetic strips—gradually gave way to digital sound recording and mixing, added to film on optical strips or synced to accompanying compact discs. This was followed by the replacement of editing on flatbed Moviolas or Steenbecks, literally cutting and splicing pieces of film together, with Avid digital editing systems. Eventually negative cutting gave way to the creation of a digital intermediate, where instead of complex chemical-dipping color-timing techniques, the digital "painting" of the image, used on such films as the Coen brothers' gold-tinted *O Brother, Where Art Thou?*, became routine.

It took far longer for the quality of high-definition (HD) digital video cameras to catch up to superior 35-millimeter cameras, which required cameramen to reload ten-minute film magazines. Film was expensive, so time was precious. And every day, the filmmakers would wait to get back the "dailies" of the previous day's shooting. In the documentary *Side by Side,* David Fincher describes feeling the day-after "betrayal of dailies" as he watched reels of film from the previous day's shooting that did not turn out the way they were planned. He is among many directors who have cheered the slow improvement in the quality of digital cameras, which can run for forty minutes, from the Sony Camcorder to 2005's widely accepted Red digital camera, followed by the Arriflex.

Both George Lucas and director of photography Anthony Dod Mantle (who shot the Danish Dogma film *The Celebration* in HD) prefer the accuracy of the instant playback that digital provides. What you see is what you get. "That's exactly the way it's going to be in a movie theater," says Lucas. Even 35-millimeter diehards like Oliver Stone prefer the pristine consistency of digital projection over worn, scratched prints. Eventually, the disruptive technology became accepted by the establishment. When director Danny Boyle hired Mantle to run through Mumbai holding small gyro-stabilized cameras for 2008's *Slumdog Millionaire,* the Academy awarded Mantle the first Cinematography Oscar for a digitally shot film.

Many major directors refuse to go digital: Paul Thomas Anderson shot his post–World War II drama *The Master* on 70 millimeter, but when the time came to release it in September 2012, he was hunting for theaters around the country equipped with 70-millimeter projectors. Most were not, so the film was either shown in 35 or digitally. He's shooting his next for Warner on 35 millimeter.

Christopher Nolan still shoots in 35 millimeter, with increasing swatches filmed with IMAX cameras. His concession to bigness is to have his films, from *Inception* and *The Dark Knight Rises* to his next, *Interstellar,* blown up into the giant IMAX digital format. But while 2012's *The Dark Knight Rises* was shot on celluloid, it was shown digitally in most theaters.

That transition took longer still, because installing digital projectors in theaters required massive and costly upgrades. Each digital projector cost from $50 to $150,000 to install, depending on quality and complexity, from lower-resolution 2K (2048×1080 or 2.2 megapixels) to 4K (4096×2160 or 8.8 megapixels). Theater chains began slowly adding digital projectors starting in 1999.

The studios had a major incentive for wanting to save money on prints and shipping: fifteen hundred dollars to print and ship each movie to some four thousand theaters around the country costs them millions a year. But even the biggest theater chains, which were prepared to go digital, balked at paying for the massive upgrades themselves. It took years, but in 2005, Disney, Paramount, Sony, Twentieth Century Fox, Universal, and Warner Bros. created a set of financing instruments—called Digital Cinema Initiatives—that they could fund in order to assist theaters to upgrade to digital projectors.

A 3-D REVOLUTION

The studio wedge with exhibitors—the real engine of the switchover to digital—was 3-D. As competition from cable, television, music, and video games increased, and marketing dollars skyrocketed as the studios tried to make enough noise with louder and bigger event movies, they needed to find exciting eye candy to lure audiences to the multiplex.

Early promoters of 3-D, which had become more viable with computer-driven digital technology, were tech whizzes Lucas, James Cameron, and Bob Zemeckis, who schlepped to the NATO convention in Las Vegas back in 2005 (with Peter Jackson appearing at the convention on video) to coax the exhibitors into making the move to digital. Lucas was an early adopter of digital cameras and computer-graphic environments at Lucasfilm, and announced that he would reformat the *Star Wars* trilogy in 3-D, starting the lucrative trend of 3-D rereleases in advance of DVD reissues.

Jackson, Cameron, and Zemeckis, all pioneers in CG visual effects, could see where the future was headed. It was in 2004 that Zemeckis's innovative live-action/animation hybrid *The Polar Express* was released in IMAX 3-D at sixty-six IMAX locations and in 2-D at 3,600 other theaters. Exhibitors noted that, remarkably, the IMAX screens delivered fully 25 percent of the total gross. For *Man of Steel*'s 2013 opening weekend in North America they delivered 12 percent.

Disney helped lead the way with 2005's 3-D animation feature *Chicken Little,* which was an expensive experiment at the time. Just three years later, the studio's *Hannah Montana & Miley Cyrus: Best of Both Worlds Concert* was a surprise hit in 3-D, as was the animated feature *Bolt.* Add several well-grossing B-horror flicks, and theater owners saw the light: they could make more money by charging premium ticket prices. That turned the tide.

In 2009, Cameron's global blockbuster *Avatar* was shot in 3-D with special side-by-side stereoscopic cameras designed by the filmmaker and Vince Pace. It was soon followed by Tim Burton's reformatted 2010 *Alice in Wonderland,* which also made scads of money in 3-D. Then the studios promptly churned out a surge of trashy 3-D movies, many of them cheaply reformatted after they were shot, such as *Clash of the Titans,* which served to dampen audience appetites for the new fad. The bloom was soon off the rose.

Plenty of moviegoers hate 3-D. Filmmakers know that they can get an easy roar of approval from the crowd at Comic-Con panels by disparaging the 3-D format. Their complaints? The premium ticket cost, the pesky glasses, and the darker screen (theaters often allow as much as a 30 percent reduction in image brightness to save money).

During the next three years, the studios had settled into a better sense of when to deploy 3-D, from high-end animation and comic-book movies to low-brow eye-poking genre fare. And filmmakers started to figure out that 3-D was a clever way to score higher budgets from studios. In 2011, even Steven Spielberg, who loves shooting in 35 millimeter, decided to learn the 3-D ropes via his collaboration with Peter Jackson on the performance-capture family film *The Adventures of Tintin,* and Martin Scorsese significantly advanced the art of 3-D with his Oscar-winning *Hugo.*

At CinemaCon in 2012, Ang Lee wows exhibitors with the first footage from his upcoming *Life of Pi*. The footage from the movie, three and a half years in the making, is nothing short of stunning and instantly generates Oscar talk. When I interview him, Lee admits that the picture might not have gotten funded if he hadn't come up with the idea of shooting the movie as a 3-D VFX epic— well before the release of *Avatar*. But that wasn't the only reason the film was stalled so long. Before 2008 the technology simply hadn't existed to achieve the tiger-in-the-lifeboat aspects of Yann Martel's 2001 bestseller about an Indian boy surviving alone on the high seas (seven million copies sold). He reminds me that this is just the beginning of learning how to use this 3-D technology.

Fox cochairmen Tom Rothman and Jim Gianopulos tell the CinemaCon 2012 exhibitors that *Life of Pi* combines their substantial R & D on *Avatar* and *Rise of the Planet of the Apes* with Lee's artistry. (Both real and CG tigers were used.) "It's an attempt to put you in an emotional space," Lee says at the presentation. An Oscar contender is born.

At an exhibitor luncheon program held during the convention, Lee and Scorsese compare notes on the aesthetics of 3-D, revealing how individual each director's approach to the technology can be. As each one discovers and pushes the limits of this filmmaking tool, which Scorsese suggests could become as "normal" as color, he or she reinvents it for his or her own use. Lee and Scorsese discuss the use of foreground and close-up, immersion and intense drama. Lee, for one, says he kept pulling his actors back. And Scorsese, a total convert to what he now considers to be the dominant new medium, makes it clear that he intends to shoot his future films in 3-D whenever he can. "There is something that 3-D gives to the picture that takes you into another land, and you stay there, and it's a good place to be," he says.

3-D seems right for a film as epic as *Life of Pi,* which features a ship in a violent storm, a zebra leaping into a lifeboat, Pi underwater watching his family sinking into the depths, and Pi's power struggles at sea with the tiger, not to mention a scene involving thousands of flying silver fish. Intimate drama, however, may not be the right place to use 3-D. In the right hands, 3-D works magic—Cameron spent $17 million to retrofit *Titanic,* and it looked superb. But I am not the only one skeptical of the CinemaCon footage of Baz Luhrmann's adaptation of *The Great Gatsby,* a movie that shows no signs of anyone pulling back. Sure enough, Warner Bros. later postpones the literary drama's opening from the high-profile December 2012 award season to a more forgiving summer 2013 berth. (It's a smart move; in that context, the film is decently reviewed and scores with audiences to the tune of $331 million worldwide without facing awards scrutiny. Remembering that theaters hang onto about half the gross, that's still not enough to make back the more than $200 million in production and marketing costs from theatrical revenues.)

At Fox's CinemaCon show-and-tell, the studio—just like everyone else—demonstrates it is surging full-steam ahead on 3-D movies, from *Prometheus, Abraham Lincoln: Vampire Hunter,* and *The Wolverine* to the animated *Ice Age: Continental Drift* and many more titles to follow.

Meanwhile, Warner Bros. uses CinemaCon to introduce another technological advance via Peter Jackson's new *Lord of the Rings* prequel *The Hobbit,* the first installment of a planned trilogy. The film was shot at the new super-fast rate of 48 frames per second (fps)—twice as fast as the standard 24. Digital cameras and projectors make this possible, although exhibitors need to enhance the software on their 3-D projectors to handle 48 fps, at about $10,000 per projector. The main boosters of this technology, Cameron and Jackson, promise that 48 fps—or faster—offers a crisp viewing experience, free of any motion artifacts such as image vibrating or juttering, shuddering, or other familiar 24 fps anomalies.

But exhibitors and media resist. Many say that the super-clear ten minutes of footage—especially the exterior sunlit scenes—look like lousy TV video. Later in July, at the fanboy convention Comic-Con in San Diego, Jackson admits that the bad reaction in Las Vegas convinced him not to present *The Hobbit* footage in 48 fps until he could show filmgoers the entire film in 3-D. Cameron had encountered similar resistance to early marketing shots of the blue aliens in *Avatar*, which only came to believable life within the 3-D world of the fictitious planet Pandora. At $237 million, *Avatar* was not only the most expensive but the highest-grossing film of all time (thanks to premium 3-D tickets), setting a high standard for 3-D films; Cameron had hoped to shoot his three sequels with a high frame rate. But *The Hobbit* at 48 fps never took off. As a concession to Jackson, Warner released *The Hobbit* on December 14 using the new format in just 450 theaters out of 4,000. The studio plans to release both *Hobbit* sequels (*The Desolation of Smaug* in 2013, *There and Back Again* in 2014) in at least some theaters in the new format.

Digital screen conversions took off between 2009 and 2010, when the number of global d-screens exploded from 16,000 to 36,000. Older projectionists were replaced by technicians who knew how to navigate the world of DVDs and Blu-rays, servers and Digital Cinema Packages (DCPs), delivered as conventional computer hard drives in plastic cases, or via satellite or fiber-optic broadband with protective time-limited decryption keys. Unfortunately, the new digital technology causes far more delays and problems, especially when used in high volume at time-sensitive film festivals, than old-fashioned mechanical projectors ever did—they were easily fixed. It's still a shock, in any case, to see a projectionist at the Pacific Theatres at the Grove in Los Angeles start a film by punching an iPad.

"Simply put," the NATO spokesman John Fithian tells lagging exhibitors at CinemaCon 2012, "if you don't make the decision to get on the digital train soon, you will be making the decision to get out of the business."

By and large the conversion process was completed by the biggest theater chains in time for the studios' late 2012 deadline, when their financial aid to theaters would end. In fact, Twentieth Century Fox declared in a November letter to exhibitors that it would soon no longer supply 35-millimeter prints to theaters: "The date is fast approaching when 20th Century Fox and Fox Searchlight will adopt the digital format as the only format in which it will theatrically distribute its films . . . We strongly advise those exhibitors that have not yet done so to take immediate steps to convert their theaters to digital projection systems."

While some indie distributors were still supplying a few 35-millimeter prints, as well as digital "prints," to smaller indie art houses and mom-and-pop theaters, by 2012 the changeover to digital was pretty much complete. The recession has made it tough for small houses that can't afford the changeover, and it has gotten harder for indie theaters to obtain 35-millimeter prints. Even overseas, digital has taken over in all but the poorest recession-hit countries. One last edge that 35 millimeter has over digital is in the area of film preservation. Many filmmakers try to sock away a 35-millimeter print of their films for safekeeping, as digital formats demand constant, expensive upgrading to the latest system.

While the theater chains are unified in their mission to hang onto moviegoers for dear life, the studios have their own conflicting agendas. They are well aware that they have many more distribution options than ever before: the global theatrical market is just the most crucial and potentially lucrative.

And the studios watched the music business lose its profit margins to rampant piracy, which was about consumers wanting to consume what they wanted when they wanted, for free, mostly. The music companies ignored for too long the signs of changing demand. It took Apple chief Steve Jobs to radically alter the economic model and devise a profitable way of selling music to buyers by the download.

Luckily for the Hollywood studios, digital piracy of feature films required far more bandwidth and was more difficult to accomplish—for a while. The question was, would the studios bend to consumer demand, giving them what they wanted, or hang on for dear life to their tried-and-true—and lucrative—ancillary windows, which required movie fans to either go to theaters or wait months for video on demand and DVD?

Here's the old paradigm: premiere a movie in theaters, then make it available three or four months later at a high premium cost via VOD, then sell and rent DVDs, then show it on pay cable, and then make it available on broadcast television all over the world.

The theaters were happy because they were the sole venue for selling movies for three to four months. They wanted a space of time so that moviegoers wouldn't think, "Oh, I'll just wait for cable." The studios were happy because they could collect revenues from every stream. But piracy was growing all over the world and eating into revenues, no matter how vigilant the fight against in-theater camcorders. Hence more studios started to favor opening films in theaters around the world ahead, or at the same time as North America, to cut that risk; 3-D was another hedge against copying.

Meanwhile, studio DVD revenues continued to plateau after the 2008 recession, when consumers stopped stocking their home video libraries. And Netflix somewhat clumsily began to encourage its customers to subscribe not only to rent DVDs via their signature returnable red envelopes, but to stream online as well. In 2012, Netflix changed the conversation entirely, competing with television directly by producing its own high-end programming. (In March 2013, after Netflix made available the entire season of David Fincher's $60 million, thirteen-episode remake of the Brit series *House of Cards*—relocated to Washington, D.C., and starring Kevin Spacey, Robin Wright, and Kate Mara—the company's stock soared and subscription services like HBO, along with the mighty networks, faced increased consumer demand for binge-viewing, the ability to watch an entire season all at once.)

Consumers, thanks to such independent companies as Magnolia Pictures and IFC Films, both owned by cable operators, were getting used to being able to download and stream via Netflix, iTunes, Hulu, TiVo, Roku, Playstation 3, and Amazon. They could even watch premium subscription VOD on their local cable system weeks before a movie hit theaters.

THE $ 11 BILLION YEAR

Every year CinemaCon rolls out the $100 Million Reel; it's a tradition to remind the exhibitors of the movies that scored in their theaters. The 2012 compilation that was shown in 2013 ran clips from the top-grossing films that totaled over $100 million domestically, from the animated originals *Brave* and *Wreck-It Ralph* and Spielberg's biopic *Lincoln* to three franchise movies—*The Avengers, The Dark Knight Rises,* and *The Hunger Games*—that broke the $400 million domestic barrier. Of the top twenty-six films of 2012, nineteen were based on some other property, eight were sequels, four were comic-book franchises, two were remakes, two were prequels, and seven were originals. (See charts at the back of the book.)

Among the $100 million gang, there was a wide range, with the PG-13 rating faring best, followed by PG. Sounding a familiar gong at CinemaCon 2013, NATO's Fithian asks the studios to make "more family-friendly fare." Eight of the $100 million films were R-rated. "Give more choices to all ages," he says. One of the reasons 2012 broke records was because there were more G, PG, and PG-13 "spread over the calendar."

Fithian cites Universal as a model for releasing films away from summer and holiday peak periods. The Denzel Washington and Ryan Reynolds original CIA thriller *Safe House* came out in February, Illumination's animated *Lorax* in March, and Tony Gilroy's rebooted franchise *The Bourne Legacy* in August. "Off months bring huge returns," Fithian says. "Distribution in the off months produced higher returns than the holiday period." He also begs for more films aimed at women and Hispanics, a growing frequent moviegoing segment, using as examples the *Twilight* series, *Brave,* and *The Hunger Games.*

Universal cochairman Adam Fogelson is only too happy to join in the chorus of how well Universal did in 2012. It was their biggest year domestically, internationally, and overall. He points out that they didn't do this with one towering blockbuster; in fact, they survived a $150 million write-off on *Battleship*. Nonetheless, six films made the $100 million club, and eight passed $200 million globally. They did this with a diversity of films turning into events, and with a range of stories to tell.

Ted was the largest-grossing R-rated comedy globally, and Mark Wahlberg's biggest hit to date. *Pitch Perfect* was a sleeper hit musical aimed at the *Glee* set, the fourth-biggest digital download in 2012. At $441.8 million worldwide, Oscar winner *Les Misérables* was a global musical hit second only to Universal's own musical *Mamma Mia!* on the all-time list.

THE PESKY TIMETABLE

Fogelson, forty-five, has been trying to convince exhibitors that changing the economic paradigm is in everyone's best interest. Back in 2011 he tried to perform a premium video on demand (PVOD) experiment with the Brett Ratner comedy *Tower Heist,* starring Eddie Murphy and Ben Stiller, by making it available three weeks after the November 4 opening via high-priced video on demand—targeting moviegoers who crave earlier access to new releases. Exhibitors and filmmakers from James Cameron to Jon Favreau are fighting to keep the theatrical window at an average of ninety days, while several studios are pushing back, under pressure to move toward a shortened window of sixty to seventy-five days.

Several theater chains, including Cinemark and Regal, refused to book *Tower Heist,* especially over the Thanksgiving holiday, which pushed Universal to abandon course. The studio could have gone straight to video and skipped theaters, but that was not the head-to-head collision it had in mind. Fogelson had hoped he had paved the way with exhibitors, all of whom were alerted to his plan in advance. But they balked instead.

With equal politesse, Fithian praises Universal for caving into the exhibitors' demands. "NATO would like to thank Universal for responding to various theater owners' concerns and canceling the PVOD test it was contemplating. They have been engaged with individual exhibitors on this test, and while it was something that many theater owners could not ultimately support, the open and collaborative nature of the dialogue is appreciated. NATO recognizes that studios need to find new models and opportunities in the home market, and looks forward to distributors and exhibitors working together for their mutual benefit."

Both sides agree that the industry model needs changing; anxiety rides high as no one wants to break what does work—building future ancillary value and branding via reviews and word-of-mouth over a theater run—while experimenting with making movies accessible to audiences as soon as advertising reaches them. Many consumers want movies for free everywhere at the same time, which won't make money for anyone.

Indies such as Magnolia and IFC already push out features such as Lars von Trier's *Melancholia* with a premium price tag months ahead of their theatrical release. Warner Bros., Universal, Fox, and Sony tried a shortened two-month window—amid a huge outcry from exhibitors—with DirectTV and a $29.99 price point that might have been a tad high. Fox's Gianopulos points out that most movies last about three weeks in theaters; there's a "dark zone" of three months when all those marketing millions go for naught. Why not go for VOD for a premium price point of twenty to twenty-five dollars?

Amy Miles, CEO of Regal Entertainment Group, agrees that theaters nab about 95 to 97 percent of revenue in the first eight weeks, but asks, "What is the impact on our business if the consumer has the perception that films go to the home on an accelerated basis? It's not just that we generate the revenue over a time period, but if the consumer understands that they have to wait to see a film in the home, we believe that helps our business."

Reducing a four-month window to two months would encourage consumers to wait to see a film at home, she insists, and various new-model experiments will not yield real results. "Success to me and success to my partner in the test may not be the same," she says. "It's hard to measure. What does that mean? Studios are a vertically integrated business, while we offer one piece of their business—theatrical. If they shift revenue from one entity to another, they're still ahead." Why not share those revenues? "In the home, a lot of people are renting content for four or five dollars. I don't want to lose a dollar and be paid a dime."

Universal is investing billions of dollars in sending people to movie theaters, Fogelson says at a panel I moderate at CinemaCon in 2013: "I say it every year; I believe it. I think when exhibition believes it as strongly as I do, then there will be wiggle room, because the fear that people would rather stay home and watch a movie on television would start to go away enough to allow for experimentation.

"The studios are losing billions of dollars a year in revenue because the DVD market has declined and has largely been replaced by much lower revenue-generating options. We are owned by public companies who demand responsible business practices. For us to continue to have enough money to make enough movies to stock all these theaters with great product, we need to be able to generate a proper return on investment, we need to claw back some of that revenue. I believe there are people who love going to the movie theaters. It is a fact that people who go to the most movies in movie theaters buy the most DVDs."

Viewing begets viewing and consumption begets more consumption, he says, citing NBC's successful experiment showing the Olympics live on various platforms before the revenue-producing prime-time shows. Overall viewership actually went up in prime time, he says, "because the experience of watching the Olympics produced by a great network in prime time is different, the way it's packaged, the way it's sold—it's different. I've been in the best private screening rooms on the planet. They are not what a movie theater is. I believe movie theaters are spectacular and special and cannot be replaced and won't be replaced. I don't know what the answer is, but I know if we don't experiment we won't find out. Everyone has a point of view. If both sides don't take responsibility for opening their minds to experimenting to find a better way to do this we're all going to suffer, large or small, some kinds of consequences."

"The biggest thing we struggle with as exhibitors," David Passman of Carmike Cinemas responds, "is if you look at the revenue stream for a feature, exhibitors get one bite of the apple." If just one patron chooses not to go because of a windows or day-and-date or an alternative method, he argues, "then the exhibitors and the studios are hurt."

Passman thinks the old windows model needs to be completely overhauled. "I think if we could sit the top ten exhibitors and seven studios down and have a two-day workshop, we actually would create a new model that would work for all our benefit."

Unfortunately, the studios and exhibitors can't do this, Fithian reminds me afterward, because the lawyers would step in to prevent any accusations of restraint of trade. Thus Fox and Warner and others are talking to exhibitors in small groups, but not to each other.

Clearly, it's in the interest of the studios and exhibitors to get along. But this standoff is not going to be resolved easily. The overt hostilities have stopped. But the theaters are dependent on robust commercial product to survive, while the studios are struggling to figure out the best way to give consumers what they want. The digital wars are not over.

SXSW

One place that brings together two worlds that are usually far apart, Silicon Valley and Hollywood, is South by Southwest, the annual spring conference each March in Austin, Texas. A raucous collision of music and film festivals (audiences sampled 132 features and 138 shorts in 2012, selected from more than 5,300 submissions), as well as an interactive gathering of speakers and panels that functions as a Silicon Valley conference, SXSW pushes together disparate groups in the halls of Austin's convention center and nearby hotels. They learn from each other, share new apps, tweet each other's panels, and congregate at various watering holes. And if they're running short on time, they can order food at entrepreneur Tim League's Alamo Drafthouse, which enforces a strict no-phone policy in their theaters.

At SXSW I first discovered the notion of sharing locations via such apps as Foursquare and sharing what I was watching via Get-Glue. It was also where I found out that both Internet Movie Database founder Col Needham and Rick Allen, CEO of *Indiewire* owner SnagFilms, had plans to provide free streaming content, and where I learned how social movie site Flixster was helping moviegoers choose what to see on their smartphones. (Kevin Tsujihara acquired Flixster and review aggregator Rotten Tomatoes for Warner Bros. while serving as the company's digital chief, before he became head of the studio.)

I heard Morgan Spurlock, whose documentary *Super Size Me* was a hit on SnagFilms, question the revenue potential for filmmakers on streaming platforms. At one indie film distribution seminar, a music business insider raised his hand and shared distribution tips that could apply to the film side. When I showed up at *New York Times* media correspondent David Carr's tweeted meet-up at the Driskill Hotel, I met Yancey Strickler, one of the cofounders of burgeoning crowdsource funder Kickstarter, which has revolutionized how movies are funded, along with Indiegogo, Slated, and Seed&Spark. At SXSW 2012 I met Nicolas Gonda, cofounder of theatrical on demand platform Tugg, which is changing the way indies book theaters based on where audiences want to see their films.

These companies, along with Netflix, Google, Apple, and Amazon, are among the digital forces that will pull Hollywood kicking and screaming into the future.

CHAPTER 4

MAY: THE CANNES INTERNATIONAL FILM FESTIVAL

AMOUR, MOONRISE KINGDOM

For new arrivals, hitting France not-so-fresh from a sleepless transatlantic flight from Los Angeles to the Côte d'Azur airport in Nice is always rough. (Ever since I heard the story of a prominent talent agent being carried off the plane still down for the count after taking too many Ambien, I've eschewed sleeping pills.) That's one reason why so many festivalgoers stop in London or Paris en route to the granddaddy of film festivals, which is celebrating its sixty-fifth anniversary in 2012.

This year, I'm sharing a tiny fifth-floor two-bedroom walk-up in Cannes with three *Indiewire* staffers; there are only two sets of keys, so we stow one in a flowerpot on the unlit landing. Luckily, my iPhone has a flashlight and the apartment location is ideal, just blocks from the wide palm-lined beachfront walkway in Cannes, Boulevard de la Croisette, and about halfway between two major meeting nexuses: the Grand Hotel, with its vast green lawn with white sofas and terrace café, and the poolside bar at the Majestic Hotel, where the festival officials and jurors stay. Harvey Weinstein stays there too, although for a period he moved out to the famed cash-only Hotel du Cap down the Riviera coast in Cap d'Antibes, where the stars and moguls hang, motoring to and from Cannes by boat. (My favorite Hotel du Cap story: a bored Charlie Sheen throwing ashtrays off the balcony onto the rocks below.) For decades, most of the major studios, including Sony, Universal, and Fox, have locked in suites at the billboard-festooned blue and white Carlton Hotel, which also reserves a tiny single for the critic of the *New York Times*.

The Europeans and indies tend to congregate at the Grand Hotel, where I used to stay in the nineties when Bingham Ray bequeathed me his tiny studio apartment in the Residences. It was right out of a Pedro Almodóvar movie, complete with olive and orange décor, shag rug, and tropical plastic toilet seat. After long hours of meetings and screenings, industry folks, often in formal wear, drift in from their evening doings to the Grand bar and terrace for drinks and info sharing. "Your BlackBerry is archaic," IMDb chief Col Needham told me sternly one year as I complained about data access in France. As soon as I got back to L.A., I upgraded to an iPhone.

The roots of this classiest of international film festivals are anything but frivolous. The Cannes Film Festival was born out of the outrage felt by French filmmakers over a slight they suffered at the 1938 Venice Film Festival. To please the fascist regime, the Venice jury passed over Jean Renoir's antiwar masterpiece *La Grande Illusion,* widely considered one of the finest films ever made. When the French government was approached to finance a French counterpart to Venice, they hemmed and hawed, concerned about alienating Italian dictator Mussolini.

But the Education Ministry prevailed, the resort city agreed to bankroll much of the costs, and the first Cannes festival was scheduled to take place on the same day that Germany invaded Poland in 1939. Appropriately for the venue that veteran *Los Angeles Times* film critic Kenneth Turan calls "the quintessential place for film," the inaugural Cannes festival president was none other than Louis Lumière, who, with his brother Auguste, patented the first apparatus for making and showing films to audiences. With the war at hand, the festival's debut was postponed until September 1946, more than a year after the war ended. By then historian Georges Huisman was at the helm. From there on, Cannes went forward every year—except for 1948 and 1950—and from 1952 onward it has been held in mid-May.

The festival itself admits that its early sessions were mainly social events from which almost all of the films went away with a major award, but in the 1950s, the presence of stars such as Sophia Loren, Cary Grant, Kirk Douglas, Grace Kelly, Brigitte Bardot, Romy Schneider, Robert Mitchum, Elizabeth Taylor, Simone Signoret, and Alain Delon on the red carpet signaled an event of international stature. And as the decades went on, the lure of that phalanx of journalists and photographers and the irresistibly photogenic backdrop of the French Riviera has remained irresistible to movie stars.

Whether you get an engraved invite in your *cassier* to one of the nightly black-tie festival dinners, cough up the bucks for Harvey Weinstein's star-studded annual amfAR Cinema Against AIDS benefit, or score access to Paul Allen's yacht or Graydon Carter's *Vanity Fair* party, there's glamour to spare. I'll never forget the night at Cannes in 1993 that I arrived at the bottom of the Palais red carpet right behind Sylvester Stallone, star of Renny Harlin's *Cliffhanger*, as he climbed the stairs to meet another star at the top, one who stood in flowing white, clutching her little dog Snowy to her ample bosom: Elizabeth Taylor.

Alongside the festival's black-tie glamour and critical prestige is the world's most robust film market, with global acquisitions executives from TV and film flocking to screenings of both finished films and rough footage. The studios use Cannes as a massive marketing opportunity to launch their pictures in the all-important global market, which has outstripped North America and now represents more than 50 percent of the film industry's annual grosses. Much of the decline in quality of American pictures can be laid at the door of the studios' push to please foreign markets with big explosions and simple formula plots.

Every day the Cannes media get invites to cover press conferences and PR stunts, from Jerry Seinfeld jumping off the roof of the Carlton in a bee costume (the 2007 animated *Bee Movie*) to lifting aloft with giant colored balloons the house from Pixar's *Up* to bare-bottomed Sacha Baron Cohen posing in a green thong with babes in bikinis, long before "Borat" was a household word.

Buyers, sellers, and press are wined and dined at nightly dinners, with talent on hand. In 1991, the Weinsteins brought Madonna to Cannes for *Truth or Dare* and threw an afternoon yacht cocktail party; all the guests boarding the yacht had to remove their shoes—except for Madonna. At the red-carpet gala, Chicago critic Roger Ebert and I watched from an apartment terrace across from the Palais as Madonna climbed the steps and whipped open her dress coat to reveal a Jean Paul Gaultier cone bra, a photo op that went around the world. At the gala after party, *Time* critic Richard Corliss went down on his knees to talk to the star. Multiple beach parties line the Croisette every night, and in the wee hours, more than one woman has removed her high heels and walked home on bare feet.

Each morning—no matter how late you got in the night before—the media make a dash up the red-carpet stairs of the bunkerlike Palais, to grab a red seat for the 8:30 a.m. press screening of that night's competition film at the Grand Theatre Lumière, which fills up early for anticipated titles. The seats are so plush that it's easy to snooze through the pokier films. Movies like Jane Campion's *The Piano* or Lars von Trier's *Dancer in the Dark* yield a theater full of tough critics moved to tears. And at the screening's end, what every filmmaker fears is the dreaded boos or, worse, the flapping of the seats in displeasure.

On the morning of the first press screening of the 2012 Cannes Official Selection, I follow the director Wes Anderson and his entourage as they ascend the escalator to embark on the obligatory gauntlet of Cannes photo call, TV interview, and *conférence de presse*. Making a bid in the ramp-up to the Oscars, Universal's specialty arm Focus Features is giving Anderson (*Fantastic Mr. Fox*) the Cannes treatment. Focus booked his latest—and, according to many critics, best—film, *Moonrise Kingdom,* as the festival's opening night world premiere for several reasons: One, Anderson, forty-three, is a Cannes virgin. There's nothing like a rousing walk up the Palais red carpet, flashbulbs exploding, to feed a filmmaker's hungry ego. (And building your foreign profile improves box office around the world.)

Focus chief James Schamus, an erudite Columbia film professor who wears bow ties and moonlights as Ang Lee's producer-screenwriter, tells me he opted to follow the Sony Pictures Classics playbook for Woody Allen's *Midnight in Paris,* which opened in Europe and America right after its Cannes debut in May 2011 and went on to win Allen his fourth Oscar. But more important, the movie was Allen's career-highest domestic grosser ($56.8 million) and the most successful indie title of the year.

Anderson had a blast, he admits to me later, walking to the top of the Palais steps and doing the ritual photo poses with Cannes general delegate Thierry Frémaux, *Moonrise Kingdom* cowriter Roman Coppola, and the cast: Bill Murray, Bruce Willis, Tilda Swinton, Jason Schwartzman, Edward Norton, and Anderson's two young discoveries, Jared Gilman and Kara Hayward. Then Anderson walked into the 2,400-seat Salle Lumière to the de rigueur standing ovation and booming announcement of "*L'auteur,* Wes Anderson!" Heady stuff.

Anderson's seven movies are utterly identifiable as his, from his 1996 debut with Texas pal Owen Wilson, *Bottle Rocket,* and its follow-up, *Rushmore,* to 2007's *The Darjeeling Limited.* Sometimes his arch artificiality is winning (*The Royal Tenenbaums*), other times, irritating (*The Life Aquatic with Steve Zissou*). In the case of his latest film, it works.

Every frame of *Moonrise Kingdom* is arranged to perfection; the dialogue is deliciously flat; the sixties period references are selected with humor and affection. This remote island family comedy, which was filmed in 16 millimeter on Conanicut Island in Narragansett Bay, Rhode Island, is packed with eager Khaki Scouts and anxious, bumbling, disappointed, and well-meaning adults. But at its heart is a budding romance between two twelve-year-old loners (Gilman and Hayward). Their powerful feelings ignite strong reactions in everyone around them as a storm rises and lightning literally strikes them twice.

Anderson's superb cast delivers precisely scripted comic moments, surrounded by such archaic 1965 props as walkie-talkies, megaphones, and person-to-person split-screen phone calls. Anderson's cowriter and frequent collaborator, Coppola family scion Roman Coppola (*The Darjeeling Limited*) describes himself as a midwife helping Anderson to deliver and shape his ideas. Onetime Boy Scout Anderson tapped into personal memories of his own childhood longings, an early crush, and finding a manual, *Coping with the Very Troubled Child*, on top of his family refrigerator. "I wasn't the only child in the household, but I knew I was the one," he told the *New York Times*. "Now it makes me laugh, because it's a funny thing to find, especially on top of the refrigerator. But it was a horrible feeling."

After the early morning press screening, many of us rush to the press room with its free Wi-Fi, café espresso, and flat-screen live stream of the photo call followed by translated Canal Plus TV interviews and the official press conferences. Anderson and his cast bask in the rapturous critical reception. The actors describe participating in a delightful family summer camp adventure; Anderson led them much the way Norton's character leads the scout troop. As a sign of the times, the movie is one of the few in the festival shot on film. Anderson admits that it may be his last, as labs like Technicolor move to digital services and stop processing celluloid film prints. "Maybe there's a great app that makes it look like film," he says, "but to my mind there is no substitute."

"The whole movie is on the shoulders of these kids," the brown-corduroy-suited Anderson tells me during our beachside interview, squinting in the sun as the blue Mediterranean laps behind him on the Gray d'Albion beach. "I love artifice and very emotional movies like *The Life and Death of Colonel Blimp* . . . I'm not actually au courant." *Moonrise Kingdom,* he says, is "the re-creation of a fantasy when I was a twelve-year-old."

As someone with vaunted auteur status, Anderson is able to score a coveted Cannes competition slot. Fox Searchlight has to settle for second-tier placement in the Cannes official selection sidebar Un Certain Regard for Benh Zeitlin's Sundance Grand Jury Prize winner *Beasts of the Southern Wild.* That's because the Cannes brass tends to be conservative and myopic about where they place their titles. Only rarely will they take the chance of putting into the official competition a Sundance entry from an unproven director who has not already entered the official auteur canon by being lavishly praised by global critics. The exception that proved the rule was Steven Soderbergh's *sex, lies, and videotape,* a non–world premiere that went on to win the Palme d'Or in 1989.

Thus Frémaux offered 2012 competition slots to Jeff Nichols's *Mud* and Lee Daniels's *The Paperboy,* both American follow-ups to prestige hits (*Take Shelter* and *Precious*) that had previously played in Cannes sidebars. Both were for sale, and both starred Texas actor Matthew McConaughey. Indie darling *Donnie Darko* didn't rate a Cannes berth in 2001, but later the festival breathlessly snapped up Richard Kelly's unfinished 2006 follow-up, the notorious *Southland Tales,* which inspired several highbrow critics at Cannes to make a case for its pretentious meanderings.

In years past, Cannes has often accorded established auteurs competition slots for their weaker films, from Terry Gilliam's drug-addled *Fear and Loathing in Las Vegas,* starring Johnny Depp and Benicio del Toro, to Nanni Moretti's prophetic 2011 Vatican-in-crisis comedy *We Have a Pope.* One reason that Cannes's Frémaux remains loyal to the world's chosen auteurs is that he may need them someday. Moretti was back in 2012 as Cannes jury president, presiding over the usual mix of global talent: actors Ewan McGregor (Scotland), Emmanuelle Devos (France), Diane Kruger (Germany), and Hiam Abbass (Israel); directors Alexander Payne (United States), Andrea Arnold (United Kingdom), and Raoul Peck (Haiti); and designer Jean Paul Gaultier (France). (In 2013, Frémaux finally bagged his long-sought-after American prize, Steven Spielberg, as jury chief.)

While studio specialty divisions Searchlight and Focus dutifully trawl Cannes to acquire films with mainstream breakout potential and often leave mid-fest, the Weinstein Company, Sony Pictures Classics, Roadside Attractions, and IFC thoroughly scour the official and market screenings for gems. The executives also pack their schedules with meetings, screen early footage, and check out the landscape for projects in the works.

SPC's Michael Barker and Tom Bernard (who navigates the fest on a bicycle) genuinely support foreign-language fare, and tend to slug it out with IFC Films for the likeliest foreign Oscar nominees. The studio subsidiary has the advantage of deep relationships with exhibitors and Sony global output deals, as well as the savoir faire to push films with art-house audiences and Academy members alike.

As a subsidiary of AMC Networks, IFC's Jonathan Sehring prefers to play with a mixed menu of limited theatrical and VOD releases, and thus releases a high volume of titles that cost little to acquire and market.

IFC has grabbed *Beyond the Hills,* the Romanian competition film from Cristian Mungiu, before the festival, sight unseen. They had handled his Oscar-nominated 2007 Palme d'Or winner *4 Months, 3 Weeks and 2 Days.* Mungiu is a rigorously uncompromising artist who shoots long unedited sequences with natural light and a nonprofessional cast.

IFC has also acquired ahead of the festival Brazilian director Walter Salles's movie version of Jack Kerouac's *On the Road,* adapted by his *Motorcycle Diaries* scribe José Rivera. Salles inherited the long-in-the-works project from Francis Ford Coppola. The film stars rising young actor and breakout hopeful Garrett Hedlund (*Tron: Legacy*) as larger-than-life Dean Moriarty, Brit actor Sam Riley (*Control*) as laconic observer Sal Paradise, and Kirsten Dunst (*Spider-Man*) and earthily sexy Kristen Stewart (*Twilight*) as the women in their lives. The strong supporting cast includes such Oscar regulars as Amy Adams and Viggo Mortensen.

IFC has paid more than usual for the highbrow film in hopes of positioning it in the awards race with a planned release during the crowded year-end period. But the Cannes reviews, while respectful and admiring, are just okay. To get into the awards race, you need near-consensus raves. IFC staffers are furious when my review, posted after the morning press screening, suggests the movie is not a likely awards candidate. Marketing chief Ryan Werner sends me an e-mail asking me not to show up at their rooftop gala after party. I was raining on their parade as passions were running high; months later, after things cool down, Sehring, Werner, and I kiss and make up. They were resigned by then to *On the Road*'s slim chances of landing Oscar nominations. And there were none.

Every morning, attendees check out the critics' star ratings chart in *Screen International*'s Cannes daily to see how each film is ranked. *On the Road* is in the middle of the pack. It's better to ignite fiery debate among critics than polite discussion. Critical controversy can help ignite interest in a cerebral provocation like David Cronenberg's competition title *Cosmopolis,* starring Rob Pattinson as a jaded Wall Street player cruising through New York in his limo. (Distributor eOne has acquired the film pre-fest.) Similarly, Leos Carax's outrageous stunt *Holy Motors,* starring Denis Lavant as a series of flamboyant characters, also generates lively online debate before it's acquired by new Dominican Republic–financed Indomina Releasing. (By year's end the company abandons the distribution business, yet another casualty of reckless overspending on small-audience pictures.)

Sony Pictures Classics arrives in Cannes having already acquired at the start of production all North American rights to the tough relationship drama *Rust and Bone,* Jacques Audiard's follow-up to his

Oscar-nominated *A Prophet*. Starring Marion Cotillard as a whale trainer who loses her legs in a terrible accident, and rising Belgian star Matthias Schoenaerts (*Bullhead*) as a rough-and-tumble fighter who helps her to recover, the movie does well with critics. "We wanted to be in business with Audiard," says Barker.

During the festival SPC also swiftly moves to acquire Cannes sidebar Directors' Fortnight film *No* from Chilean filmmaker Pablo Larrain (*Tony Manero*), which winds up in the final five nominated for a foreign film Oscar. Starring gifted Mexican producer-actor Gael García Bernal (*Y Tu Mamá También*), the film is set during the regime of dictator Augusto Pinochet and depicts the advertising men behind the "no" campaign to vote him out of office.

While Barker and Bernard grew up in different neighborhoods in Dallas, Texas, both men were politicized by the films of the sixties and seventies, from *The Battle of Algiers* to *The Conformist* and *Z*. When they saw *No*, says Barker, they "talked about its borderline-radical film techniques that look at the politics of a world in a way that no other medium could. It reaches you and explains complex issues."

They also go into the fest with Austrian filmmaker Michael Haneke's French-language *Amour,* starring iconic octogenarians Jean-Louis Trintignant (*Z, A Man and a Woman, The Conformist*) and Emmanuelle Riva (*Hiroshima Mon Amour*). In 2009, SPC had released Haneke's Palme d'Or–winning *The White Ribbon*, which earned Oscar nominations for Best Foreign Language Film and Cinematography.

It's a formidable pickup. Written and directed by Haneke, *Amour* stars Trintignant and Riva as long-married intellectuals coping with the crushing effects of her debilitating stroke. Isabelle Huppert, unforgettable as Haneke's masochistic *Piano Teacher* (2001), plays the couple's self-involved grown daughter. In a business that relies on trusted partnerships forged over time, SPC has enjoyed a decades-long relationship with the film's producers, Stefan Arndt, Veit Heiduschka, Margaret Ménégoz, and Michael Katz.

On the night of the gala premiere at the Grand Lumière, there's a torrential downpour. "The red carpet was like a sea of umbrellas," says Barker. "In the photos of the stars, everyone was drenched. We tried to keep the actors from getting wet. I've never seen a storm like that for a movie opening. It was hard to keep everyone's composure. With the two older actors, everyone had to be careful getting them up the stairs and into the theater."

After the credits roll, there's a long silence as the deeply affected audience absorbs the ending, and then the thunderous standing ovation begins. "When Tom and I saw the final film," says Barker, "we talked about the potential. What knocked us out was that the critics and exhibitors were unanimous."

That SPC scored the heartrending drama ahead of the festival was no fluke. The relationship with Haneke dated back to *Caché* (2005), a mystery on slow-burn starring Daniel Auteuil and Juliette Binoche, which SPC picked up as soon as they saw it at Cannes; it garnered Haneke that year's Best Director prize. He told Sony about his plans for *The White Ribbon,* which triumphed at Cannes four years later, but because it was a chilling black-and-white vision of pre–First World War Germany (a kind of ritual punishment is exacted on the children of a small fictitious village as mysterious deaths occur), Sony waited to see an early screening from Haneke before buying it. With *Amour,* again, the producers gave Sony first crack at the finished film, but they wanted the studio to be confident in the picture before making an offer for it.

"It felt preordained," Barker later tells me on the phone. "It's a subject, caring for parents, that we're all having to live with in the culture." He compares the film to Ingmar Bergman's 1973 *Cries and Whispers,* which was nominated for five Oscars, including writing, directing, costume, and picture, and won cinematography for Sven Nyqvist. "Bergman had been making wonderful films and people thought it was his moment. We wanted that for Haneke."

It had been fourteen years since Trintignant had starred in a movie, and he was in frail health. But Haneke, a tall, somewhat intimidating Austrian, tells me in an interview at the Four Seasons Hotel in Los Angeles that it didn't take much convincing for the beloved veteran actor to take the role of Georges. He had narrated for Haneke the French version of *The White Ribbon*. Haneke says, "He was so enthusiastic about that film that he said yes when I asked him to work in *Amour*."

As for Riva, she, along with several other actresses, auditioned for the role of Anne, who like her husband, Georges, is a retired, highly cultivated piano teacher. Haneke says even before they met, he sensed that she and Trintignant would make a good couple. "Of course, as a young man I had seen her in *Hiroshima Mon Amour* and been smitten with her, but after that I lost her from view." At the audition, Haneke says, "immediately I knew that she was the one for [the part], because she was so good, but also because they fit together so well, they play to each other so well."

A seamstress, poet, and photographer, Riva has enjoyed a long and happy career as an actress, still working in theater until 2001. Unmarried and childless, Riva, who lives alone in Paris, exploded on the world scene at age thirty, starring as a French actress simply named "She" in Alain Resnais's 1959 esoteric classic of the French New Wave that had so haunted Haneke, *Hiroshima Mon Amour*.

"I liked the roles I had both on the stage and in cinema," Riva writes to me in an e-mail. "Going from one role to the other is a healthy exercise; no time for them to leave any mark on us. It is others who leave a mark on us. And I don't want to be a prisoner of any part, or to specialize in any genre. I don't want to cultivate my image (how boring!). I would rather always feel the freshness of something newly born."

Because both actors were octogenarians, Haneke deliberately scheduled a slower shoot of eight five-day weeks. "You can't demand that they shoot a string of ten-hour days. If it had been a production involving two forty-year-old actors, we probably would have planned for a six-week shoot." He arranged for his production designer Jean-

Vincent Puzos to create an apartment at the studio for Riva to live in during the shoot so that she wouldn't have to travel to and from set.

The exacting atmosphere on the set paid off in masterly, once-in-a-lifetime performances. At the press conference at Cannes, both actors suggest that Haneke was very demanding. The director acknowledges that he insists on getting what he wants when he shoots a scene, and sometimes that takes a while. "The scenes with the pigeon were particularly demanding and difficult physically [for Trintignant], and shooting those two scenes took a long time . . . It's hard to direct a pigeon."

THE HARVEY FACTOR

True to form, Harvey Weinstein has already made his mark on Cannes 2012 before the festival even begins. After decades of throwing his weight around at film festivals, the wily New York indie mogul is, as usual, ahead of his competitors.

Even though they are flying high off back-to-back Best Picture Oscar wins (*The King's Speech, The Artist*), that doesn't mean the Weinstein Company (TWC) is in robust financial shape. Harvey Weinstein and his brother Bob launched the company in 2005 after a brutal breakup with Disney, which twelve years before had acquired their company Miramax—home of such Oscar winners as *The Crying Game, Pulp Fiction, Shakespeare in Love, The Hours,* and *Chicago.* After raising a billion dollars in equity and debt financing in 2005, the Weinsteins went on a buying spree, seeking to become an entertainment empire with arms in fashion, book publishing, television and film production, video games, and home entertainment. Only after their investors forced the Weinsteins to refocus on their core business—the producing, acquiring, and releasing of low-budget independent movies—did the brothers start to right the ship.

"The first four years had nothing to do with movies," Weinstein said to a room of producers and a few reporters at a Producers Guild breakfast at Sundance 2013. "I was so dissatisfied. I was the worst CEO for the twelve companies we bought, I was so blatantly incompetent and stupid, about almost every decision. It wasn't my passion to do this. Okay, I had a fight with Michael Eisner at Disney. I was angry at them that they didn't do *The Lord of the Rings* when I brought it in. I was angry about *Fahrenheit 9/11* [Eisner insisted he give the movie to another distributor to release]. We were going to buy Bravo and AMC, monster gigantic improvements to my company to bring in, worth billions to Disney. It would have made Miramax one of the great labels and taken forward that vision of independent film . . . I was frustrated, I thought I could do what Michael Eisner can do. You taste bottom in this business. When you fail, you pick yourself up and get yourself back, whether with one movie or two. It's not over, just keep going."

Arriving in Cannes 2012, the Weinsteins are on the path to recovery. In 2011, before that year's festival slate was announced, Harvey had flown to Paris to check out what Vincent Maraval had up his sleeve. Maraval's maverick foreign sales company, Wild Bunch, had financed and produced such daring work from indie auteurs as Darren Aronofsky's heart-tugging Oscar contender *The Wrestler*, starring Mickey Rourke, and Steven Soderbergh's four-hour Spanish-language biopic *Che*. Maraval had something special to show the American distributor. *The Artist* was a black-and-white silent film set in 1920s Hollywood. It was directed by Michel Hazanavicius and starred his wife, Bérénice Bejo, and comedian Jean Dujardin, who had costarred in the director's successful series of comic capers. Weinstein listened to Maraval and screened the film.

Weinstein knows one thing better than anyone on this planet: what the 5,700 voters in the Academy of Motion Picture Arts and Sciences will like. He instantly made a bid on the movie and called his friend, Cannes official Frémaux, who decides where movies in the Cannes Official Selection will play, and asked him to move *The Artist* into the 2011 main competition. That Frémaux did.

With TWC behind it, *The Artist* was the buzz title to see on the Croisette well before the opening-night film had even screened.

Sure enough, at festival's end, Dujardin wound up winning the Palme d'Or for Best Actor, which put the film on the road to a long string of wins on the awards circuit, including five Academy Awards: Best Picture, Director, Costume, Score, and Actor in a Leading Role, which Dujardin became the first French actor to win (after nominations for Maurice Chevalier, Charles Boyer, and Gérard Depardieu). A grinning Frémaux attended the Weinsteins' glittering Oscar after party on the Sunset Strip along with Meryl Streep, whose gold dress matched her Oscar for playing Margaret Thatcher in the Weinsteins' *The Iron Lady*. He was basking in the first-ever Best Picture Oscar win for France.

Cannes helped to make that happen. But so did Weinstein, and the French knew that he had done much to push their films at the American box office. He also picked up French crowd-pleaser *The Intouchables* well before its star Omar Sy beat *The Artist*'s Dujardin for the Best Actor César in February. After TWC turned *The Intouchables* into a summer American specialty hit, the French Oscar selection committee picked it as their official French submission for the foreign Oscar. *Rust and Bone* would have been the other obvious choice, but Audiard had already had his crack at the Academy with *A Prophet*. It was time to give someone else a chance.

Clearly, after *The Artist,* Weinstein has plenty of sway with the Festival de Cannes, and so, in 2012, he leverages two genre flicks into the competition lineup before they disappear into the ether of box-office disappointments. Frémaux is willing to accept a weak movie—even in the main competition—as long as it boasts a respectable auteur and several stars worthy of the massive Palais red-carpet photo op.

Two stylish films from Australian directors fit the bill. John Hillcoat's $22 million period gangster film *Lawless* boasts a sprawling global ensemble including Brits Tom Hardy and Gary Oldman, Americans Shia LaBeouf and Jessica Chastain, and Aussies Mia Wasikowska, Guy Pearce, and Jason Clarke. And Andrew Dominik's *Killing Them Softly* offers golden star Brad Pitt, fresh off his triumph the year before in Terrence Malick's *The Tree of Life*.

That he could be counted on to walk the carpet with Angelina Jolie doesn't hurt.

Lawless started out its life in development with husband-and-wife producers Doug Wick and Lucy Fisher's Red Wagon shingle at Sony. Screenwriter-musician Nick Cave and director Hillcoat, who had collaborated on outback western *The Proposition,* adapted *Lawless* from Matt Bondurant's 2008 novel *The Wettest County in the World,* loosely based on the author's grandfather and two great uncles running booze in Virginia during Prohibition.

But *Lawless* is among the many films these days that no longer fit inside Hollywood's reduced studio parameters; Sony passed. "It had heart, but it was violent," Fisher tells me in a phone interview before Cannes. "Ten or fifteen years ago a studio would have made it in a second."

So Wick and Fisher, producers responsible for such high-end fare as *The Great Gatsby, Memoirs of a Geisha, Stuart Little,* and Oscar-winning *Gladiator,* did what many studio producers are doing these days. They went indie. With a strong ensemble cast led by LaBeouf—"who was in from day one," says Fisher, "up or down he was always there"—plus Hardy, Chastain, and Wasikowska, Wick and Fisher lined up overseas financing. Glen Basner's FilmNation presold individual overseas territories at Cannes 2011, showing early footage to buyers. And CAA brought in financing from Annapurna, owned by Silicon Valley master of the universe Larry Ellison's twenty-six-year-old billionaire sprig Megan Ellison. The final piece of the package: the Weinsteins acquired North American rights.

Weinstein's other competition offering, also backed by Annapurna, is Dominik's stylish *Killing Them Softly,* adapted from George V. Higgins's 1974 crime novel *Cogan's Trade* and set in post-Katrina New Orleans in 2008. Pitt plays aviator-shaded Jackie Cogan, a hit man who arrives to investigate a Mob-protected poker game that has been looted. The lowlife culprits are Frankie and Russell (Scoot McNairy and Ben Mendelsohn), who are trying to pin the blame on the game's overseer, Markie Trattman (Ray Liotta), who once successfully organized a heist of his own card room. Cogan is supposed to wipe them all out, and hires an old crony (James Gandolfini) to do the job. But he's out of shape, drunk, and washed up. Cogan must do the job himself. Softly or not.

Pitt has remained loyal to Dominik since he starred in his lofty, too-long 2007 artful western *The Assassination of Jesse James by the Coward Robert Ford,* which failed at the box office. Pitt believed in Dominik's take on genre violence in *Killing Them Softly,* which added a conceptual layer of political resonance to the equation. "I like violence in movies," Dominik explains at the Cannes press conference. "The most dramatic expression of drama is violence. Jackie is . . . concerned with violence not being cruel to the victim . . . Crime films are about capitalism. With this movie genre it's perfectly acceptable for all the characters to be motivated by money. We were in the middle of an economic crisis when it all came together."

As jaded, practical, cool-as-ice Cogan, Pitt earns strong reviews, better than the film. But even though the world media tend to adore America-bashing (hence the rapturous Cannes reaction in 2004 to Michael Moore's *Fahrenheit 9/11*), Cannes critics aren't buying Dominik's heavy-handed political pedantry. As a movie star in front of a press conference microphone and video cameras in a viral world, liberal Pitt also recognizes that he can't afford to espouse the politics of the movie, even if they're his own. "I love America and find it an exciting place to be right now," he states carefully. "Innovation, fairness, and justice are ideals to be protected. Violence is an accepted part of the gangster world, murder is accepted as a possibility when dealing with crime. Playing a racist would be more difficult for me."

The film's neophyte backer Megan Ellison makes her own mark on Cannes, having financed three projects via Annapurna that are selling in the Cannes market through her foreign sales company Panorama. They might not have gotten made without her, including one film she rescued from development limbo that wasn't ready in time for Cannes: Paul Thomas Anderson's $35 million post–World

War II drama *The Master.* Sitting on a hotel terrace overlooking the Mediterranean, FilmNation CEO Basner, who built Weinstein's foreign sales operation before going out on his own, tells me, "She's smart, straightforward, and interested in film. She has good taste."

Top-dog talent agency CAA has packaged all of fledgling Annapurna's projects, helping the young producer to put together *The Hurt Locker* director Kathryn Bigelow's $45 million bin Laden drama *Zero Dark Thirty* (released through Sony), which luckily wound up earning enough global coin to pay for Annapurna's losses on such also-rans as *The Master* and B-movie producer Randall Emmett's 2011 Anchor Bay release *Catch .44.* Hollywood doesn't want to make dramas anymore, the ones Warner Independent and Paramount Vantage used to handle—movies in that mid-range between $10 million and $50 million that aren't presold brand names or tentpoles—and Ellison does.

Even though she paid for the movies, Ellison did not have an easy time working with the intimidating Weinstein on *Killing Them Softly, Lawless,* and critics' favorite *The Master,* which all stalled out at the North American box office. *The Master* took a rather unorthodox opening berth in September, skipping the fall festival circuit altogether because it previewed in seven cities around the country in 70-millimeter presentations—ahead of the Telluride Film Festival, which refused to play the film as a result. TWC supported an Oscar campaign for *The Master,* which was beloved by critics and the Academy actors' branch—Joaquin Phoenix, Philip Seymour Hoffman, and Amy Adams all secured nominations.

While some reported that Ellison would never work with the mogul again, in a reminder of Hollywood's "never say never" adage, Weinstein wound up acquiring her Wong Kar-wai martial arts epic *The Grandmaster* right before it opened the Berlin Film Festival in February 2013; it was released that summer. Annapurna also backed David O. Russell's holiday 2013 Washington scandal drama *American Hustle,* reuniting *Silver Linings Playbook* stars Bradley Cooper and Jennifer Lawrence (Columbia Pictures), and has invested in

Anderson's next, an adaptation of Thomas Pynchon's novel *Inherent Vice*. Ellison is also partnering with her brother David Ellison's Skydance Productions (*Mission: Impossible—Ghost Protocol*) on a movie for which she spent $20 million for the rights: the fifth *Terminator* film, to be scripted by Laeta Kalogridis (*Avatar, Shutter Island*) and *Dracula 2000* director Patrick Lussier.

But *Lawless* and *Killing Them Softly* aren't all that Weinstein is selling at Cannes 2012; before the festival he also scoops up (for some $4 million) market title *Quartet,* Dustin Hoffman's directorial debut starring Maggie Smith, Michael Gambon, and Billy Connolly as three people in a home for aging opera stars.

And right on the eve of opening day, he acquires most territories for the out-of-competition official selection *The Sapphires,* directed by Aboriginal actor and theater director Wayne Blair, and written by Keith Thompson and Aboriginal playwright Tony Briggs, whose mother and aunt were part of the late-sixties all-girl pop group of the title. The entertaining period musical is shot by Warwick Thornton (previous winner of the Camera d'Or at the Cannes Film Festival for *Samson and Delilah*) and stars Aboriginal actress Deborah Mailman (*Radiance*), Aussie pop star Jessica Mauboy (*Bran Nue Dae*), and *Bridesmaids'* rising Irish funnyman Chris O'Dowd. When the film fails to incite much interest in Cannes, the Weinsteins hold it for release the following spring. (It grosses $2.5 million stateside.)

Stateside acquisitions execs were crossing their fingers in the hope that Weinstein would leave them with something else to buy. "TWC has everything," says one buyer as he finalizes his company's "black book" schedule of screenings and meetings. Out of the Cannes market, TWC also nabs James Gray's unfinished New York period drama (later entitled *The Immigrant*) starring Joaquin Phoenix, Marion Cotillard, and Jeremy Renner. (It goes on to play in competition at Cannes 2013.)

But Weinstein knows that so far none of the 2012 crop of TWC Cannes films is Oscar fodder. And so he has other fish to fry. He arranges a demonstration that is designed to say to the American press, "Here's what I really have up my sleeve." He invites the festival media to the Salon Diane at the Majestic Hotel in order to introduce preview footage of the real diamonds in his late-year lineup, three upcoming Academy Award hopefuls that aren't yet ready to unspool on the Croisette, but that he plans to push all the way to the Oscars.

He shows five minutes of planned September release *The Master;* two and a half minutes of Russell's Philadelphia family comedy *Silver Linings Playbook,* starring Cooper, Lawrence, Robert De Niro, Chris Tucker, Julia Stiles, and Jacki Weaver (November 16); and eight minutes of Quentin Tarantino's western by way of the antebellum South, *Django Unchained,* starring Jamie Foxx and Christoph Waltz (a global partnership with Sony slated for December 25).

The media like what they see. Weinstein has won Best Picture two years in a row with *The King's Speech* and *The Artist,* and he's poised to enter the awards fray again with all three films, which take very different routes getting there.

Designed to show off the acting prowess of its stars, the Cannes promo footage from *The Master* gets the media excited about the Oscar prospects of this visually stunning, well-acted period drama about a troubled alcoholic World War II veteran (Phoenix) who falls under the spell of a charismatic cult leader (Hoffman). His wife (Adams) isn't so sure that her husband's mission to "fix" this lost soul has merit. It's clear that Phoenix and Hoffman are on some kind of collision course. Which one is the master is the question.

After the Cannes press is teased with a small taste of *Silver Linings Playbook,* Russell's follow-up to Oscar winner *The Fighter,* the prognosis is less clear. Russell adapted the script from Matthew Quick's novel and does not seem to have the tone nailed; the footage plays as a romantic dramedy, and it doesn't necessarily translate in a few-minute clip. We can see that Cooper had lost his marriage, his mind, and his meds; Lawrence seems similarly addled. (Russell and editor Jay Cassidy tinker with it right up to the Toronto festival deadline.)

Spaghetti southern *Django Unchained* is still in mid-production—it won't wrap until the first week of July—and there's a real question as to whether it will finish in time for its planned release. While the film certainly isn't as sensationally exploitative as its 1975 predecessor *Mandingo,* it's provocative, steering into sensitive, little-explored areas of America's slave past. Tarantino is playing with volatile material that has the potential to both dismay and wow critics and smart-house audiences. Not to mention the Academy voters.

The *Django* footage reveals that Weinstein is selling a bang-up western packed with physical comedy, bloody action, and hell-bent revenge, a film shot in the classic widescreen tradition of Sergio Leone, even if the setting is New Orleans and Mississippi two years before the Civil War. Sophisticated German Dr. King Schultz (*Inglourious Basterds* Oscar winner Christoph Waltz) approaches a chain gang and attempts to buy one of the slaves. When the guards don't go along with this idea, he shoots them both and literally releases Django (Foxx) from his chains. He is now a free man.

While Schultz poses as a dentist, with a big molar swaying on top of his horse and buggy, he's actually a bounty hunter. He needs Django to identify some pretty nasty slave drivers he knows only too well, and the ex-slave is eager to help him. They find the men on the plantation of Big Daddy (Don Johnson); watching Django stalk across the grounds to shoot one of the men who abused him is chilling. He whips another to death. He also wants to find his wife, Broomhilda (Kerry Washington), who is owned by evil plantation owner Calvin Candie (a beefy Leonardo DiCaprio with long greasy hair).

Schultz, appalled by southern America's racist ways, tries to protect Django, who blooms under his tutelage and turns out to be a pretty good shot. Tarantino is taking the revenge western to a whole new level as the two bounty hunters shoot their way through the unsuspecting South. It looks like the first Leone-esque section of *Inglourious Basterds,* and it's about fighting injustice, except this time it's not Brad Pitt against the Nazis in World War II—it's an angry black man getting his own back from racist white southerners before the Civil War.

This is the challenge faced by Weinstein. This is not your ordinary movie to sell overseas or domestically—or to the Academy. But when Tarantino breaks the rules with style and panache, critics and audiences follow, as Oscar-winning *Pulp Fiction* and *Inglourious Basterds* have proved.

THE CANNES RESULTS

Lo and behold, Benh Zeitlin's Louisiana bayou drama *Beasts of the Southern Wild* does well at Cannes: it takes home both the International Federation of Film Critics (FIPRESCI) Prize for best film in Un Certain Regard and the Camera d'Or for best first film. (And it goes on to score $12.8 million at the summer box office, which gives it a good start on the year-end awards race.)

In a surprise on Cannes awards night, *Beyond the Hills'* nonpro actresses, Cristina Flutur and Cosmina Stratan, share the best actress prize, while *On the Road* comes up empty-handed. (The $25 million *On the Road* does not fare well at the North American box office, either, yielding just $720,000 in limited release toward a worldwide total of $9 million.)

Rust and Bone, perhaps because it is aimed at a younger audience, also comes up empty-handed. Each jury has its vagaries; others in the past refused to give prizes to such eventual Oscar winners as the Coen brothers' *No Country for Old Men* and Clint Eastwood's *Mystic River.*

As expected, Haneke scores his second Palme d'Or in four years with *Amour,* bringing his two stars up to share the glory on the stage. I'm not the only attendee at Cannes who feels both Trintignant and Riva deserve to win the top acting prizes, but ironically, that is prohibited due to a change of rules that occurred as a result of Haneke's previous award winner, *The Piano Teacher.* Says Haneke: "There was a great division in the jury. Some members wanted [*The Piano Teacher*] to be awarded the Palme d'Or or, at the very least, all the other prizes. [They said,] 'We'll give him the Grand Prix de

Jury, the Jury Award, and the two acting prizes.' As a result of that, the rules of the festival were changed so there couldn't be that concentration of awards [for one film]."

"The Palme d'Or was a very moving and very strong moment for all of us," Riva later writes me in an e-mail. "Each good film corresponds to a stage in our life, and thus seems gratifying. *Amour* happened as I'm approaching the last stage of my life. I was not expecting it at all. The film's success makes all of us happy. The awards are pouring into our hands. One feels like we are truly sharing our lives. We all have several lives, and this very moment in my life is, for me, the most gratifying."

SPC's strategy for *Amour* through the summer and fall, after the trifecta of the Telluride, Toronto, and New York festivals, is to get as many Academy actors, writers, and directors to see the film as possible. They want to create an aura around it, making it a film voters feel compelled to see. It's not a given that the Academy voters will respond well to *Amour*'s excruciating end-of-life subject matter. SPC creates a tasteful and restrained Oscar campaign for the film, which wins one award after another on its road to the Academy Awards. In the end, the greatly moving, elegantly wrought slice-of-life builds solid voter support, and both Haneke and Riva become serious Oscar contenders.

TWC's *Lawless* doesn't fly with the media at Cannes. When it opens stateside in August it does better with critics—who rate it 68 percent fresh on review aggregator Rotten Tomatoes—and with audiences who are drawn to the attractive cast. Weinstein manages to get the film to a decent $37.4 million domestically, even though it is too talky for mainstream male action fans and too violent for art-house seniors.

Because Pitt stars in *Killing Them Softly*, the Weinsteins hold back the stateside release until post-Thanksgiving November, one of the worst times to bow a movie, when it scores 75 percent fresh on the Tomatometer. But the movie flounders at the box office against competing films with adult appeal, including such powerful well-marketed entertainments as *Argo* and *Lincoln*, and it tops out at $15 million.

Focus's strategy of opening *Moonrise Kingdom* around the world after its Cannes launch works like a charm: the movie plays all summer (total gross: $68.3 million worldwide) and heads into Oscar contention. But Anderson does not participate in Oscar rituals: by the fall he's in Europe prepping his new film *The Grand Budapest Hotel*—starring Edward Norton, Bill Murray, Tilda Swinton, Ralph Fiennes, Jude Law, and Owen Wilson—rather than participating in the long slog of public appearances required of an Oscar campaigner. His laconic cowriter Coppola is left to hold down the fort.

Anderson comes out ahead, though. He has now been entered into the ranks of Cannes auteurs. He'll be back.

Bingham Ray and me on Main Street, Park City, Utah, in the early 1990s.

Benh Zeitlin, the director of *Beasts of the Southern Wild*,
with his star Dwight Henry at the 2012 Cannes Film Festival.

Mark Duplass and John Hawkes at an Indie Spirits brunch.

Helen Hunt and John Hawkes get intimate as sexual surrogate and patient in Ben Lewin's *The Sessions*.

Beasts of the Southern Wild's Quvenzhané Wallis was six years old when she played Hushpuppy, who learns how to survive below the levees in New Orleans, and nine when she became the youngest-ever Best Actress nominee.

Singer-songwriter Rodriguez and *Searching for Sugar Man* director Malik Bendjelloul.

Documentary filmmakers Heidi Ewing and Rachel Grady opted to self-distribute *Detropia*, their portrait of the deteriorating Motor City.

Filmmaker Kirby Dick's documentary *The Invisible War* brought to life shocking cases of sexual assault in the U.S. military.

Elizabeth Banks as Effie Trinket, Woody Harrelson as Haymitch Abernathy, and Jennifer Lawrence as District 12 fighter Katniss Everdeen in Gary Ross's successful launch of the *Hunger Games* franchise.

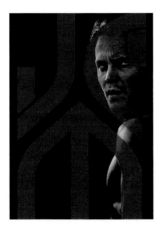

Disney's generic early teaser poster for *John Carter*.

In *John Carter*, Taylor Kitsch plays the title role, a Civil War soldier who gains superhuman strength when he is magically transported to Mars. Here he is pitted against two hulking Barsoom beasts.

At CinemaCon, eye-popping preview footage from Ang Lee's *Life of Pi* and Tom Hooper's *Les Misérables* wowed the convention audience. TOP: After a shipwreck drowns his family, Pi (Suraj Sharma) is stranded in a life raft on the Indian Ocean with a Bengal tiger (created by combining computer graphics with footage of live tigers). BOTTOM: Anne Hathaway's passionate, beautiful singing of Fantine's song, "I Dreamed a Dream," was filmed live in single takes.

Emmanuelle Riva and Jean-Louis Trintignant with director
Michael Haneke (*center*) on the night *Amour* won the Palme d'Or at Cannes.

Cannes Festival virgin Wes Anderson sits for a *Moonrise Kingdom* interview
and photo shoot on the beach in Cannes.

Cannes veteran
Harvey Weinstein.

Tom Bernard and
Michael Barker
of Sony Pictures
Classics at the
Carlton Terrace,
Cannes.

Fanboys and -girls flock to San Diego each July to attend Comic-Con.

The Avengers writer-director
Joss Whedon.

Django Unchained stars Christoph Waltz and Jamie Foxx pose for an
LA Times photo shoot at Comic-Con.

Daniel Day-Lewis channeled President Abraham Lincoln, never stepping out of character on the set of *Lincoln*.

Steven Spielberg's *Lincoln* received twelve Oscar nominations, including Best Director.

Ben Affleck played the real-life CIA agent Tony Mendez in *Argo*, a true story about a mission to save State Department employees hiding in Tehran.

Ben Affleck.

John Goodman and Alan Arkin provide comedic relief in *Argo* as two Hollywood producers who pretend to back the fake film project mounted by the CIA.

Kathryn Bigelow, Jessica Chastain, and Amy Pascal at the *Zero Dark Thirty* premiere.

Annapurna chief Megan Ellison.

Actress Geena Davis, director Paul Feige, Regal Entertainment CEO Amy Davis, Fox Animation president Vanessa Morrison, and producer Nina Jacobson talked on a CinemaCon panel about women in media.

Kathryn Bigelow and Mark Boal on the set of *Zero Dark Thirty*.

Quentin Tarantino directing *Django Unchained*, in which he played a bit part.

David O. Russell backstage at the Indie Spirit Awards.

Ben Affleck, Grant Heslov, and George Clooney accept
the Best Picture Oscar for *Argo*.

The four Best Actor winners wave their statuettes backstage at the Oscars.

Ang Lee takes congratulations after winning the Best Director Oscar.

CHAPTER 5

JULY: COMIC-CON AND THE FANBOYS

DC vs. MARVEL

Back when nerds wore pocket protectors and geeks were beat up by bullies after school, reading comics was something many of us did under the covers with a flashlight.

When I was a kid in New York City, every weekend I bought the latest comics: Marvel's *Thor*, *Spider-Man*, and *The Fantastic Four*, and DC's *Superman*, *Batman*, *Wonder Woman*, and *Supergirl*. As I grew up, I moved on to Frodo and Gollum and the odysseys of Homer, Arthur C. Clarke, and Stanley Kubrick.

But generations of Peter Pans never relinquished their youthful devotion to *X-Men* and *Star Trek*. And George Lucas made it easy for fans to feed their appetite for all things *Star Wars* after he launched the franchise in 1977. Thanks to his insistence that he hang onto multiple rights to the *Star Wars* and *Indiana Jones* franchises, Lucas was able to build his sprawling Bay Area Lucasfilm empire over the next thirty-five years, complete with the industry's top-ranked VFX, sound-editing facilities, and licensing and merchandising divisions. In 2012, after he passed the leadership to Kathleen Kennedy, he was able to sell that legacy to Disney for $4.05 billion.

Lucas refined the art of playing to a large fan base, nurturing fan clubs with updates and newsletters on sequels and prequels, and offering them the *Young Indiana Jones Chronicles* TV series, *Star Wars* spin-off novels, video games, and collectible art and action figures. Lucasfilm was among the first of the movie companies to self-promote directly to fans and actively hawk its wares at San Diego's Comic-Con International—the premiere comic-book convention and showcase for genre properties in the world.

Back in the early eighties, my film critic husband, David Chute, who inhaled comics and graphic novels, introduced me to the small-scale convention called Comic-Con, originally founded in 1970 by a group of San Diego aficionados thrilled to welcome three hundred guests to their first gathering, then called the Golden State Comic Book Convention, at the U.S. Grant Hotel. Over the years, David introduced me to curmudgeonly dweeb Harvey Pekar, whose autobiographical *American Splendor* comics inspired the 2003 film of the same name starring Paul Giamatti, and to virtuoso underground comic writer and illustrator R. Crumb, who wore a seersucker jacket and fedora. And I met the man who took Batman to the dark side, *The Dark Knight Returns* writer Frank Miller, who, with artist Lynn Varley, also dramatized the Spartans' Battle of Thermopylae in the gorgeous graphic novel *300* and went hard-boiled noir with *Sin City*. All became hit movies.

Over successive Comic-Cons, attendance expanded to fill the San Diego Convention Center's capacity of 130,000 and draw thousands more to numerous satellite sites in nearby parks and hotels. Comic-Con, held every July, became the city's biggest convention ever. The Hollywood studio presence increased over the years as filmmakers and marketers figured out that many collectors and buyers of comics and art and action figures were also huge movie enthusiasts—a built-in, easily targeted core audience for genre fare. The circle closed when studios locked their tentpole strategy into mining already proven beloved characters from comics for big-budget franchises aimed at the fan faithful, who would help guarantee a return on investment. Ironically, the bashful comic book fanatics, who never asked a girl to dance at the high school hop, became the most desirable figures on the dance floor.

Warner Bros., which acquired DC Comics in 1969 and therefore movie and television rights to the jewels in the DC crown, *Superman* and *Batman,* discovered in the early eighties that many fans of the comics were attending Comic-Con—and would come to see their movies. Soon the promotion of movies inspired by comic books expanded to genre films and eventually just about anything aimed at the studios' sweet spot, the young male demo.

Most fans must wait in ridiculously long lines to get into the studio presentations inside the Convention Center's cavernous Hall H, which holds 6,000 people. They line up just outside and, for the must-attend panels, sleep under tents in sleeping bags overnight, sometimes on concrete. One fan waited seven hours and still didn't get in, as the line was cut eleven people ahead of him. So once they get into Hall H, people camp there all day. Getting sustenance and keeping appliances charged are a serious issue. (*The Wrap* editor Sharon Waxman and I have almost come to blows over the limited electrical outlets.) Press people work hard to get access to VIP passes—for each separate panel—so they can skip the queues.

At Comic-Con 2012 (Thursday, July 12, through Sunday, July 15), fan anticipation for the fifth and last installment in the *Twilight* series is so high that a lengthy queue of Twihards starts camping out the Sunday before the opening. Tragically, on Tuesday, one woman eagerly awaiting the Thursday entry to the *Breaking Dawn—Part II* panel in Hall H leaves the line and, in her rush to regain her place, runs against traffic and falls into an oncoming car; she later dies from head injuries.

Inside the convention, at the last Comic-Con *Twilight* press conference and panel, you'd never know that Kristen Stewart has eyes for a man other than on-and-off-screen swain Rob Pattinson, who plays her vampire lover, Edward Cullen, given the way the couple plays their roles as real-life lovebirds to the hilt. They, author Stephenie Meyer, and the rest of the *Twilight* cast bid farewell to the series of five movies that has given them enough "fuck you" money to last the rest of their careers.

The team expresses their sadness at having to say good-bye to the series and to their onscreen family, with whom they have worked for the past four years. After the last week of shooting, "I was sad not to be able to hang out with these people," says Meyer. "This is the last question, the last press conference," adds a smiling Pattinson, whose fans in the hall are still screaming. Director Bill Condon sends a video message from London, where he is scoring the film. Taking up where the fourth film left off, he opts to preview the first seven minutes of its follow-up, which starts with Bella Swan opening hard yellow vampire eyes—and learning how to embrace her inner action hero.

There's plenty more than movies going on at Comic-Con, where *Game of Thrones* and other TV series have crashed Hall H. The real attraction is the blocks-long exhibition floor spanning letters A through G, with Hall H at the end of the building and more halls and meeting rooms up above on the second floor. The exhibition covers more than 525,000 square feet of contiguous space on the ground floor (about ten NFL playing fields), where fans cruise with their giant Warner Bros. tote bags looking for cool stuff to buy, from T-shirts and bobble-head dolls to signed graphic novels. As marketing hype threatens to overwhelm the Con, its beating heart still resides with the artists and collectors. I get a kick out of the lovingly crafted costumes—from steam punks and Wonder Woman to Little Bo Peep, *Walking Dead* zombies, and the Joker in nurse garb—that allow fans to embody their own image of who they want to be.

The studios use the convention as a massive viral marketing opportunity. The colorful blitz includes signings, roving billboards, elaborate stunts, public appearances, and interactive treasure hunts, complete with clues, prizes, and rewards. The studios no longer rely on TV and print ads and in-theater trailers to reach moviegoers; they have sophisticated online marketing departments planting viral memes, games, and video and tracking social media and awareness.

In a world where the once mighty *Newsweek* has been superseded by TheDailyBeast.com, moviegoers no longer need to wait for stories planted by publicity departments in print editions of the *New York Times* and *Rolling Stone.* They're seeing blog posts on *Vulture, Slashfilm, Collider,* MSN.com, the *Huffington Post,* MTV.com, and EW.com; following their favorite media outlets and influencers on Twitter and Facebook; and seeing trailers, interviews, and reviews via Flixster, Rotten Tomatoes, IMDb, Metacritic, and Criticwire.

Thus Comic-Con is an irresistible generator of instant buzz. Fans and major media all perch in Hall H eager to communicate with the outside world via laptop and smartphone. If a director breaks news on a release date or shows new footage, reaction hits the Internet in seconds. Studio chiefs attend their show-and-tells, such as the one for Peter Jackson's *The Hobbit,* which, the director first hints to Comic-Con media, will be a trilogy. (Tellingly the footage is not shown at 48 fps.) Execs also attend the presentations of their competitors. All the while, ears are pricked to see how footage and materials play with fans.

Just before the huge exhibition floor opens its doors to thousands of fans, many of them in costume, I tag along with a gaggle of press covering an AMC *Walking Dead* event: the unveiling of next season's survival car, a souped-up Hyundai Elantra GT complete with rhino guards and whirring spikes. "It's a one-of-a-kind engineering marvel!" gushes the PR rep. "The ultimate zombie-proof survival vehicle!" Comic-book creator Robert Kirkman (celebrating his hundreth issue) had described the black car, which was then realized and built to his specifications by Gary Castillo of Design Craft Fabrication, who claimed, "The car is 100 percent zombie-proof!"

It's a delight wandering around Disney's museum-style Art of *Frankenweenie* exhibit, which features Tim Burton's drawings and miniature sets for the black-and-white stop-motion expansion of his 1984 *Frankenweenie* short. But later, at Disney's Hall H show-and-tell, the response to the movie is muted. Sure enough, when *Frankenweenie* opens in October, it's a box-office disappointment, topping out at $35.3 million domestic. (Another more contemporary, colorful, and comedic stop-motion horror feature, Laika's *ParaNorman*, plays better both in Hall H and in theaters.)

After the Con closes down each evening, talent, executives, and media swing by a series of hotel parties, many of them poolside at the Hard Rock Hotel. At the Lionsgate-Summit *Twilight* fete, Summit chiefs Rob Friedman and Patrick Wachsberger, now running Lionsgate's motion picture division, admit they are applying the same approach to *The Hunger Games* franchise as they did to the *Twilight Saga*: don't waste any time getting the sequels up and running.

The indies have also discovered the benefits of Comic-Con. If self-promoter Kevin Smith can market B-fare such as *Zack and Miri Make a Porno* directly to his fans (without help from critics) via raunchy stand-up routines, as he did in 2008—one young fan got down on one knee and proposed to his intended during one of Smith's Q&As—why not take *Django Unchained* to Comic-Con? The Weinstein Company follows up its highbrow Cannes media intro with a

Quentin Tarantino panel for the fans in San Diego at which they show footage of the film. They also hold backstage press round-tables with stars Jamie Foxx, Christoph Waltz, Kerry Washington, and Walton Goggins. (Smart move: the film won't be finished and screened for press until right before it opens December 25.)

No longer a convention just for fanboys, fangirls now flock to Comic-Con, thanks in part to Summit bringing the first *Twilight* movie to the Con in 2008 and luring thousands of women who might otherwise not have gone. That year many regulars were aghast when piercing screams filled a darkened Hall H the first time unruly-haired Brit Rob Pattinson opened his plummy mouth on the panel dais, projected on giant video screens. If Summit needed proof that it had a winner, that was it. *Twilight* scored a total $392.6 million worldwide. "It's the world's largest focus group," journalist Scott Mantz tells filmmaker Morgan Spurlock in his 2011 documentary *Comic-Con Episode IV: A Fan's Hope.* "Studios realize this is the place to get grass-roots awareness," adds actor Seth Green.

But make no mistake: playing well at Comic-Con is no guarantee of success, as the studios have learned the hard way. Comic-Con hits from Edgar Wright's *Scott Pilgrim vs. the World* to Jon Favreau's *Cowboys & Aliens* have crashed and burned. The fan demo is just a slice of the wide mainstream audience that big-budget studio movies need to pull in. Zack Snyder's innovative $60 million sword-and-sandal actioner adapted from Frank Miller's *300* played well in Hall H and went on to be a $456 million global hit in 2006. His 2009 follow-up *Watchmen,* adapted from a complex, interlocking Alan Moore graphic novel that had been deemed unfilmable for years, played equally well—but cost too much ($138 million) to make a profit in release ($185.3 million worldwide).

The general rule of thumb is that a movie needs to gross double its production cost to come out ahead. Given that Warner Bros. spent at least $50 million in global marketing costs and that returns from theater owners were about half of worldwide ticket sales,

Watchmen was a write-off for the studio—even with earnings from TV licensing and DVD sales (down 20 percent from their 2004 peak). In 2012, for the first time, online revenue grew enough to offset the seven-year drop in DVD sales and rentals.

An earlier disappointment for Warner had been Bryan Singer's out-of-control 2006 reboot *Superman Returns,* which cost close to $250 million and yielded just $391 million worldwide. It also caused an uproar among fans who complained that it was too much of an homage to the original 1978 Dick Donner *Superman* and didn't have enough action. They were dismayed that Superman (Brandon Routh) and Lois Lane (Kate Bosworth) had spawned a kid and were facing too-familiar villain Lex Luthor (Singer regular Kevin Spacey). The problem with the square-jawed orphan from Krypton is that he's an invulnerable big blue Boy Scout, with no weaknesses except kryptonite—and his feelings for Lois. But Superman doesn't have to be squeaky clean, many fans argued: the origins of the character are darker and more complex.

In late 2009, one Warner exec told me that, after many false starts, the studio was again seeking to find the right direction for the superhero: "We're working on a strategy for DC. Superman is the trickiest one to figure out."

With its franchise stalled out, Warner inevitably turned to the indie filmmaker who had saved its bacon with *Batman Begins* and was coming to the end of that $2.5 billion trilogy with 2012 release *The Dark Knight Rises*: Christopher Nolan. At Comic-Con 2012, the studio introduces a teaser for Nolan and writer David S. Goyer's latest Superman iteration, *Man of Steel,* which visual stylist Zack Snyder is directing with young Brit Henry Cavill (*The Tudors*) in the starring role, Russell Crowe as his father, Amy Adams as Lois Lane, and Michael Shannon as archvillain General Zod.

When a fan asks Snyder if he'll be using John Williams's iconic *Superman* score, he explains why not: "We had to act as if no film has been made. When we approached it, we had to say, 'This is

Superman for the first time.'" Veteran composer Hans Zimmer got the gig.

Unlike DC, whose properties have remained under the control of Warner, Marvel decided to take control of its destiny. After partnering with various studios on *X-Men* (Fox), *Spider-Man* (Sony), and *Iron Man* (Paramount), Marvel took itself independent—for a time—by taking over management, production, and ownership of its films. The results have been extraordinary. Because it was invested in controlling over the long term its characters as well as the universes they inhabit, Marvel developed a five-year plan and put Kevin Feige in charge. An ardent comic-book fan who lives and breathes and fights to protect Marvel characters, he knew the Marvel world inside and out and understood both moviemaking and fandom.

New Jersey native Feige, forty, studied film at the University of Southern California and interned for producer Lauren Shuler Donner, whose husband, Dick, had directed the *Lethal Weapon* series and the first two Christopher Reeve *Superman* films. When she produced *X-Men* at Fox, Feige became her assistant and an *X-Men* associate producer because of his vast knowledge of all things Marvel. Since joining Marvel in 2002, he has supervised all their in-house films; he became president in 2007.

After proving his prowess with various Marvel studio pictures, Feige was heading toward an ambitious goal. He laid the groundwork first in singular hero movies by introducing Iron Man (Robert Downey Jr.), Captain America (Chris Evans), and Thor (Chris Hemsworth), as well as several other supporting characters such as Black Widow (Scarlett Johansson) and Hawkeye (Jeremy Renner). Once established, Marvel could proceed and assemble them, along with the Hulk, into one supercharged Marvel hero ensemble movie: *The Avengers*.

But who had the skill and chops to artfully blend all these worlds into one, and not have the whole thing devolve into a shouting match? Feige turned to writer-director Joss Whedon, son of two generations of Manhattan TV writers: father, Tom, and grandfather John Whedon. (His mother, Lee Stearns Whedon, my best-ever English teacher at St. Hilda's and St. Hugh's School, taught me Shakespeare.) An unapologetic comics maven, Joss Whedon went to Hollywood, where he moved from TV success with *Buffy the Vampire Slayer* to the writers room of the Oscar-nominated *Toy Story* to cult status with the short-lived TV series *Firefly*, later incarnated as the underwhelming film *Serenity*.

In fact, Whedon was one of those writer-directors who was respected within the industry for his writing chops, but who hadn't quite scored as a commercial director. He labored for a long time on DC's *Wonder Woman* without success—in fact his idiosyncratic smarts had never flourished inside the studio system—but he had scored with Marvel on a comic-book run of *The Amazing X-Men*. Feige had the sense to pull him into Marvel's vortex to deliver *The Avengers*. Whedon had nourished an enormous fan base over the years, who always turn up to his panels in droves. "This is the place where they can say, 'are we not dope, are we not amazing for being this obsessed with something?'" Whedon told Spurlock.

While *The Avengers* had plenty of visual effects and noisy whiz bang action sequences, it wouldn't have worked if the cult leader of the *Firefly* fans known as the browncoats hadn't understood the characters, from Robert Downey Jr.'s snarky Tony Stark to Mark Ruffalo's surprisingly sympathetic Bruce Banner/Hulk, and how they related to the mission: defeating super-super villain Loki (Brit rising star Tom Hiddleston).

At Comic-Con 2011, months before *The Avengers* started filming, Ruffalo stumbled out onto the Hall H stage like a deer in headlights with the long chorus line of the cast, having woken up in the morning at his farm in upstate New York knowing that if a limo pulled up to his door, he had landed the part.

Sure enough, with a mighty Disney marketing campaign and rave reviews, *The Avengers* April launch turned into a box office juggernaut that lured happy comics lovers of every generation, easily rising to the top of the 2012 box office with a global $1.5 billion total.

By Comic-Con 2012, Marvel is ready to celebrate the success of *The Avengers* by showing a pump-up reel and a promise of another Joss Whedon installment to come in May 2015. Downey Jr. makes a grand entrance through the hall, joined by his *Iron Man 3* costars Don Cheadle, Jon Favreau (now in acting mode), Gwyneth Paltrow, Rebecca Hall, Mia Hanson, Guy Pearce, Ben Kingsley as The Mandarin, and new writer-director Shane Black (*Kiss Kiss Bang Bang*).

Three other Marvel movies in the works besides *Iron Man 3* (May 3, 2013) are *Game of Thrones* director Alan Taylor's *Thor: The Dark World* (November 8, 2013) shooting at London's Shepperton Studios with the entire cast returning; *Captain America: The Winter Soldier* (April 4, 2014) starring Chris Evans, Scarlett Johansson, and Robert Redford and set to start filming in 2013; and *Guardians of the Galaxy* (August 1, 2014), starring Chris Pratt, Zoe Saldana, and Benicio del Toro and based on the Marvel comic (which ran from 1969 through 2008). Also, Comic-Con fave *Shaun of the Dead* writer-director Edgar Wright is looking to apply the latest technology to *Ant-Man* (July 31, 2015) who "will kick your ass one inch at a time," he says.

When *Man of Steel* finally opens in June 2013, it grosses a respectable but not stellar $630 million worldwide. The following month at Comic-Con, Warner announces it will add the character of Batman to the next Superman movie from Goyer and Snyder, and a month later says Ben Affleck will play the new Batman. Reaction ranges from fan cheers to fears that this is a desperation move to compete with Disney's Marvel.

That's because, for the rest of the industry, Marvel has set the bar very high.

CHAPTER 6

THE FALL FILM FESTIVALS

ARGO, SILVER LININGS PLAYBOOK, LIFE OF PI, LINCOLN

Any movie looking to earn multiple Oscar nominations has to meet a high standard. Getting there is a long hard slog. You need more than merit and luck to go all the way. Your handlers must do everything right—and be willing to spend.

First, assuming that a movie is perfectly mounted, it must have the right stuff to break through—with serious marketing and publicity know-how and resources behind it—and to make noise and grab attention from the media during a crowded period when it's easy to be drowned out by other films' thunder.

What magic alchemy of screenplay, direction, visual beauty, and performance—yielding some level of emotion in the beating heart of viewers—will sustain moviegoer attention long enough to wind up on the screener stacks of critics, guild members, and, finally, Academy voters? And not at the bottom of the pile but at the top? That's the decision that distributors have to make.

As it stands, the big six studios avoid taking undue risks on more than a handful of movies for grownups; these pictures must be brilliantly executed, after all, to get the boost from critics and word-of-mouth they need to lure audiences. The fall season offers the chance to take a few films that have turned out really well for a test drive. It's the fall festivals that will tell the filmmakers, distributors, and studios what they need to know, that will provide them with the serious contenders heading for the late-year Oscar corridor. The festival programs will be packed, with many of the best films already well-reviewed by critics and audiences at the first wave of festivals—beginning with Sundance in January and going through SXSW in March, Tribeca in April, and Cannes in May—which start the buzz on the better movies. If the movies pass muster with audiences and press at these earlier festivals, they'll land slots on the fall circuit. And if they score at one or more of the fall festivals that act as launchpads for award campaigns, they're off to the races. If not, their distributors will pull back and reconfigure their release plans.

The critics perform a valuable role, as their reviews start the drumroll that can turn a film into a must-see; year-end ten-best lists and critics' group awards also contribute to the snowball effect of a repeated winner.

But a critics' fave does not always an Oscar contender make—many critics and actors hailed Paul Thomas Anderson's *The Master,* but art-house audiences and the Academy at large gave the handsome but intense drama a pass. And while most Oscar contenders need to earn at least some critical respect, movies like *Crash, The Green Mile, Chocolat,* and *The Cider House Rules* landed coveted Best Picture slots without being consensus picks by critics' groups; in 2005, *Crash* took home the ultimate prize. Winning a SAG Award or a Golden Globe is great, but it's still not the Gold Man.

The Academy of Motion Picture Arts and Sciences, known as the Academy, is six thousand voters strong. While most are based in Los Angeles and other California environs such as Santa Barbara and the Bay Area, followed next by New York and London, they live all over the country and the world. They have all been recommended and voted in by their peers in each branch; the Academy invites about 130 new nominees and winners every year. They're voted in by seventeen branches of varying sizes: the actors are by far the largest group, with some twelve hundred members; producers and executives number in the four hundreds; writers, publicists, and directors in the three hundreds; while other crafts are quite small.

The execs, publicists, and actors tend to have more mainstream tastes than the more sophisticated writer, director, and craft branches. But there's also a steak-eater contingent of old-school males in the Academy who vote for such movies as *Gladiator, Silence of the Lambs,* and *Braveheart,* and against gay romance *Brokeback Mountain,* which by most signposts would ordinarily have won Best Picture against *Crash.* (Ang Lee did take home Best Director for *Brokeback.*)

Movies of scale and scope have an advantage for the Best Picture award, especially if they are expensive period pictures with massive sets and visual effects. Think *The Last Emperor, Master and Commander, Gandhi, The Lord of the Rings,* and *Inglourious Basterds.* But the Academy doesn't go for avant-garde or messy, no matter how gorgeously mounted a film like *Cloud Atlas* may be. And expensive blockbusters such as *Star Wars, The Dark Knight,* and the Harry Potter films tend to wind up sequestered in the Academy's technical categories. They're often rewarded for their individual craft accomplishments—and punished for their populism. Festivals lent a mainstream movie like *Argo* some gravitas, and helped to boost an indie drama like *The Sessions* into the limelight.

Effective manipulation of a festival takes both legwork and oodles of money, but there's a risk involved. You stick your chin out when you are weighed as a possible award contender. You could be found wanting. Reviews could go south. And you don't want to seem presumptuous. During the summer of 2012, Roadside Attractions was debating whether to take Richard Gere to the Toronto International Film Festival for Sundance hit *Arbitrage.* Would screening it there tip their hand, signaling Oscar hopes? Would their film get lost in the noisy scrum? Were they better off spending their money on the release? They opted not to go.

Four prominent fall festivals are on the awards watch list—Venice, Telluride, Toronto, and New York. The first three are held practically within days of each other in late August and early September, with the New York Film Festival following in late September and early October. These festivals are the effective gatekeepers for winnowing the list of serious contenders going forward into the height of Oscar season. The 2012 season yielded an unexpected garden of riches. At the end of July, as the programs began to be announced, some thirty movies were lining up for possible awards consideration.

First up at summer's end is Italy's Venice International Film Festival (August 29–September 8, 2012), which at age sixty-nine is the oldest in the world. I went to this glamorous old-school European gathering in 2010, and interviewed Darren Aronofsky for *Black Swan* and Sofia Coppola for *Somewhere*. Celebrities love this low-key festival because it makes fewer demands on them than others do. They're treated like royalty at this romantic Italian tourist hub, and while they do have to alight gracefully from water taxis, they don't have to do a lot of press. The Venice Fest takes place on the island of Lido, where visitors zip around on bicycles and pile into a series of world-class restaurants between screenings. Unlike Cannes, this fest is a relatively quiet, safe place to unveil a world premiere without generating too many stateside reviews, as few American critics attend beyond *Time* magazine's Richard Corliss and the trades. Ang Lee (*Brokeback Mountain*), George Clooney (*Good Night, and Good Luck*), Joe Wright (*Atonement*), Stephen Frears (*The Queen*), and Darren Aronofsky (*The Wrestler, Black Swan*) all launched successful Oscar campaigns at Venice.

But while the Weinsteins took Paul Thomas Anderson's *The Master* to Venice in 2012, it failed to win the festival's top prize, the

Golden Lion. (That went instead to Kim Ki-duk's *Pieta,* the eventual South Korean foreign film Oscar entry.) Instead, Anderson took home the Best Director Silver Lion prize, and the movie shared a Best Actor prize for its stars Philip Seymour Hoffman and Joaquin Phoenix.

THE TELLURIDE FILM FESTIVAL: *ARGO*

Because it does not announce its programming in advance, the thirty-nine-year-old Telluride Film Festival (August 31–September 3, 2012) mounts de facto "world premieres" high in the Colorado Rockies and takes place at the same time as Venice, over a four-day stretch covering Labor Day weekend. Some filmmakers with stamina like to jet straight from Venice to prestigious Telluride in advance of the more sprawling Toronto Film Festival, because it allows for an early spotlight and for buzz to build ahead of the noisier big-city ten-day fest. Every year a growing list of players return with or without their latest film, just to enjoy the relaxed summer camp atmosphere, among them directors Ken Burns, Alexander Payne, Werner Herzog, Mark Cousins, Allan Arkush, and George Lucas; producers Ron Yerxa, Albert Berger, and Bill Pohlad; theater director Peter Sellars; and actors Gael García Bernal, Michael O'Keefe, and Laura Linney.

Per usual, several distributors bring award hopefuls to Telluride in 2012, because the intimate festival has earned a reputation over the past decade with its consistent Oscar track record: Danny Boyle's *Slumdog Millionaire,* Jason Reitman's *Juno* and *Up in the Air,* Michel Hazanavicius's *The Artist,* and Tom Hooper's *The King's Speech,* to name a few.

Just before every Labor Day weekend, the L.A. contingent assembles at LAX to board the charter plane to Montrose, Colorado, and shuttle jitneys to Telluride. Critics Todd McCarthy and Leonard Maltin, lawyer Linda Lichter, Paramount marketing exec Megan

Colligan, ICM agent Ron Bernstein, and San Francisco chef Alice Waters are eager to grab the Telluride *Watch* as they settle into their seats and plan their schedules.

We soon discover that Telluride has not only booked Ben Affleck's *Argo* but several future foreign Oscar contenders, including Sony Pictures Classics' Cannes entry *Amour* and Magnolia's Berlin prize-winner *A Royal Affair,* starring Mads Mikkelsen. "We show the best films from around the world," says Telluride codirector Gary Meyer at the opening day press conference, joined by codirectors Tom Luddy and Julie Huntzinger, "and if the films get Oscar nominations and awards, that's great."

Argo has already been getting strong advance word in Los Angeles. Affleck scoped out Telluride in 2011, when his wife, actress Jennifer Garner, came to the sleepy Rocky Mountain town with political satire *Butter,* in which she played a ruthlessly competitive butter carver. The film did not amuse audiences and was soon pulled from the Weinstein Company's 2011 release schedule. But Garner and Affleck loved the intimate festival, which allows relatively free movement away from the usual paparazzi craziness. With his sights on the big prize with *Argo,* Affleck understands that the impeccably programmed art-film-lovers festival, attended by top critics and ardent cinephiles from all over the country, is a classy way to establish his commercial Mideast thriller as both serious-minded and entertaining.

Affleck was happy to world-premiere the movie at Telluride, where people come to see movies, as opposed to hunching in hotels talking about them. On Friday afternoon, he tells the crowd at the mountain ski resort's Chuck Jones Cinema, accessible by swaying gondola: "You're the first paying people to see the movie. It was a labor of love."

At the end of this screening the audience roars its approval, the first of many to applaud Affleck's taut, fact-based drama, his third film behind the camera (after *The Town* and *Gone Baby Gone*). It is directed with a screw-tightening efficiency that would make Michael Mann proud.

DNA from the films of Martin Scorsese, Sydney Pollack, Sidney Lumet, and Alan Pakula infuse *Argo*, which was produced by Affleck with George Clooney and Grant Heslov's Smokehouse, and distributed by Warner Bros., which had championed *The Town*. Clooney and Heslov developed a script by Chris Terrio about the CIA's declassified involvement in rescuing six hostages in Iran in 1979. The screenplay is based on selections from ex-CIA agent Antonio J. Mendez's book *The Master of Disguise* and a 2007 *Wired* magazine article by Joshuah Bearman.

Affleck was looking hard for the right project to do after *The Town*, and had turned down several studio directing projects, including *Man of Steel*. He got hold of Terrio's script and persuaded Clooney—who had obviously also recognized potential in the property—to let it go and produce it with him. Terrio's screenplay was so strong that Affleck, who after all had won an Oscar with pal Matt Damon for writing *Good Will Hunting*, saw no need to do his customary script overhaul.

Affleck, like fellow actor-directors Clooney and Clint Eastwood, sees the value of staying hands-on with a modest ($44 million) budget. Like them, he views playing the lead as efficient. After years of watching directors work, from Gus Van Sant (*Good Will Hunting*) to Terrence Malick (*To the Wonder*), Affleck is a strong and confident director who knows what he wants. "I maybe have matured," the onetime star of *Gigli* and *Pearl Harbor* says of his pursuit of smart, quality, modest-budgeted movies designed to stand the test of time—like the seventies classics he reveres.

The star delivers a solid, naturalistic performance as CIA agent Tony Mendez, who specializes in pulling people out of tight situations. Nothing could be tougher than Iran, as angry American flag-burning mobs call for the return of the shah, who has sought asylum in the United States. Painfully slowly, as the Iranians literally piece together the identities of the missing embassy personnel, Mendez, his CIA boss (Bryan Cranston), and others in the administration get the go-ahead to create a fake B-movie production based on the sci-fi fantasy script *Argo,* using it as a cover to extricate the group.

The tone shifts to enjoyable Hollywood insider parody as ace comedic actors John Goodman and Alan Arkin take the lead as, respectively, a makeup artist and Cannes award-winning producer on the downslope; they pretend to be actually producing *Argo* as cover for the escapees. The six hostages are to impersonate a filmmaking team on a location scout in Tehran. The idea is outrageous—and lives are definitely on the line.

Cinematographer Rodrigo Prieto (Oscar-nominated for *Brokeback Mountain*), who shot the Alejandro González Iñárritu films (such as *Babel*) that Affleck admires for their gritty naturalism, did outstanding work on location in Turkey, Los Angeles, and the Ontario, California, airport. Prieto and a group of cameramen carrying 8-millimeter and 16-millimeter cameras did such a convincing job shooting the opening mob scene that Affleck and Michael Mann's longtime editor William Goldenberg (who also edited *Gone Baby Gone*) didn't need to use any stock footage. Throughout the film, Prieto's handheld cameras "make everything feel grabbed and accidental," Goldenberg tells me during an interview, "finding things and pieces, like the film accidentally landed there."

Affleck admits that he shoots a lot, trying many performance colors—for himself as well as his editor—and figures out the movie in the editing room. Affleck is his own toughest critic, says Goldenberg: "He is brutal." That shot of Affleck removing his shirt (revealing a six-pack) was originally written as Mendez emerging naked and vulnerable from the shower and wrapping a towel around himself. Affleck self-consciously pulled it back a tad (and later good-naturedly took his shots on *Saturday Night Live*).

Goldenberg wound up competing with himself in the year's

awards race, as he also edited *Zero Dark Thirty*. He and Affleck expertly navigated *Argo*'s tricky tonal balance: the director admits that lines like Arkin's classic "If I am doing a fake movie, it's going to be a fake hit" are hilarious, but Affleck insists that he cut any laughs that undermined the film's fabric of reality. "I'll never go for comedy," he says, "I'll go for realism."

They admittedly made the final escape more thrilling than it actually was. In real life, Mendez and the six "houseguests" wound up stranded at the airport as their flight was delayed for three hours; the CIA agent kept them calm. "Tonally each part of the film meshed together," says Goldenberg. "This time we got it right."

While Affleck knew that the film would be timely—unrest in the Middle East has not dissipated over the decades—he could not have anticipated that a September 11 mob assault on a U.S. consulate in Benghazi, Libya, would make news headlines three days after his film's debut in Toronto, the week after the Telluride premiere. *Argo* is "a tribute to the diplomats who work overseas," he says. And recognizing the Canadian sensitivity to his rewrite of history, he swiftly moves to change a card at the end of the movie so as not to undercut the heroism of Canadian ambassador Ken Taylor. At the Toronto after party, Affleck celebrates with cast and crew, producer Heslov, and buddy Damon, as well as Warner president Jeff Robinov, who after *Gone Baby Gone* chased after Affleck to direct when nobody else did.

At the film's post-Toronto premiere at the Academy's Goldwyn Theater in Beverly Hills, the industry audience accords the retired Mendez a standing ovation. Being able to cheer a real American hero—as well as Hollywood ingenuity—clearly helped *Argo* to ride the zeitgeist, not only at the box office but in the awards race. Movies that tell us something both about us and our world tend to do well with Oscar voters.

Affleck's only Oscar nomination was that 1998 Original Screenplay win with Damon for *Good Will Hunting*. Since then his best performances have been in his own films. Multiple nominations were clearly inevitable for *Argo* after Telluride and Toronto, as the film surged to the top of early Oscar contenders lists and went on to deliver strong opening weekend numbers and a rare A-plus Cinemascore from audiences.

The trick was to hang on through the thick and thin of the most competitive Oscar field in years. One obvious rival, Kathryn Bigelow's *Zero Dark Thirty,* tackled another timely topic, the capture of Osama bin Laden, not to mention other perceived front-runners Steven Spielberg (*Lincoln*), Ang Lee (*Life of Pi*), Quentin Tarantino (*Django Unchained*), and Tom Hooper (*Les Misérables*).

THE TORONTO INTERNATIONAL FILM FESTIVAL: *SILVER LININGS PLAYBOOK*

Another arch competitor swiftly becomes apparent at TIFF, the Toronto International Film Festival (September 6–16, 2012), where David O. Russell's *Silver Linings Playbook* is given its world premiere by the Weinstein Company and immediately earns raves. Harvey Weinstein's preview footage at Cannes had not captured the poignant depths of the full-length family dramedy, which reached its final form after a series of audience previews and some down-to-the-wire editing-room tweaking.

Russell first broke out at Sundance 1994 with taboo-breaking first feature *Spanking the Monkey.* He went on to build his reputation for pulling strong comedy performances from his actors with family ensembles *Flirting with Disaster* and *I Heart Huckabees*, taking a detour into the heart of darkness with the Iraq war film *Three Kings,* during which he managed to alienate his usually affable leading man Clooney, who publicly protested Russell's rough treatment of extras on set. Russell returned to family dysfunction in 2010 with *The Fighter,* based on a true story. Out of seven Academy Award nominations, including Best Picture and Best Director, the gritty

Lowell, Massachusetts–based dramedy picked up two supporting Oscars: for Christian Bale, who plays a meth-head former boxer, and for the actress who played his hard-as-nails mom, Melissa Leo.

It was in 2007 that producer-directors Sydney Pollack and Anthony Minghella showed Russell the manuscript for Matthew Quick's novel about another addlepated working-class family, this time from Philadelphia. (Alas, both Pollack and Minghella succumbed to cancer before seeing the film come to life.) Russell related to the struggles of Pat Solitano (played by Bradley Cooper), a young man with bipolar disorder who is trying to recover his equilibrium at home with his parents after four years in a mental hospital.

Russell, whose own bipolar son Matthew was then twelve, was at the time actively searching "for a film that would make my son feel like he was part of the world," he told the London *Telegraph.* "Because my son has wrangled with many of the same challenges as the Bradley Cooper character . . . There were so many ways to get it wrong. Because mental illness shouldn't be the whole focus of the thing. It's really just a part of the fabric of life, and it resonates with how we all are."

Russell, who adapted the novel himself, originally planned to cast as his two romantic leads Vince Vaughn and, as Tiffany, who deals with her policeman husband's death by sleeping with most of the men in her office, Zooey Deschanel. He wound up with two bankable names with franchises behind them, *The Hangover*'s Bradley Cooper and *The Hunger Games*' Jennifer Lawrence.

When Russell first met Cooper after *Wedding Crashers* "he seemed like a palpably angry person to me," he told one interviewer. "A scary angry person. So I knew that was good for *Silver Linings Playbook*, because it wasn't fake, it wasn't nice, it was just intense . . . I asked him about that. His answer told me that he could do this role because his answer was very self-revealing. His answer was that he had been unhappy at the time when he made *Wedding Crashers*. His life was not as fulfilled. He was thirty to forty pounds heavier like the character in the movie, he was hiding behind it, but really he was scared. So already you're getting so much depth and it's very much in the world of the character—he's a very open, emotional guy."

For Russell, directing is about fighting against fakery at all times. So he gets in his actors' faces for multiple takes lasting twenty minutes—without yelling "cut"—until he gets to the raw realness he's seeking.

Silver Linings joins the front-runners for the Oscar as soon as the film wins the coveted TIFF audience award, which has been nabbed previously by such crowd-pleasing Oscar winners as *The King's Speech, Precious,* and *Slumdog Millionaire.*

Other Toronto players still in the Oscar pack include *Argo,* Sundance hits *Beasts of the Southern Wild* and *The Sessions,* Palme d'Or winner *Amour,* and *The Impossible,* Summit's tsunami disaster drama starring Naomi Watts. But front and center in the Best Actor and Actress race are Cooper and Lawrence as two lost, emotionally damaged yet attractive people who draw comfort and kinship from each other. Russell, who has said he admires Billy Wilder's tough and unsentimental approach to romance, delicately fine-tuned a relationship comedy that is both funny and moving. Even in this cynical age, we root for these two characters in pain to heal each other, win their dance contest, and find true love.

Cooper is in ebullient spirits the day after *Silver Linings'* rousing debut. Russell approached him early on in the casting process, Cooper tells me, and then circled back to him right before production. Cooper, having already read the script, said yes without batting an eyelash, even though he was terrified. "I know how demanding David is," he says. "It's really no-bullshit acting. You have to be real. I go, 'God, I don't know if I can create a character that can take this audience on the arc of this movie and introduce them to all these different characters.' I gave all that fear away and looked him in the eyes and said, 'If you believe that I am the guy, then I will go down this road with you, because I have never seen a bad performance out of anybody in any of your movies.' I decided I was just going to roll the dice."

Cooper was willing to match intensity with Russell on set. "Any director worth their weight in gold is intense, because it's an intense atmosphere," Cooper says. "It can manifest itself in a calm way, or in a high-octane, infectious energy way. David has all of those colors. He has a very soothing voice. It worked with Jen and Bob, the three of us, it just clicked. We were all there for each other. There are chunks of truth that are born out of love that resonate in the book and script."

Russell had two cameras going at all times, either a 35-millimeter camera, a Steadicam, or a handheld; the cinematographer lit the sets so that he could turn the cameras 360 degrees around at any time and shoot anywhere. "Love is what David brings, it comes from love, and there's zero ego, he's a collaborator," says Cooper. "The only thing he requires of you is to really show up; don't bring your 'bedroom perfect' take on character or the scene. If you do that, it's not going to work, you're going to have a hard day. You show up for work, take all your clothes off, get naked, and bomb! You have to get ready to rock on rehearsal: 'Okay, camera! Ready? Cry here, cry, okay, come on, come on, come on, what's happening? Everybody standing around, get out of your head, now!'

"Creatively, I love the way he works. Anyone who can bring you out of your comfort zone and can get you in a place quickly—he's interested in what's happening now, that's all he cares about."

Russell also coaxed the best performance in years out of De Niro, who plays obsessive-compulsive bookie Pat Solitano Sr., the father of Cooper's character. "David is a wonderful director, and writer, a combination of that," De Niro tells me later at the Academy nominees luncheon. "When we're moving around in a scene, he puts the camera on a Steadicam or handheld, on you or on the next character that speaks, back to you, around here, throwing a couple lines at you here and there. But the core material is what you've worked on. It's spontaneous, that energy and controlled chaos, it helps the immediacy."

Cooper drove down to the set in Philadelphia before production to rehearse the dance contest with Lawrence. They had three weeks to nail it. "She's twenty-two years old, she has this quality, like Bob, that is really powerful," Cooper says. "It's not so much that he's a great actor, which he is, but he has this quality, as does she. She's a chameleon, but I do see this similar quality in all her work. She's forty-five and twenty-five at same time, and so much so that when I hang out with her I realize she's just a kid. Physically she's built like a throwback movie star. She doesn't look like a child; she moves like a beautiful woman."

As strong as Kentucky-bred Lawrence has been so far—from her Oscar-nominated role in *Winter's Bone* to her turn as iconic action heroine Katniss Everdeen in *The Hunger Games*—she came into her own in *Silver Linings Playbook*. An actress who relies on her own instincts on how to read a character and make her real, Lawrence blossomed under Debra Granik's tutelage on *Winter's Bone* and proved she was not a one-trick pony when she also popped in Jodie Foster's *The Beaver*.

After landing the coveted *Silver Linings* role via a Skype audition from Louisville, Lawrence embraced Russell's hardboiled directing style, she tells me in Toronto. If he told her something sucked, she did it again. And yes, she memorized the scene-stopping monologue that drew cheers at Toronto's Roy Thomson Hall—even if she got her sports teams mixed up at first. (She and Cooper not only go on to costar again in Susanne Bier's period drama *Serena*, but rejoin De Niro in Russell's 2013 FBI sting drama *American Hustle*, which also stars Christian Bale and Jeremy Renner.)

THE NEW YORK FILM FESTIVAL: *LIFE OF PI* AND *LINCOLN*

Following Toronto on the fall fest calendar circuit is the prestigious New York Film Festival (September 28–October 14, 2012). The

NYFF is a classy, smaller-scale Oscar-launch venue for the studios and the independents, with cred. The highbrow selection committee only picks about twenty-five top movies for the main program, with three or four key slots going to studio debuts, such as David Fincher's *The Social Network* in 2010 (Sony), and a work-in-progress screening of Martin Scorsese's 3-D *Hugo* in 2011 (Paramount).

Life of Pi

In 2012, Twentieth Century Fox booked its $120 million epic *Life of Pi* to open the NYFF. Fox 2000, a quality label run by veteran Elizabeth Gabler, had pushed for a decade to adapt Yann Martel's international bestselling novel. For years it was considered impossible.

Life of Pi marked a high-degree-of-difficulty dive off the high board for director Ang Lee. And given the technology required to achieve the ambitious computer-graphic visual effects, the film couldn't have gotten made any sooner than it did. Lee wasn't even sure he had pulled it off when he was finishing up the print of the 127-minute 3-D movie he was going to show at Lincoln Center. "Three days before the New York Film Festival, for the first time, I had all the images rendered, music done, and mixing," he tells me in an L.A. interview before the opening. "And I see it put together, I started to cry. I think it worked! It's emotion, you know?"

Lee, more than any director working today, is a filmmaker for the world. He left Taiwan and moved to America to make such independent art films as *The Ice Storm*, and his three great love stories—martial arts romance *Crouching Tiger, Hidden Dragon*, gay love tragedy *Brokeback Mountain*, and Jane Austen's *Sense and Sensibility*—were accessible to multiple cultures. He's capable of a wide range of storytelling, from Marvel comic-book movie *Hulk* to NC-17 period romance *Lust, Caution*.

And with *Life of Pi*, Lee fashioned a love story that transcends borders. In this case, it's love between a seventeen-year-old young man (nonpro Suraj Sharma) from India and a Bengal tiger. The movie asks, is it possible for a wild animal to love a human being? And vice versa?

A universal story that resonates in a world where religion can tear people and societies apart, Martel's story of a Hindu/Christian/Muslim who is the sole human survivor of an ocean shipwreck reminds us that film can both heal and inspire. But it is also a stunning technological triumph. Conceived a decade ago, long before the 2009 arrival of the 3-D *Avatar,* this movie is a live-action/animation hybrid, as major characters like the threatening tiger and sublime phosphorescent Pacific seascapes could only be created by artists in the digital realm.

The 3-D film boasts scenes of breathtaking beauty: a simple shot of the tiger in the moonlight, several surreal mergers of sea and sky, fully realized scenes (that had previewed months earlier at CinemaCon) of Pi watching the ship—and his family—going down, a luminescent whale breach, and silver fish in whirring flight. Lee mastered the aesthetics of 3-D, considering every detail in terms of its impact on the viewer. Never have spatial relationships been more dramatic: Pi maneuvers with an oar and a large tiger in a small lifeboat on a huge ocean.

The film's $120 million final cost far exceeded its planned $70 million budget, partly because Lee insisted on shooting in 3-D. "I just have this hunch against everybody," he recalls, "including Fox, that 3-D might pull this off. I don't think it could be 2-D. They were like, 'It's a literature property! Why do you want to spend that money? If it was an action movie, we'd push you to do it, but it's like $25 million more dollars! What are you talking about?'"

Lee told them: "I just have this feeling, with this movie." He thought, "It might open up the space. Your mind-set is different. Because 2-D is so sophisticated, you're so used to it, it doesn't open up the imagination and it doesn't bring the extra innocence or whatever. And also I have to wow the audience because there's this talk about the power of God. When you talk about God, the first thing that comes along is not love, it's fear. You have to fear, and be in awe. You have to be scared."

In fact, Lee's longtime editor Tim Squyres, who had never worked in 3-D before, decided very early on that in cutting the film, they would do everything in 3-D. So from the first day of assembly they only ever worked in 3-D. "We cut it thinking, this was a 3-D movie," says Squyres. He never saw the film any other way.

The movie begins with a stunning series of shots of animals in their natural glory at a zoo in Pondicherry, India (one of the film's shooting locations, along with a huge water tank in Taiwan). The movie revels in the lush colors and textures of India as Lee sets up his through-lines. His narrator, the adult Pi (Irrfan Khan of *Slumdog Millionaire*), tells his improbable survival story to a young Canadian novelist (*Anonymous* actor Rafe Spall, who replaced Tobey Maguire mid-film—Lee admitted that he realized the *Spider-Man* star was too well known and would be distracting in the role).

We meet Pi's family, who doesn't understand his attraction to three of the world's religions—Hinduism, Christianity, and Islam— and we encounter the fierce zoo tiger Richard Parker, who ravages a goat in front of Pi's eyes. Pi's belief in both God and the soul of a tiger play out as he uses his wits (and a shipwreck survivor instruction manual) to outsmart Richard Parker on a lifeboat for 227 days. "Thank you, Vishnu, for introducing me to Christ," says Pi at one point. "God wasn't finished with me yet," he says at another.

Fox cochairman Tom Rothman (who left the studio before the film was released), Gabler, and producer Gil Netter (*The Blind Side*) all accept credit for standing behind Lee's quest to make the film. "It has a gigantic visual effects component," Gabler told me as she was trying to convince Fox to give it the green light. "You can't put a live tiger in a boat with a child. It has elements of *Cast Away*, when the kid is alone in the boat. You don't need language to convey what's on the screen. We need to make the movie for the whole world." That they did.

THE SCREENPLAY

After ten long years of painstaking development, *Life of Pi* finally made it to the screen. There were many times when Gabler, who optioned Yann Martel's bestselling novel right after it was published in 2001, did not think that it would happen. Only when Lee came along in 2008 did it become possible. The device of using the older Pi as the window into the story came from screenwriter David Magee, who was hired on the basis of his moving Oscar-nominated screenplay for the J. M. Barrie biopic *Finding Neverland,* which "was a good adaptation," Gabler explains in an interview. "It had adult and child protagonists. It was mystical to a large degree, very dramatic and emotional."

Lee and Magee had almost worked together years earlier on a project. They met for the first time three and a half years ago at a Manhattan sushi restaurant. "We had a great conversation," the writer tells me on the phone. "Ang ended the meal by saying, 'Okay, then. Let's do it.' He can say that. In our first dinner he and I had agreed on one thing immediately: this was a story about storytelling. It's about religion, how stories get you through life."

So theater grad/actor-turned-screenwriter Magee took on the challenging adaptation. He credits his work as a voice actor on books-on-tape for turning him into a screenwriter adept at adaptations. He'd often record both the full-length and abridged versions of books, and began to feel he could do abridgements that were better than some of the ones he was reading. So he wound up abridging eighty books over five years. That became training in structure, as he whittled books that were 100,000 to 300,000 words down to 29,500 words so they could be read in a three-hour period. These shortened scripts were stripped of their descriptive passages and heavily reliant on dialogue, and like most screenplays of a similar length they focused on strong action.

The two men would hang out at Lee's Soho loft and throw around ideas and talk through scenes. The source of the movie's emotion,

Magee admits, is that "the entire second act of a boy on a boat with a tiger is not just dealing with the conflict between them. We had to find a way to express what's going on with Pi's inner journey. We used voice-over of him looking at a journal. We tried a number of different things. We wrote the second act silent, with ouches and grunts and groans. But it was apparent that certain things were not coming out—the emotional and physical strain of it. We were not getting his coming of age, the realization that his relationship with the tiger was changing who he was, so we had to find a way to do that."

Luckily the filmmakers tracked down Maine writer Steven Callahan, who had written *Adrift*, a book about his true experience of sixty-nine days at sea in a lifeboat. "We learned that he was a sailor," says Magee. "For him the only way to stay sane was to focus on the details of his journey, even though he couldn't control where the boat was going: measure speed, latitude, the part of ocean. He kept a meticulous journal in his survival manual, writing with the smallest letters. That became a jumping-off point, the writing notes in the survival manual. Without words to hang onto he was lost, he would lose his mind. Reading aloud became Pi's secret voice-over."

Lee brought a sophisticated global cultural sensitivity to the project. "What made him good for this story is his sense of heightened reality and wonder," says Magee. "It has to be grounded in meticulously believable reality. There's an incredible amount of detail he thinks about when putting together his films. We had worked with Callahan to figure out the wind speed on any given day, where the sun would be, what the waves would look like where in the Pacific Ocean. The audience doesn't need to know any of that. The accuracy gives it a believability you're not going to find when someone is concerned with flash first and reality later."

Finding the film's bookend structure was essential, says Magee. "We could potentially have done without the bookends. We debated endlessly leading up to preproduction, shifting things around and trying different ways to see if another way would work better."

Lee came up with an ingenious method for developing the first and third acts of the screenplay: they literally split the page down the middle, so that everything going on in the apartment as the adult Pi tells the story was on one side, and the other side was everything going on in India years ago. They rearranged both sides of the page in different ways to play the imagery off the narration and went back and forth, says Magee. "In the first act, essential things in the modern story begin the journey."

The second act on the ocean was largely silent, with little dialogue, while during the first act the film flowed back and forth between the two worlds, returning to that mode in the third. Further into production, certain visuals were deemed unnecessary and dropped, as was the voice-over of less important narration. "It was about trying to pare it down to essentials," says Magee.

Finding the right balance for the spiritual themes in the story was tricky. "Spiritual things in context were very difficult to lay out simply," he says. "We didn't want to turn the film into a lecture about comparative religion. It was important to us, as Martel says in the book, that an atheist has a story he believes in too. We weren't taking sides on which religion, we were not trying to prove God exists, or what we care about. Everyone uses a different narrative to get through life. The ending is a Rorschach test asking you to respond to the movie. It says more about how you view the world than how Pi does. He is a religious character, but that doesn't mean you have to accept the story the way the writer does."

Understanding multiple world religions helped Lee to deal with this complex material, says Magee. "Lee has the perspective of someone who is not quite an outsider but stands at the edge of the crowd. He was raised with the Christian faith in Taiwan, but by the same token he has an understanding of Eastern culture, including Indian culture, relationships between men and women going from religion down through daily custom, the formality in the way people speak to one another."

For his part, Lee felt like a video game programmer making the movie, he says. "And you gotta play. Because it talks about the strength of storytelling. God is just a red herring, or even faith, for that matter. It's different than religion. The book didn't take religion that seriously; it takes God more seriously. So what is God? How is God at work? Is it his fatherness? I think that the book treats God more as this otherness that creates us—then we have a conversation. But I come more from the East, and how we talk about that is different. It could almost be the most introverted, sub-mystery that we look in, that we don't know what is at work."

THE PRODUCTION

Preproduction took place in Lee's home country of Taiwan, where Lee and Magee did scene rewrites up to the start of production. There were a hundred days of shooting; it was a great machine that had to roll forward, and it included many scenes in the wave tank. Most of the film's ocean vistas were created digitally with specific moods in mind.

For Lee, working hands-on to coach acting novice Suraj Sharma was key. With his longtime casting director Avy Kaufman, Lee went through a long search involving four or five thousand kids in six or seven different cities, including London, Vancouver, Montreal, New York, L.A., and Mumbai. Lee was hoping to find somebody who was born and reared in India.

Sharma didn't intend to audition. The eighteen-year-old student tagged along on his younger brother's tryout for the film in Mumbai. He read the survival manual for the casting director, as well as some scenes in which he trains the tiger. Each time, Sharma would make the cut. Lee narrowed it down to ten people.

At the fourth and final audition in Mumbai, Sharma finally met the director. He had to read the four pages in the hospital-bed finale as part of his audition. "He made it extremely real," Sharma tells me in an interview. "He made me go back and find memories that made me feel real emotions. So the second time, I don't know what happened but I started crying . . . or anyway, I teared up. They seemed to like it a little bit." Lee immediately and deeply felt, "He's the guy."

Under extraordinary duress, as shipwreck survivor Pi alone on the ocean, Sharma delivers a performance that would have been daunting for any professional actor. He expresses grief, fear, anger, and depression, mostly acting in a giant tank buffeted by wind and water and pretending to fight off a Bengal tiger—who wasn't there. He had to buff up from 150 pounds to 167, and then drop down to 130; he had to learn how to swim and to hold his breath underwater.

The actor was put through his own tortures, buffeted by the elements, standing there, in the storm, screaming. He got through it with months of training. He became devoted to master director Lee, learning how to work a boat, tie rope, act, do yoga, and speak Mandarin. He also gained a new goal in life: to be a film director. The performance will likely be his last. He has no intention of acting again.

The visual effects were pushing the edge of what was possible. Lee admits that just five years ago he wouldn't have known what to do, but he also recognized that he learned a lot from shooting the VFX movie *Hulk*. It gave him experience to build on, to know what was possible. He found the work so intense that it gave him nightmares.

Animation supervisor Erik-Jan de Boer was in charge of animating sixteen to eighteen animal species, of which five were main characters, including the tiger, zebra, and orangutan in the boat. Most of the boat scenes were shot dry in a parking lot in Taiwan against a blue screen. When we see the tiger in the movie, fewer than 10 percent of the shots are live-action. Eighty-four percent of the tiger is digital, 84 percent of the rain is digital, and all of the orangutan is digital. The real tiger was used in some of the shots in the boat, when he's a fair distance from Pi with an oar between them. Having a real tiger gave L.A.-based visual effects firm

Rhythm & Hues an incredible reference; their attention to detail made the difference. The scene where Pi trains the tiger with the stick is about half real and half CG.

"So we would shoot it with the real tigers," cinematographer Claudio Miranda tells me at a Q&A for various craft guilds in Los Angeles. "And the real tigers did stuff that we never would have anticipated. There's that shot where the tiger's sharpening its claws on the bench. That wasn't scripted—that's just something the tiger did. I sat with the tiger trainer, and he explained that that's a nervous tiger saying, 'See, I'm not nervous.' That kind of behavior was very interesting, so we shot that first, planned it all, and then, three weeks later, shot it in CG."

Having a trainer was an advantage. "Our trainer had worked with tigers for thirty years," adds producer David Womark at the Q&A. "And he had an insight into their thought processes and manners. A lot of details—the tiger trying to prove he's not scared, for instance—came from him. In the shot when Pi pulls the tiger into his lap, he told us that while tigers are aggressive animals, he had an experience with one that was older and sick, and said that in that moment, on her deathbed, she craved comfort and nuzzling."

Rather than trace frame-by-frame shots (or rotoscope) of live tigers as they performed for a given camera angle, de Boer chose to use pure hand-to-eye key frame animation—working with an experienced crew of forty-seven animators in four teams under four supervisors in Mumbai, Hyderabad, and Los Angeles. "It was about trying to stay as close as possible to the animal," he says at the Q&A. "We would go back and look at what the tiger is doing in the surrounding live action shot. We would put that into our animation and the look of our tiger to make sure we had a seamless integration."

Standing over their shoulders was their demanding leader, Lee. The first thing he said to the visual effects crew in Taiwan: "I want to make art with you."

"Ang also felt that the entire process of making the film was parallel to Pi's journey," says Miranda. "He really thinks like that, and when you have a director that feels that way, it informs everybody."

But Lee was making a movie that he knew could have an impact on audiences, and he struggled in the editing room with Squyres to find the right balance of emotion and spirituality. For Lee, that's the key difference between his movie and the book. "The book is not emotional, it's thought-provoking," he says. "But for the movie, you have to make emotional connections, and I think religious thought, or your relation to faith, can be emotional. It's not just a thought process. In the movie that's how it comes to big images, with human expression. It has to be emotion.

"So my biggest change [from the book] is how the emotional connects to the process. In the beginning, middle, and end, all three parts, I have to make emotional connections . . . For that, I think Pi's relationship to the tiger is like to God. It's unrequited. I think that can be really heartbreaking. It's not like with a beast and a man it goes both ways. It's unrequited. Because the tiger has tiger's emotions, he's not a human being. He has feelings, but it's not a human view."

The filmmakers knew that the moment when the tiger leaves Pi was the heart of the movie. "Pi's journey is about being raised in a zoo in a safe environment where everything is taken care of, and he believes in God, he goes on a journey that tests his will and his strength," explains Magee. "The beast that was safe and majestic in the zoo becomes frightening. Pi has to come to terms with his relationships. His father taught him that the tiger is not your friend no matter what you see in his eyes. The tiger is your enemy; the tiger is of a different nature. Because you build a relationship with a tiger doesn't mean the tiger is your pal who hangs around you. That is the journey he has. We're all different. We're all creating narratives to come to understand that larger universe we can never know fully. So we come up with imperfect stories to try and express it."

Lee admits that the third part of the film, the showdown between

Pi and Richard Parker, was "the hardest, tough as hell. People talk about water, kids, animals, 3-D, but this movie is totally illusion. How do you examine the illusion within the illusion? In a movie, you can't take people out, you can't pull a rug from under them."

Not bringing in the alternate version of the story—where Pi reluctantly gives investigators the other alternate reality—was off the table. "It doesn't matter if I consider it or not, it's not an option," Lee says. "That's the book, you have to do it. You get stuck. I struggled and I couldn't move for a year and a half. It was the most painful experience to make the movie, how to pull that ending off. How do I bring on the second story? And at the end—we try so many ways—I found both stories need to have emotion. You have to treat them equal, so people can make a choice. And I was like, 'God, it's so hard to do.' I make movies for a long time. It doesn't get easier. You just have to be humble. Five years ago I don't think I could do this."

The movie wowed critics, audiences, and award-givers all over the world. It had the right elements: globally popular literary source (7 million copies sold), heartwarming family story from an A-list Oscar-winning director, and epic scale and scope.

In a less competitive year Sharma would have been a shoo-in for a Best Actor nomination. But he faced Daniel Day-Lewis, Hugh Jackman, John Hawkes, Bradley Cooper, Denzel Washington, and Joaquin Phoenix. *Life of Pi* did become a leading contender for Oscars, and not only for its extraordinary technical accomplishments.

Lincoln

A late entry to the NYFF lineup was the world premiere of Steven Spielberg's *Lincoln*, which had a second premiere at November's AFI Fest in Los Angeles. Every year AFI, held in the heart of Academy country, adds a few late-breaking Oscar contenders to the mix. I attend an earlier *Lincoln* screening, and the thing that strikes me on first viewing Spielberg's historical epic about the last four months in the administration of the sixteenth president of the United States is how unconventional it is. It's organic, grown from several chapters in Doris Kearns Goodwin's eight-hundred-page Lincoln tome *Team of Rivals,* nurtured over five years by Tony- and Pulitzer-winning playwright Tony Kushner, and shaped by Steven Spielberg and actor Daniel Day-Lewis into something we've never seen before. This alchemy of a torrent of words, well-researched history, and the powerful personality of the world's most popular American president yields a magical biopic that swiftly moves to the front of the Oscar pack.

The movie plays well both in New York at Lincoln Center and in Hollywood for its Chinese Theatre opening night, which is preceded by a party attended by the cast and crew at the Roosevelt Hotel. A later Academy screening draws rousing applause, enhanced by the presence of Spielberg and Day-Lewis, who do a Q&A, something that is rare for both of them. Some members have to be turned away from the packed 1,000-seat auditorium, and several days later the same thing happens to producers who show up late to the Producers Guild of America (PGA) screening.

"They picked a story within the story," Goodwin tells me at the premiere, commenting on the film's focus on the crucial month of January 1865, when Lincoln maneuvered Congress into passing the Thirteenth Amendment to the Constitution, which ended slavery in America. "It had a beginning, a middle, and an end. The important thing is that they got Lincoln: his stooped walk, his high-pitched voice, his humor. All the things that I cared about in eight hundred pages were compressed into two hours. It feels more than right."

Spielberg, who hasn't test-screened a movie to get audience reaction since he directed *Hook* in 1991, tells me at the premiere that on *Lincoln* he decided he wasn't going to try to play it safe after obsessing about the film for nine years. "At a certain time in your life you get to where it's not about risk," he says. "It's about trying to stay interested in the entire medium by not going back to the same recipes again and again. It's about caring so much that if you totally fail at something that is experimental in terms of narrative, I can at least be proud that I tried."

Spielberg had "always wanted to tell a story about Lincoln," he tells *60 Minutes* anchor Lesley Stahl. "I saw a paternal father figure, someone who was completely, stubbornly committed to his ideals, his vision. I think the film is very relevant for today . . . I think there's a sense of darkness . . . with him. He was living with two agendas, both of which had to do with healing . . . First, to abolish slavery, end the war. But he also had his personal life, and I think there's darkness in there."

The project began life at Universal with Liam Neeson attached. After nine years of sporadic development, Neeson dropped out, feeling he was getting too old for the role. When Universal finally passed as well, Fox and Participant joined Reliance-owned Dream-Works and distributor Disney to back the production. It took a while to line up the financial partners and presales in territories overseas, though, and Spielberg at one point thought he'd have to make it at HBO.

Angels in America and *Caroline, or Change* playwright Kushner, whose screenplay for Spielberg's *Munich* was Oscar-nominated, gave five years of his life to *Lincoln,* Spielberg says. "He licked it, after three years of real struggle, then two when he was on a roll."

Kushner started with a five-hundred-page script that needed whittling down; it was more than four times the length of an average two-hour screenplay. Spielberg helped Kushner figure out which slice of Lincoln's life to choose; he wanted to show audiences the president's human face. Spielberg was the one who saw as the potential dramatic focus of the film the last months of Lincoln's life, when he fought to pass the Thirteenth Amendment and worked to wind down the Civil War. The most daring sequence in the movie shows Lincoln berating his cabinet for fighting him on the amendment, an eight-minute scene that Day-Lewis insisted on shooting in one uninterrupted take.

One of the bold decisions the filmmakers made on *Lincoln* was not to dumb down Kushner's script. *Lincoln* is an unapologetic smart person's movie. At its center, underpinning the entire film, is a speech that no self-respecting screenwriter would have included. Kushner knows he broke the rules. "I ducked it in a way because I'm a playwright primarily," he tells me in an interview. "And so this wasn't so long for a speech in a play. You can get away with it. I've written longer monologues. I've written an hour-long monologue in *Homebody/Kabul*."

In March 2006 the writer had started detailing the last two years of Lincoln's administration, from September 1863 to the end. "I couldn't find a way to condense it, to speed it up; the material was overwhelmingly rich," Kushner recalls. As he was writing, Spielberg would tell Kushner, "That's going to leave people in the dark," or, "They won't care about it." "Spielberg liked this scene or that scene, but I started getting panicky. He was patient. I thought maybe it was impossible to do."

The Writers Guild strike gave Kushner permission to put the script away, and he stopped reading about Lincoln. When the strike was over, Spielberg asked him to come out to L.A. and sit down and talk through things and see where they were. "Two days before I got on the plane I suddenly thought, 'If I just did the last four months . . .' In all the reading beyond *Team of Rivals*, several themes kept reappearing on the central conundrum Lincoln faced. So I wrote this speech. I just said, 'He's a lawyer.' I found the little story about this old lady that's a great illustration of this question of the gray areas of legality. And then I, in as lawyerly a fashion as I could, using the terms Lincoln would have used, tried to work my way through the issue. The speech was quite long."

For years, Spielberg had been trying to convince a recalcitrant Daniel Day-Lewis to take on the role of Lincoln. But the two-time Oscar-winning actor wasn't convinced he could do justice to this quintessentially American icon. (After the movie opened to triumphant success, Spielberg released to the media one of Day-Lewis's rejection letters.)

After years of demurring, it was Kushner's script—and the chance to work for the first time with Spielberg—that tipped the scales. But not before Day-Lewis invited Spielberg, Kushner, and producer Kathleen Kennedy to his home in Ireland so they could talk in person and meet the actor's family.

Day-Lewis put them up in a quaintly beautiful inn in the Irish countryside near the old, wisteria-covered farmhouse in the Wicklow Mountains outside Dublin where the actor lived at the time with his wife, filmmaker and author Rebecca Miller, and their two children. Kennedy told *People* magazine that for the first several hours of that meeting, the filmmakers simply stood in the kitchen, getting to know the kids.

Kushner, meanwhile, had to plow ahead with the script not knowing whether Day-Lewis was on board. "I sent in the draft after Steven and Daniel and I had met for the first time in Ireland," says Kushner. "So I was writing a draft with the possibility that Daniel, who I always wanted, was actually maybe going to do this. He hadn't said yes, but he was waiting for the rewrite to see if he felt that he could do this."

Spielberg himself sets the budget for each of his movies, in this case $65 million, and forces everyone around him, including Kennedy, to meet it. "They have no choice," his DreamWorks cochairman Stacey Snider tells me in an interview. "Steven is not used to anyone saying no."

Luckily, Day-Lewis finally stopped saying no to Spielberg. The British actor may not appear to be a marquee movie star, but audiences are starting to get the idea that when he does a movie—and he picks them carefully, willing to wait years between roles—they should check it out. At a time when many actors risk overexposure, grabbing all the roles they can while interest is hot, Day-Lewis steps back and keeps himself grounded in his family and waits for the muse to hit him.

He's a draw for moviegoers because when he steps up, when the match is perfect between director and role, when it feels right, he gives his all. He embraces a role so totally that it consumes and overtakes him. He loses himself in the part throughout production. It's fair to say that Day-Lewis *is* Abraham Lincoln, and that people went to see the movie because the actor was in it.

From the start of his career, he showed a penchant for muscular, angry, and violent roles, from Stephen Frears's *My Beautiful Laundrette* and Jim Sheridan's *My Left Foot, In the Name of the Father*, and *The Boxer*, to Michael Mann's *The Last of the Mohicans*, Martin Scorsese's *Gangs of New York*, and Paul Thomas Anderson's *There Will Be Blood*.

"I spent most of my time on the front line of London street life," he tells the *Hollywood Reporter*'s Scott Feinberg at a Santa Barbara Film Festival tribute in February, "playing soccer, fighting on the school playground, and rebelling against authority and the British class system." His socialist father, the poet laureate of England Cecil Day-Lewis, died when Daniel was fifteen. "He had more than enough chances to see me screw up," Day-Lewis says. At the Bristol Old Vic Theatre School he embraced the Stanislavski method, and he learned via three films with Sheridan that steeping himself over time in a role, with familiarity, worked best for him: "If I was going to carry on doing this, I could only work in this way."

Day-Lewis admits that he can't do the work without the "reclusive need to withdraw from that. These two things are mutually dependent upon each other. I cannot do the work I love to do unless I take time away from it. It's the time taken away from it when, God forbid, I reengage with life, that allows me to do the work in the hope that I would bring something of my experience to it, not lurching from one film set to another."

"But the life that we bring to our work has to come from elsewhere, it has to," he continues. "So as much as I love the work, so I love to stay away from it, and that time away, I am always engaged in some kind of skullduggery that allows me to come back to it. I don't know what allowed this little kernel of self-knowledge at such an early age, but without it I would have given up this work a long time ago, because I would have exhausted my capacity or desire to do it. It's not an endlessly regenerating compulsion. It has to be recognized and honored when it comes. If it's not there you should be occupied doing something else . . . Without that personal need, that curiosity that is unleashed out of some compulsive need to explore some field of human experience, there are no arts. That's all there is."

On November 19, 2010, DreamWorks finally announced that two-time Academy Award winner Day-Lewis was starring as the sixteenth president of the United States in *Lincoln*. Day-Lewis worked in complete seclusion on his Lincoln voice, a reedy tenor: the higher the pitch the more travel power a voice has. Kushner believes it's one of the reasons that Lincoln's voice worked effectively: "Daniel finally sent Steven a recording of himself doing the voice in a little tiny battery-operated tape recorder so he could hear it. I got to hear it a few months before we started filming, when he and David Strathairn [who played Secretary of State William Seward] read a couple of scenes together. I got to sit behind Daniel and listen. But Steven called me after he first listened to the voice and said, 'I just listened to Abraham Lincoln.'"

The remarkable eight-minute speech Kushner devised, concerning the reasons why the Emancipation Proclamation wasn't enough—it had to be bolstered by the passage of a law—was the first "dialogue" scene Day-Lewis filmed on location in Richmond, Virginia. Kushner was afraid it would never make the cut. It was not only densely written, but extremely long. "Steven really wanted me to address the issue of the Emancipation Proclamation in the screenplay. I sent him the draft before I sent it to Daniel. But I thought that he was going to say, 'The speech is ridiculously long and you can't do this and it's so hard to follow.' But he loved it. He was more excited than he'd ever been by anything I'd written."

Day-Lewis asked Spielberg prior to the first take if they could just go through the entire scene once, then break it up, Kushner recalls. There was no on-set rehearsal. "Well, Daniel sat down, and they did the whole attack on him, 'Why are you doing this? What are you doing?' And then Daniel walks into the thing and went through it word-perfect. It was one of the most amazing things I have ever seen in my life, and everyone just had their jaws on the floor. The reactions of the cabinet were real. Everyone just thought, 'How is he doing this?' He came in with this pencil, he was just whittling, and I thought, 'That's not in the script. Why does he have a pencil and what is he doing?' And then at the end he pulls it out—he's going to sign the amendment and he has a pencil in his hand."

The action seemed completely spontaneous, Kushner says. "I have never seen anything like it. Steven forgot to call 'cut.' It just sort of stopped and there was a stunned silence. And David [Strathairn], who I have known for a long time, was just sort of shaking. You know it was like being with Lincoln. It was just astonishing."

The *Lincoln* set was "a cathedral, an almost sanctified place," says Snider. "And everyone simply dived into history." Day-Lewis stayed in character throughout the shoot, addressed by all as "Mr. President."

On the *Charlie Rose* show, Strathairn, one of a "wealth of New York actors" on the film (which features 140 speaking parts), admits that Day-Lewis set the tone on the set. "We were in 1864," he says. "You could choose to be there, or if you didn't want to be there, you'd remove yourself from the energy of the room. It brought focus, something very precious, to investing in this man at this moment. Lincoln was a man of the highest resolve and will and humility, Machiavellian, with a force of will, in combination with his cleverness. And the movie gives a window into his sadness."

As he admitted in an unusually frank chat with the BBC during the height of the Oscar race, Day-Lewis himself is reticent to talk about this aspect of his craft. "I always feel like I'm digging my own grave. I will seem self-important, adding to the fairly comprehensive impression that people seem to have that I'm strange when I work." But wasn't it extremely draining to be Abraham Lincoln, nonstop, for months?

"Part of my job is to be drained," he says. "It's logical for me to remain within that world. But it's also my pleasure, because that's where the work is. You're not discovering anything when you're having a tea and a laugh with the grips, as tempting as that would be, because there are a lot of great people on a film set. I wore myself out the first couple of movies I was in. The thing that wore me out was the socializing on the set."

Kushner says that Day-Lewis's extreme focus enabled him to come up with many of his own bits of business, including a moment during a story Lincoln tells to break tension during the assault on Williamsburg. As everyone anxiously awaits the sound of the telegraph, he pours himself coffee and describes someone relieving himself. Yes, Spielberg used an old-fashioned riser to make Day-Lewis look taller. And he wasn't afraid to let there be silence amid the rush of Kushner's dialogue.

The writer provided some comic relief in the form of three guys chasing votes—by hook or by crook. Tommy Lee Jones also lightened the somber mood as the windy Great Commoner, antislavery activist Thaddeus Stevens, who was portrayed as a monster in previous films such as *The Birth of a Nation* and *Tennessee Johnson*.

Goodwin says that Sally Field nails the role of the president's high-strung wife, Mary Todd Lincoln, who has been portrayed in so many differing ways over the years: "She is semi-manic-depressive, but she's fierce, she's strong, she's smart, and she's a little crazy." Kushner was trying to amend the bad rap given to her. "There were certain bipolar features in there," he says. "One of her cousins said she was always either in the attic or the cellar. She was a very difficult person, but she was a brilliant woman and she danced with Lincoln as a lawyer in Springfield. The first night she met him and right after dancing with him she turned to her cousin and said: 'I've just danced with the greatest man of his time, and he's going to be president of the United States.' And this is a woman to whom all three candidates for president in 1860 had proposed marriage."

Production designer Rick Carter, who shared an Oscar for his work on *Avatar*, says the crew leaned on Lincoln's detailed diaries— they knew exactly what he was doing on any given day, and could even re-create the content of the papers strewn on desks. During an interview on *Charlie Rose*, Goodwin marveled at the re-creation of the newly constructed 1864 White House, from the wallpaper and maps to first-edition books and carpets. "Here's my Lincoln!" she marveled. "He's back again!"

Cinematographer Janusz Kamiński, who won Oscars for Spielberg's *Schindler's List* and *Saving Private Ryan,* tried to use natural light whenever he could on *Lincoln,* taking full advantage of Richmond's historic buildings. Who knew the nation's Capitol had a black dome back then?

And eighty-year-old John Williams—who has composed muscular scores for *Star Wars* and every Spielberg film since *The Sugarland Express*—sticks to a delicately minimal period-inflected score. "He never borrows from himself," says Snider. "Everyone stepped up their game."

There are few visual effects, as Spielberg was less interested in battles than in human-scale emotions—but Spielberg went CG on Lincoln's surreal dream and the Battle of Williamsburg. As for the 150-minute running time: "It was what it needed to be," says Snider.

After the AFI Fest premiere, Day-Lewis, Field, and Jones were all instant shoo-ins for nominations—not to mention Spielberg, Kushner, Kamiński, Carter, editor Michael Kahn, and Williams.

Day-Lewis was vying for his third Oscar (after *My Left Foot* and *There Will Be Blood*), which would mean winning more Best Actor Oscars than any actor in history. Several lead actors, including Fredric March and Jack Nicholson, have two; Nicholson also won a supporting statuette for his role in *Terms of Endearment* as astronaut

Garrett Breedlove. Katharine Hepburn holds the leading actress record: four.

Even though films featured in the fall fests get a major boost on their road to the Oscars, there are also ones not finished in time that come out at the end of the year and have another advantage: they're fresh in voters' minds. Take, for example, Clint Eastwood's *Million Dollar Baby* or Sandra Bullock vehicle *The Blind Side.* In 2012, the late arrivals skipping the festival circuit were Kathryn Bigelow's *Zero Dark Thirty,* Tom Hooper's *Les Misérables,* and Quentin Tarantino's *Django Unchained.*

CHAPTER 7

WOMEN, POLITICS, AND *ZERO DARK THIRTY*

From the start, Kathryn Bigelow and Mark Boal's ripped-from-the-headlines drama *Zero Dark Thirty* was a different species than its predecessor, *The Hurt Locker.* In order to make that film, the director and her writing and producing partner had raised independent financing to fund their tough, stylish $15 million Iraq war movie starring Jeremy Renner, Anthony Mackie, and Guy Pearce.

The earlier film, an intense thriller, debuted at the Toronto International Film Festival in September 2008, was swiftly acquired by neophyte film company Summit Entertainment, and toured the international festival circuit before its eventual release in June 2009. *The Hurt Locker* persevered through award season, riding a swell of year-end praise to win six Oscars and beat out Bigelow's ex-husband James Cameron and his mighty *Avatar* for Best Picture and Best Director.

That year, several factors swayed the Academy in Bigelow's direction. One, *The Hurt Locker* was an anomaly—a rigorously intelligent, well-made, male-friendly, underdog war film that just about every branch of the Academy could admire. And two, Bigelow offered the right opportunity for the liberal-leaning, politically correct Academy to remedy an historic oversight—never before awarding Best Director to a woman. Bigelow deserved it, but she also stood in for all the other women directors who had not received their due.

In its history, the Academy's largely male directors' branch had nominated only three other women directors—Italian Lina Wertmüller (*Seven Beauties*), New Zealander Jane Campion (*The Piano*), and American Sofia Coppola (*Lost in Translation*), daughter of Oscar-winning *Godfather* creator Francis Ford Coppola.

Gender politics in Hollywood—as everywhere else—are complex, layered, often unconscious, and difficult to parse. One can argue that things are slowly improving for women in the film industry, but they are still woefully underrepresented in too many areas, from hiring, especially as directors, to roles onscreen.

In 2012, female representation in popular movies hit its lowest level in five years, according to a study by the University of Southern California Annenberg School for Communication and Journalism. That was despite a steady succession of high-profile box-office successes starring women over the decades, from *Silkwood* and *The Rose* to *A League of Their Own, 9 to 5, The First Wives Club, Sister Act, Mamma Mia!, Bridesmaids,* and two recent mighty franchises, *The Hunger Games* and *Twilight*.

Among the hundred highest-grossing movies at the U.S. box office in 2012, the USC study reported, 28 percent of speaking characters were female. That marked a drop from 32.8 percent three years ago—even though, as actress Geena Davis pointed out at Cinema-Con 2013, 51 percent of the moviegoing audience is female. In the United States, 40 percent of managerial jobs are held by women, but in Hollywood, the much lower proportions have stayed the same for at least twenty years: in both the Directors Guild and the Writers Guild, only 13 percent of members are women.

According to Martha M. Lauzen, executive director of the Center for the Study of Women in Television and Film, of the top 250 grossing films for 2012, women accounted for only 9 percent of directors. That's a boost of four percentage points from 2011, but dead even with the percentage of women directors working in 1998. Significantly, Lauzen, a leading researcher in the field who teaches at San Diego State University, titled her 2012 report "The Celluloid Ceiling."

At the same CinemaCon at which Davis revealed the latest research findings from the Geena Davis Institute on Gender in Media, which she founded in 2004, *Hollywood Reporter* editorial director Janice Min assembled and moderated a panel titled "Driving Financial Success: Women + Movies = Bigger Box Office" that included Davis, director Paul Feig (*Bridesmaids, The Heat*), producer Nina Jacobson (*The Hunger Games*), Amy Miles (CEO of Regal Entertainment Group), and Vanessa Morrison (president of Fox Animation Studios). They addressed a few of the myriad issues concerning women and Hollywood, both behind and in front of the camera.

Clearly, despite all the evidence over the years showing a consistent number of box-office hits aimed at women, from *Thelma and Louise* to *Sex and the City*, the Hollywood studios would rather chase after young men—who account for an average of 44 percent of the opening weekend crowds—with big-budget VFX than feed even modest-budget pictures to the underserved, starving women's audience. "There is an overwhelming belief in Hollywood that women will watch men but men won't watch women," says Davis. "Which is like the Bible or something. You cannot go against it. It's a myth that keeps getting propagated, but it's just not true."

And yet while young men can be counted on to show up on opening weekends, they are not the most frequent moviegoers, according to MPAA research. Adults twenty-five to thirty-nine are. "There's this pursuit of the young male, the most distracted demographic, between video games, sports, and girls," says Jacobson. "There's a lack of diversity overall which excludes many people as we obsessively pursue a demographic that's the most elusive of them all. And there's room for franchises to be made of many different sizes. It does not have to be a $200 million movie where a lot of things blow up. The remedy for a lot of the issues that afflict female representation in movies is also the same remedy for the marketplace."

A reflection of the industry itself, the Academy of Motion Picture Arts and Sciences also skews to older white males. A 2012 *Los Angeles Times* study found that nearly 94 percent of Academy voters are white, 77 percent are male, and Academy members have a median age of 62. Blacks make up about 2 percent of the Academy, and Latinos less than 2 percent.

The reasons for Hollywood's myopia about women—despite consciousness-raising efforts from groups such as Women in Film and Davis's Institute—are many. But they mostly come down to the entrenched studio habit of making movies by men for men, and of more willingly entrusting male directors with multimillion-dollar budgets. The studios accept the conventional wisdom that movies aimed at young males tend to open and perform better around the world than movies aimed at women, which they consider to be execution-dependent (in other words, women wait for good reviews and higher quality) and hit or miss.

Women directors are often assigned modestly budgeted romantic and family films, which tend not to get as much marketing support. While there are plenty of women who produce and function in behind-the-scenes roles such as editing, casting, and costume and production design, there are fewer movies made for women, written by women, directed by women, or starring women in the lead role. It's a vicious cycle.

And while there's still a (shrinking) list of male marquee movie stars who get paid $20 million to guarantee opening weekends (the list includes Will Smith, Denzel Washington, Johnny Depp, and Robert Downey Jr.), few actresses carry solo films. Most are relegated to romances, or to supporting roles as appendages to male leads, bitch-bosses, fussy mothers, or girlfriends—and they don't get to topline big-budget global action films the way their male counterparts do. Angelina Jolie is the major exception, followed by Sandra Bullock, Cameron Diaz, and Jennifer Lawrence.

Men have the advantage of a much longer shelf life not defined by their looks: as they age into masculine authority in their forties and the decades beyond, still making love to scads of constantly replenished sweet ingenues in their twenties and thirties, women age out, with few exceptions. Sixtyish character actress Meryl Streep remains eminently bankable because she's an Oscar perennial. But she is also an anomaly.

Sony chairman Amy Pascal insists that she hires women directors when she can, such as commercial romantic comedy writers Nora Ephron (who died June 26, 2012) and Nancy Meyers, who despite a robust box-office track record (*Something's Got to Give, What Women Want*) still struggles to get her glossy big-budget relationship comedies funded. Inside the studio system, directors like Ephron and Meyers who can write and/or produce their own mainstream projects tend to fare the best. Pascal has begged Bigelow to do a Spider-Man or Bond film, but she refuses. Women have to survive scads of rejection and still fight for what they want, like getting to make a big-budget studio movie, Pascal tells Forbes: "It's about women saying that's what they want and not saying no. The whole system is geared for them to fail."

Foreign countries nurture far more world-class women directors—New Zealand's Campion, Denmark's Susanne Bier, Poland's Agnieszka Holland, and France's Agnès Varda and Anne Fontaine, to name just a handful—but their films command relatively small budgets. More men move on from film schools to direct films than do women, who tend to wind up in lower-budget indie and television production. Many talented women serve the visions of their male bosses, as did the late production designer and producer Polly Platt, with Peter Bogdanovich and James L. Brooks.

In Hollywood, the barriers remain incredibly high for women hoping to direct, unlike the music or publishing industries, points out Pascal, where it's relatively easy for exploitable talent to show what it can do. Men are permitted a few mistakes, where women are not. Movie stars Barbra Streisand and Angelina Jolie did not earn much respect for their directing on *Yentl* and *In the Land of Blood and Honey,* respectively. The list is long of women who have directed one or two films. Women directors with bona fide big-budget movie careers like Ron Howard or Barry Levinson? Rare.

Pascal runs a studio, as many women have done, from Columbia's late Dawn Steel, retired Paramount chairman Sherry Lansing, and Universal's Stacey Snider—who left to run DreamWorks with Steven Spielberg—to Universal's current cochairman Donna Langley. They have all taken the occasional flyer on women's material, but they always weigh their risks; they still have to meet the same bottom-line demands as their male studio peers. However, Pascal was able to scoop up Bigelow's *Zero Dark Thirty* in a multipicture deal with Annapurna.

After starting out as a painter, hanging with the likes of Andy Warhol, Philip Glass, and Richard Serra in New York, Kathryn Bigelow came to realize that movies were a more accessible medium able to reach far more people. In Los Angeles, she built industry respect with a solid résumé directing robust, stylish genre films: *Near Dark, Blue Steel, Point Break, Strange Days,* and *K-19: The Widowmaker.* Her interests run to smart action films, not rom-coms. Bigelow, who is just under six feet tall, likes being one of the guys, and has studiously avoided being singled out as a female director. ("Would Michael Mann be described as a male director?" she asks.) *The Hurt Locker* star Jeremy Renner raved to me about how Bigelow—who was logging long hours and miles on large-scale sets in 110-degree heat in Amman, Jordan—was, at age fifty-five, in better shape than he was.

Bigelow first met journalist and screenwriter Mark Boal via an article he wrote for *Playboy* about an undercover female cop at a high school. Later, she admired Boal's script for Paul Haggis's war-at-home military family drama *In the Valley of Elah*. Bigelow knew Boal was embedding in Iraq, which she considered an underreported war. She asked him to collaborate. Bigelow was hoping he "might come back with some really rich material that would be worthy of a cinematic translation, and that's what happened," she told *The A.V. Club*.

They started working on the *Hurt Locker* script in 2005, and raised the money in 2006. They worked on their own, devoid of outside financial support, and filmed in 2007, because that's "the way one works if you want to do a piece that is a passion project, uncompromised," she told me when *The Hurt Locker* was first unveiled at the Toronto Film Festival in September 2008. "We made it completely independently, cast it as it should be cast, with these extraordinary actors."

Away from the studio development and casting process, which demands certain dramatic character arcs and well-known stars, Boal and Bigelow were able to create a boots-on-the-ground experience for viewers: gritty, realistic, stripped of varnish. The director wanted Renner's bomb-defuser to "put a human face on this combat situation, to give you a look at a conflict that would otherwise be abstract. He gives it heart."

The movie sends an Iraq bomb-disposal unit out over thirty-eight days to disarm and dismantle improvised explosive devices (IEDs), treating each day's mission as another day at the office. "That's the war, that's the conflict, not air, not hand-to-hand, that's the signature weapon of the insurgency," Bigelow said. "These are the stories Mark brought back. Obviously, there's great drama in what these men do."

She wanted Renner to be "a fresh face in a tense film where your landscape alone provides a tremendous degree of lethality; you don't know who's going to live and who's going to die. He was a relative unknown, so the audience was not coming to the character with any preconception on [his] destiny. Anything could happen, which compounded the tension."

Obviously, Bigelow was proven right—*The Hurt Locker* grossed a modest $17 million domestically but scored $32 million more around the world. So on her next go-around, she and Boal collaborated again on researching a real drama: the hunt for Osama bin Laden. Only this time, real events caught up with them. Preparing to shoot a movie about how he eluded capture by U.S. Special Forces in Tora Bora, they had to stop in their tracks when news broke that bin Laden had been killed by the Navy's SEAL Team Six on May 2, 2011.

Bigelow and Boal prepared a new script for *Zero Dark Thirty* and again obtained independent financing, $45 million from Annapurna with distribution from Sony. Pascal is gung-ho on the film's "observational journalism," she tells me at the film's premiere. At the same the time that various authors were researching nonfiction books on the subject, Boal used his sources in the intelligence community to re-create for film the CIA's decade-long search for bin Laden.

So in this rare case, a Hollywood screenwriter wasn't waiting to use the book as a basis for the movie—as with *All the President's Men,* to take one example. No, Boal was skipping that step. He was dramatizing his shoe-leather journalism into a two-and-a-half-hour fiction feature, which offers more leeway when it comes to pesky fact-checkers and legal vetting. But he was also claiming a high degree of verisimilitude.

The opening title card of *Zero Dark Thirty* reads: "based on first-hand accounts." One thing that Boal discovered about the decade-long post-9/11 pursuit to track down Osama bin Laden was that several women were key players. This makes the movie groundbreaking in more ways than one. The filmmakers were in touch with the real CIA agent who is the basis for Jessica Chastain's Maya, who is still working undercover—and making waves inside the agency. After the CIA complained that the movie gave too much credit to the one agent, the *Washington Post* verified that she in fact does exist, and very much the way she was described in the film.

"We started getting the idea to capture history in the context of the drama of the capture at this moment of time in American life," says Boal in the Q&A session after one of the first industry screenings in Los Angeles during Thanksgiving weekend. The packed audience of Screen Actors Guild members at the Pacific Design Center theater in West Hollywood is clearly stunned by the two hour and thirty-nine minute film. The industry is eager to finally get a gander at this long-withheld movie, which has skipped the film festivals in order to stay out of the election fray. The marketers don't have much time to get the film seen and promoted before the opening December 19, and Oscar nomination ballots are due January 3. At the Q&A, an exhausted Bigelow admits that she had signed off on the final mix just four days before this screening: "We wanted to make something that stands up to the test of time."

Bigelow adds that having the film feel real and contemporary was important; the actors had to perform "in a narrow bandwidth not using conventional Hollywood tropes, working within the rigorous confines of history." Though never explained in the movie, the title is military jargon for thirty minutes past midnight, the exact time—12:30 a.m.—when the Navy SEALs first stepped into the bin Laden compound in Abbottabad, Pakistan.

The film starts by dropping young CIA agent Maya (Chastain) into the thick of the action in Pakistan as her agent colleagues (Jason Clarke of *Lawless* and Jennifer Ehle of *Contagion*) and the local CIA chief (Kyle Chandler of *Friday Night Lights* and *Argo*) are deep into the investigation of bin Laden's terrorist network. They are interrogating and torturing suspects. Bigelow does not spare us here: from pain and choke collars to waterboarding, the first twenty-five or so minutes of the film show CIA agents, desperate for leads in the case, brutalizing a detainee.

Maya arrives with a reputation: "She's a killer." She becomes obsessed with one courier and his link to bin Laden. When other people get distracted, she does not. When politics intervene, she won't let anyone forget her single-minded purpose: to kill bin Laden. "I'm gonna smoke everybody involved in this op," Maya declares after one particularly destructive terrorist attack eliminates several of her close colleagues. "And then I'm gonna kill bin Laden." It's a chilling moment.

Chastain is tough, steadfast, and foul-mouthed as Maya, and does little to make her charming or accessible. There's no backstory and, thankfully, no love interest. Like many male heroes in movies, she is her work. That's it. What you see is what you get. In one crowd-pleasing scene she is the only woman in a room full of suits taking credit for her long hours of labor, the crucial discovery of bin Laden's compound. CIA chief Leon Panetta (James Gandolfini) asks, "Who's the girl?" She responds, "I'm the motherfucker that found this place, sir."

While a top CIA officer (Mark Strong) lets a room full of CIA agents have it after yet another terrorist event—the movie reminds us of the real-life cost and sacrifice brought by the war on terror—it's nothing compared to the fury unleashed by Maya in pursuit of her cause. "I've learned from my predecessor that life is better when I don't disagree with you," says one of her bosses. These men are terrified of her. And they put up with her because she's that good. "She's smart," one CIA exec says to Panetta. "We're all smart," Panetta snaps back.

The movie is as relentless as its heroine, laying out the hard facts and details without flinching from its purpose, which is to make real the daily headlines. Bigelow deploys 120 speaking parts—her cast includes a Venezuelan (Édgar Ramírez), Australians (Clarke, Joel Edgerton as the leader of SEAL Team 6), and Brits (Strong, Ehle, Stephen Dillane)—and three to four roving cameras to catch the unfolding action in locations from India, Egypt, and Jordan to London and Washington, D.C. "You shoot it, you do it," says Clarke. "You bust your ass. The long takes give vitality."

Even during production, in a November 12, 2012, brief filed in federal court, the conservative group Judicial Watch sought details about the identities of four CIA operatives and a Navy SEAL who met with the filmmakers, complaining that "selectively providing nonpublic information to some filmmakers while refusing to release it generally . . . crosses a line of appearance."

Bigelow and Boal admit that the publicity around their supposed access to inside CIA information made it difficult to get military cooperation and cost the production untold thousands of dollars. The last section of the movie makes a satisfying finale, with real tension building before an unseen President Obama finally gives the green light to order the Navy SEALs to fulfill Maya's mission. The irony, concludes Boal at the panel, is that "the leader of al-Qaeda was defeated by the specter he feared most: a liberated Western woman."

In January 2012, *Zero Dark Thirty* editor William Goldenberg met in a Studio City editing room with Bigelow and Boal, who were just back from Jordan, where most of the film was shot. He was coming into the process late, joining top-flight editor Dylan Tichenor, who was well under way with three hours of footage edited on an abbreviated schedule. To ensure the film was finished on time, the two editors handled different sections of the movie. Goldenberg took on the last sequences filmed: the tricky car/cellphone courier tracking scenes and the SEALs' raid on bin Laden's compound.

Goldenberg had to tackle an overwhelming amount of archive material—the raid alone had forty hours of untouched, uncalibrated dailies, he tells me in phone interview, "enough to make a movie on its own. On my hard drive was a bunch of unorganized stuff. I put it up on my laptop and I couldn't see any image. They didn't tell me anything about the night vision. I see they're SEALs in there. Some shots are brighter than others."

The enormity of the responsibility for cutting that sequence and the logistical difficulty of the hours of footage was overwhelming, even for the experienced editor.

So Goldenberg did what he learned to do a long time ago, he says. "You have to go into a room, keep your head down, work on the shots in front of you, and not think about how this is the definitive hunt for bin Laden, costing many millions of dollars, and the responsibilities of money and time schedule. If you do, you'll freeze up and not be able to do anything."

He started with the beginning of the raid, with the Blackhawk helicopters arriving at the compound, and looked at four or five hours of dailies a day. "I'd mark and pick the pieces I liked, cut three to five of those, go on to the next day and do the next section and piece it together," he says. "The first cut took a month." The result: an assemblage of around forty minutes.

Goldenberg had to struggle with the tension between getting this pivotal moment in American history right, exactly the way it played out in real time, and giving it enough tension to keep people glued to their seats—even when they already know what happened. There was a temptation to do the more conventional action beats building to explosive climaxes, he says. "Action/beat explosion to explosion—that's more exciting. Kathryn and I had to fight against that, saying to each other, 'This is not a traditional action sequence. That's not what this is about.'"

According to Goldenberg, Bigelow wanted to show how this is "what these guys do for a living, and not what you expect, like picking up briefcases and going to work. There were at least twelve other raids that night. 'They methodically go in, it's a wave of death,' is how Kathryn used to explain it. These guys are killers. That's what they do, professionals. Their job is to go into these raids and capture or kill someone. This happened to be a raid on bin Laden's compound. It could have been any raid on any night."

Goldenberg created a quiet raid with a lack of action highlighted by unexpected bursts of energy and sound. When a guy shoots through a door, he says, "we lull the audience . . . with sound, blasts, knowing they don't know what's around each corner, or if a person has a gun."

They didn't adopt the Paul Greengrass *Bourne* handheld point-of-view approach, either; we're watching the SEALs from outside.

Bigelow had to shoot everything twice for the different lighting situations and night vision, so that the sequence would resemble that pitch-black moonless night. "We wanted the audience to experience what that looked like," Goldenberg says. "The SEALs lost in darkness, a sniper on the rooftop, cut to his POV with night vision, juxtaposed with what it was really like for the people in the compound without night vision."

Then Goldenberg addressed the tracking of Abu Ahmed's cell phone and finding the white SUV that led the CIA to the bin Laden compound. Just watching all the footage shot by four to six cameras from different angles took three days, he recalls. "It takes tremendous experience to figure the way to tell that story."

The trick was to speed up the information by doing two things at once with sound looping and overlapping, while still keeping everything clear. Shots of satellite maps, call tracking via phone lines, and computer banks were added in postproduction to impart more information in fun visual ways. A sequence like this isn't as straightforward as talking heads, Goldenberg explains. "When you have an enormous section that is free form, it's more of a challenge to tell an exciting story."

What was Boal's role? "He did the best thing a producer can do. He stayed away. He'd come in to screenings and was able to maintain the big picture in his mind, and solved some big problems. He was able to have objectivity, did what a producer does: 'This is your problem, here.'"

Bigelow and Boal make a great team, Goldenberg says. "Whatever happens with them, as partners the whole is greater than the sum of the parts. Some magic happens between the two of them; they are destined to work together."

Goldenberg also edited *Argo*. The two films are very different, he admits. *Argo* was more of a crowd-pleaser: "You leave *Argo* feeling exhilarated. Although it was a complicated ending, you feel when they get rescued a sense of exhilaration, so that you applaud in the theater. That's an amazing feeling as an editor, when you see the movie and tear up. It still works after you've seen it fifty times at least. Leaving *Zero Dark Thirty* is more like being punched in the stomach. It's a different animal."

Predictably, as critics praised the movie's disjunctive cutting style and organic reported drama—which do not hew to narrative conventions—as well as Chastain's performance as Maya, they couldn't resist comparing the director to her central character.

Casting Maya was key for Bigelow, because the actress "had to be able to handle with verbal agility the comprehensive and complex dialogue," says the director, who had admired Jessica Chastain's poised performance in Ralph Fiennes's challenging Shakespeare film *Coriolanus*.

When Chastain left her theater training at Juilliard and started landing movie roles, she got a gift. For various reasons, none of the movies came out right away. The delayed openings meant that Chastain remained a hot actress—and a blank slate. Nobody projected her last movie onto what they thought she could do. She was able to be a chameleon.

Then, in a flurry, seven films hit in the year 2011. She played a dramatic actress in Al Pacino's theatrical *Wilde Salomé,* and in John Madden's Mossad thriller *The Debt,* she was a tough-as-nails assassin. She earned raves as brassy southern blonde Celia in summer lit-hit *The Help,* for which she would become one of the five actresses nominated by the Academy for Best Performance in a Supporting Role. In *Coriolanus,* she stood her ground against both Ralph Fiennes and the magnificent Vanessa Redgrave. She portrayed a sweetly luminous idealized fifties mother in Terrence Malick's mystical *The Tree of Life,* and the concerned wife of Michael Shannon in the ominously atmospheric drama *Take Shelter.*

When she was approached for *Zero Dark Thirty,* Chastain decided to ditch her role opposite Tom Cruise in the $120 million sci-fi adventure *Oblivion* to take part in Bigelow's $52 million indie. At noon the day after she took her grandmother to the Academy Awards ceremony in Hollywood (the Oscar went to her *Help* costar Octavia Spencer), Chastain was on a twenty-five-hour flight to Chandahar, India, to start shooting the movie that she described as her most difficult to date. They called her straight to the set, threw robes on her, and sent her into a bustling market with a cell phone. It was surreal, she tells me. "I remember thinking, 'Yesterday I was at the Oscars with my grandma.'"

Chastain is adept at charming press. Even before the movie is screened, word begins to leak out to the Oscar blog community that she has a juicy lead role in this film shrouded in secrecy. Though no one in the media has seen *Zero Dark Thirty*, the on-the-rise actress is already a front-runner for an Oscar nomination, her second, although it is frustrating not being able to tell the press what role she's playing. She later says when she was faced with speculation that she was playing a Navy SEAL wife, "every time I bit my cheek." She couldn't reveal that she was actually the film's hero. "No, there's this woman who is incredible! I did some long lead press, but 'I can't talk about the movie.'"

Released from her gag order once the movie is in preview, Chastain loves to talk about it. "I didn't know women played such a central role in the hunt for Osama bin Laden," she admits. "When we look at lead female characters in movies, they're defined by men, as girlfriends or victims of the villain of the piece. Maya is not a victim, has no boyfriend. She's a servant to her work, capable, she doesn't have any mental issue, she's a hero. She's not messed up. She's the smartest person in the room all the time, she was smarter than her parents and the other kids. She doesn't have many friends. There's a frustration that no one believes in you."

"And yet she's a woman, she didn't have to become a man," says Jason Clarke.

"I loved being a woman in a boy's world, holding on to that, not becoming a man," she says.

She did her homework. She had to learn the real meaning of the agency lingo, sitting down with Boal to go over every line. She discovered her character when she and a group went to tour a mosque. While the men were allowed in, the three women—Bigelow, Chastain, and producer Megan Ellison—had to cover themselves fully with balaclavas, exposing only a small slit of their faces. "I felt invisible," she says. "It was not hard to leave this role. It was so intense making this movie."

At the premiere at Hollywood and Highland, the movie's assertive heroine seems to play better for women than men. Sony marketers are trying to figure out how to best position the picture for a public that was expecting a Navy SEAL adventure—an all-male TV ad actually played opposite network football—as opposed to a brainy and deliberate CIA procedural closer to *Carlos* and *All the President's Men* than to *Act of Valor*. Thus they have to cover their target demos with different TV spots.

Because Bigelow and Boal purport to dramatize what really happened in the manhunt for the al-Qaeda leader, as soon as it's screened in late November, *Zero Dark Thirty* generates controversy, with various interested parties questioning its veracity. Bigelow and Boal find they can't have it both ways, dramatic freedom *and* perfect accuracy.

The main issue is the film's presentation of waterboarding as a means to extricate information vital to bin Laden's capture. Among the first to see the film at an early D.C. preview are former Connecticut senator Chris Dodd, now head of the MPAA, and California senator Dianne Feinstein, chair of the Senate Intelligence Committee. Feinstein jumps up and walks out after the early torture scenes; Dodd convinces her to return to the screening room.

During the George W. Bush administration, which sanctioned torture in the post-9/11 era, U.S. foreign relations around the world were seriously damaged. While Obama publicly backed away from torture and his reluctance to use it is depicted in *Zero Dark Thirty*, Feinstein is appalled that the movie failed to explicitly condemn the practice. For her part, Bigelow studiously avoids taking political stances in her films. Yet, she says in a *Time* magazine story, "I think that it's a deeply moral movie that questions the use of force. It questions what was done in the name of finding bin Laden."

Within days after the film opens on December 19, 2012, three U.S. senators—Feinstein, Armed Services Committee chairman Carl Levin, and Armed Services Committee ranking member John McCain—issue a statement decrying the depiction of torture in the film as not accurate, expressing "outrage" over the film's scenes that imply "enhanced interrogations."

CIA acting director Michael Morell states that the film "takes significant artistic license" and "creates the strong impression that the enhanced interrogation techniques that were part of our former detention and interrogation program were the key to finding" bin Laden. But, he says, "that impression is false."

Rather than espouse the use of torture in the hunt for bin Laden, the movie establishes that it took place—and makes the audience experience its horror. The Senate Intelligence Committee begins a review of the contacts between *Zero Dark Thirty* filmmakers Bigelow and Boal and CIA officials to determine if inappropriate access to secret information was given.

On December 21, respected documentary filmmaker Alex Gibney, who won an Oscar for the torture documentary *Taxi to the Dark Side,* lays out his case against the film in a damaging article in the *Huffington Post.* He writes that "the film conveys the unmistakable conclusion that torture led to the death of bin Laden. That's wrong and dangerously so, precisely because the film is so well made." He states that old-fashioned shoe-leather reporting, not torture, led to the capture of Bin Laden, which is suggested in the movie, and criticized the filmmakers for a "lost dramatic opportunity" because "no main characters in the film ever question the efficacy or corrupting effects of torture." The filmmakers' access to certain CIA sources may have colored their take on the story, adds Gibney in a phone interview, but Bigelow and Boal "walked into trouble by saying, 'This is true,' instead of saying, 'This is based in reality.'"

Liberal actor Ed Asner approaches Gibney by e-mail asking him to join a protest against the film's depiction of torture. Asner, Martin Sheen, David Clennon, and others ask Academy members not to vote for the film, eventually issuing a press release that states: "One of the brightest female directors in the business is in danger of becoming part of the system." Gibney declines the invitation. "They were coming from a political place," he tells me on the phone. "They didn't expect the attack to come from the left."

"The information that Maya gets that leads her on the trail is not from torture," Chastain tells me. "It comes from sitting down over hummus and tabbouleh. To say the film says that torture is necessary is absolutely untrue. Mark's stance is that the most important thing is that they tell the most accurate story possible, and unfortunately that's part of the truth."

Gibney scoffs at this, saying, "That's a stupid argument. That's not how torture works. You don't answer questions when you're gurgling with water."

Feminist writer Naomi Wolf goes so far as to compare Kathryn Bigelow to Nazi propaganda filmmaker Leni Riefenstahl. "In a time of darkness in America," writes Wolf in a column in the *Guardian* on January 4, 2013, just weeks before the Oscar nominations are announced, "you are being feted by Hollywood, and hailed by major media. But to me, the path your career has now taken reminds [me] of no one so much as that other female film pioneer who became, eventually, an apologist for evil."

Boal and Bigelow go on the press circuit explaining how they reported the movie. Boal hires lawyers, scared that he's being targeted. The Christmas break, however, creates a dead zone in Hollywood and Washington that makes it difficult to move quickly to counter the attacks. But the season also creates a box-office boom. Controversy sells. Curiosity about *Zero Dark Thirty* drives audiences to check it out, as they did back in 1976 with *All the President's Men*.

The movie opens at number one when it goes into nationwide release on January 11, 2013.

Sony cochairman Amy Pascal's statement supporting her filmmakers soon follows: "*Zero Dark Thirty* does not advocate torture. To not include that part of history would have been irresponsible and inaccurate. We fully support Kathryn Bigelow and Mark Boal and stand behind this extraordinary movie. We are outraged that any responsible member of the Academy would use their voting status in AMPAS as a platform to advance their own political agenda." By the time Bigelow and Boal fight back by speaking at the New York Film Critics Circle Awards and planting essays in the *Los Angeles Times* and other publications, the damage has been done. The superb film reviews are undermined by the bigger debate about the use of torture as a weapon in our fight against terrorists, and by criticism of the filmmakers for not disapproving of its use in their storytelling.

The question asked by many in Hollywood: who orchestrated this Beltway campaign against the movie? The timing is too perfect. Rumors and speculation fill the air. Is Connecticut resident Harvey Weinstein, who hobnobs with Dodd and Feinstein and other prominent Democrats, pulling strings to eliminate a potential rival for the Oscars he was seeking for *Django Unchained* and *Silver Linings Playbook*? (Gibney says that Pascal wrongfully assumed that he had been put up to his *Huffington Post* article by Weinstein.) Or are Steven Spielberg and David Geffen working their many Washington contacts in favor of *Lincoln*?

On the weekend of the Golden Globe Awards in mid-January, Weinstein approaches a chilly Bigelow at the annual tea party hosted by the British Academy of Film and Television (BAFTA) saying, "I'm not the anti-Christ!" He then goes up to producer Kathleen Kennedy and promises to "leave *Lincoln* alone." And yet, it is remarkable when a Connecticut congressman suddenly figures out that Tony Kushner made some errors in his abridging of the final state-by-state votes on the Thirteenth Amendment in *Lincoln*.

Connecticut voted *for* it, not *against* it, as the movie portrays. Many believe it's a Harvey leak.

The mogul is well-known for his heavy-handed Oscar campaign tactics, from the successful *Shakespeare in Love* assault against Spielberg front-runner *Saving Private Ryan* to his smear campaign against Ron Howard's *A Beautiful Mind* in an attempt to favor *In the Bedroom*. One Weinstein spokesman insists that for those reasons, Weinstein carefully kept his hands clean this time.

But Weinstein was openly upset that he had failed to acquire a piece of *Zero Dark Thirty* when Ellison was not favorably disposed toward him after the release of *The Master* did not go well. Sony was partnered with Weinstein on *Django Unchained,* handling the international release. He had wanted to land the foreign piece of *Zero Dark Thirty,* which went to Universal instead. When he was rebuffed, Weinstein joined forces with producer-financier Nicolas Chartier, who had mortgaged his house to help pay for *The Hurt Locker* but had since fallen out with Boal. Chartier had been interested in working with Boal and Bigelow on the bin Laden film, and when they turned him down, he spitefully rushed through a low-budget quickie production by B-movie director John Stockwell called *SEAL Team Six: The Raid on Osama bin Laden,* which was shown on the National Geographic Channel before the presidential election—to dismissive reviews. For their part, Bigelow and Boal felt strongly that *Zero Dark Thirty* should be held under a cone of silence and released well after the election had come and gone. There was no comparison between the two films.

As the various critics groups and guilds make their picks during the award season leading up to the Oscar nominations, *Zero Dark Thirty* is in the fray. It comes out of the box strong with two of the earliest critics groups, winning Best Picture, Director, and Actress from the National Board of Review and Best Picture, Director, and Cinematography from the prestigious New York Film Critics Circle. Critics rave, from *Time* to *Entertainment Weekly* to the *New York Times*. The movie lands a Producers Guild nomination, Boal lands a Writers Guild nod, and Bigelow is nominated by the Directors Guild. But clearly, it's one thing to award a top-notch woman director an Oscar for a small indie film like *The Hurt Locker* that never grossed much at the box office; it's another for her to play in the big show. And despite the accolades, she's getting slammed.

Sony may have gone too far with marketing this movie as a true story. Yes, Boal is a bona fide journalist who reported in the trenches alongside newspaper staffers and nonfiction authors. But as he said during his and Bigelow's interview on *Charlie Rose,* he didn't have to lay out his sources and back up his quotes. He was writing a fictionalized account, as many Hollywood writers have done. This one was much closer to recent history, however, and therefore carried political baggage. As Bigelow and Boal found out the hard way.

On the other hand, *Atlantic* writer Mark Bowden argued that "No, *Zero Dark Thirty* Is Not Pro-Torture." Bowden, himself an expert on the subject (his most recent book is *The Finish: The Killing of Osama bin Laden*), wrote that "torture may be morally wrong, and it may not be the best way to obtain information from detainees, but it played a role in America's messy, decade-long pursuit of Osama bin Laden, and *Zero Dark Thirty* is right to portray that fact."

While it's to be expected that Washington politicians and even Gibney, who is open about his anti-torture views, would step up to present their version of the facts, the more damaging story, in terms of the film's Oscar standing, was the one Kim Masters wrote for the *Hollywood Reporter*: "The Unorthodox Relationship Between Kathryn Bigelow and Mark Boal."

The story reported that on the set of *Zero Dark Thirty,* the cast and crew "were frustrated not only by the difficult subject matter and a challenging, secretive environment but also by sometimes-conflicting instructions from director Kathryn Bigelow and writer-producer Mark Boal," who is described as "so abrasive that sources say Chastain, who plays CIA operative Maya, once considered leaving the project," which was of course disputed by Chastain herself. And Ellison too "was upset at Boal's treatment of her," Masters reported.

While Boal admitted to some "spirited discussions" on the set and to having "sharp elbows," he insisted that his relationships with Chastain and Ellison are now good. "The duo [Bigelow and Boal] simultaneously seem to seek and repel Hollywood's embrace," Masters wrote. "They are widely admired for their talent and have created one of the most exciting film partnerships in recent memory. But, with Boal more comfortable out front, they also have a reputation for antagonizing cast and crew and alienating important allies."

About the Bigelow-Boal relationship, Masters wrote, "There has been speculation in media reports that they were romantically involved, but they have declined to discuss it, and even those on the sets of their films say they saw no outward signs. The duo is said to have split as production of *Zero Dark Thirty* got under way, but they have revealed nothing—even to associates. 'Even if you know them really well, you don't go there,' says one.

Asked to characterize their partnership, Boal hesitates. 'I don't know,' he says, adding, 'Look, to me, it's been the creative collaboration of a lifetime . . . It's been a huge gift.' "

It was fascinating to see, after the *Hollywood Reporter* piece ran, how often discussions of the duo's on-off romantic relationship and Boal's supposed bad behavior on the set came up in casual holiday cocktail conversation. In Hollywood's insular community, these viral memes can be lethal. Clearly, Bigelow and Boal were no longer the scrappy indies that could.

CHAPTER 8

THE HOLIDAY DRAMAS

LES MISÉRABLES, DJANGO UNCHAINED

What a difference an Oscar season makes. Back during the crash of 2008, when the indie market was in free fall, a new set of rules took hold: no one was willing to take a chance on dramas. That's how a little movie called *The King's Speech* was turned down by most Brit and Hollywood distributors, except for UK's Momentum and Harvey Weinstein, who didn't need to get anyone's approval. He knew a likely Oscar contender when he saw one. The 2010 period drama about a prince-turned-king with a profound stutter scored four Oscars for Best Picture, Director, Actor, and Screenplay, and grossed $430 million worldwide.

Another producer who has the luxury of being able to listen and act according to his own taste is New Yorker Scott Rudin. Like his archrival Weinstein, Rudin likes to chase Oscar-worthy quality films, often literary adaptations. He has trimmed his expectations in the new landscape, closing his L.A. office and pitching his diverse projects at strictly modest budget levels to Sony's Amy Pascal, with whom he has a deal, and to other studios and their specialty labels. (He has also maintained a second career as a top-flight

Broadway producer of such hit shows as *The Book of Mormon* and the revival of August Wilson's *Fences,* starring Denzel Washington and Viola Davis.)

Rudin has produced a slew of Oscar contenders in the past decade, including the Coens' Best Picture winner *No Country for Old Men* and remake of *True Grit;* theater/film director Stephen Daldry's *The Hours, The Reader,* and *Extremely Loud & Incredibly Close;* David Fincher's *The Social Network* and *The Girl with the Dragon Tattoo;* and Wes Anderson's *Fantastic Mr. Fox* and *Moonrise Kingdom.*

Weinstein and Rudin are among the chosen few who still have enough clout to execute smart dramas. Also in that elite group are producers Tim Bevan and Eric Fellner of Working Title, a boutique production company that since 1999 has been partnered with Universal, which competes with Weinstein and Rudin for the top directors and literary properties. Based in London and Beverly Hills, Working Title, with a staff of thirty, has risen to the top of the British and American movie industries by delivering a mix of globally commercial titles and smart movies, many of them Oscar winners.

They produced Stephen Frears's *My Beautiful Laundrette,* starring the young Daniel Day-Lewis, and Stephen Daldry's *Billy Elliott,* which spawned a global musical smash, as well as their own set of Coen brothers movies (*Barton Fink, Fargo, Burn After Reading,* and *A Serious Man*). They cast the young Cate Blanchett in Shekhar Kapur's *Elizabeth* and its sequel, and produced the intense Tim Robbins drama *Dead Man Walking,* starring Oscar winner Susan Sarandon and Oscar nominee Sean Penn. Their go-to writer is Richard Curtis, who penned the Hugh Grant vehicles *Four Weddings and a Funeral* and *Notting Hill.* Another Working Title favorite is Joe Wright, who directed the literary adaptations *Pride and Prejudice* and *Atonement,* both starring Keira Knightley.

After 2008 when Universal was frowning on dramas, Working Title survived on a diet of franchises such as Curtis's *Bridget Jones's*

Diary, Rowan Atkinson's *Mr. Bean* and *Johnny English,* and Emma Thompson's *Nanny McPhee.* Instead of greenlighting the modest-budget dramas Working Title does best, Universal went ahead with Kevin Macdonald's pricey but unmemorable American remake of the superb Brit TV series *State of Play,* with Russell Crowe filling in at the last minute for Brad Pitt, as well as Paul Greengrass's $130 million Iraq War movie *Green Zone,* featuring his *Bourne* star Matt Damon. Audiences shied away from both movies, which, while well made, were not produced on a budget. Both could have made it into the black had they had cost far less.

After the Weinstein Company's four *King's Speech* Oscar wins and $414 million worldwide gross, things started to look up again for dramas. "Now everybody wants *The King's Speech,*" Fellner tells me during an interview at WT's Beverly Hills office. "The bigger problem is that the people who are able to get these films made aren't thinking about the long-term health of our industry. There's so much competition for leisure time—more than ever. If we don't make good films as opposed to short-term marketable ones, attendance will continue to go down. Somebody has to invest in creating the movies of the future."

Universal exercised its first-look option on StudioCanal's $18 million John le Carré adaptation *Tinker Tailor Soldier Spy,* directed by *Let the Right One In* director Tomas Alfredson, with a top-flight cast including *King's Speech* Oscar winner Colin Firth, Tom Hardy, Benedict Cumberbatch, and Gary Oldman as George Smiley. Universal gave the film a December 2011 release with a major Oscar campaign.

The studio also greenlit Joe Wright and Tom Stoppard's adaptation of Leo Tolstoy's *Anna Karenina,* which reunited Wright with *Atonement*'s Knightley, costarred Jude Law and Aaron Taylor-Johnson, and was targeted for award season 2012. And after two years of development with British impresario Cameron Mackintosh, who produced the original show on the stage twenty-seven years earlier, and screenwriter Bill Nicholson (*Gladiator*), the studio approved WT's film version of the long-running musical *Les Misérables*, with *The King's Speech*'s Oscar-winning director Tom Hooper at the helm.

LES MISÉRABLES

The British director became officially involved in the *Les Mis* project just after he won the Academy Award in 2011. Admittedly not a fan of the score, when he went to see *Les Misérables* on stage, it moved him. He wanted to "try to find a story as, or even more, emotional," he says in a later interview. "That way of energizing people is so satisfying. *Les Misérables* is a story where you feel the music with a heightened emotional reality. Live singing became a passion of mine."

Intrigued by Nicholson's script, which featured spoken dialogue as well as songs, Hooper agreed to meet with Universal cochairman Donna Langley a few days after the Oscars. The two had breakfast together at the Chateau Marmont. "Okay, what's next?" she asked him. Her agenda: Hooper wasn't leaving that breakfast until he said yes to *Les Mis*. Which he shortly did.

Langley thought Hooper was the right person for this project not only because he is able to "get incredible performances out of actors," she tells me in an interview, but because his films, from small UK drama *Longford* and sprawling HBO miniseries *John Adams* to *The King's Speech*, demonstrate that he is "an incredible storyteller, both visually and narratively. He has great respect for the material, but he is an entertainer. He's interested in finding the right way to tell the story, in the most entertaining way, but elevating it and doing it in the most sophisticated way."

Les Mis also needed a visual style. Langley was impressed with Hooper's approach to *The King's Speech*, which could have been a TV movie and was in fact dismissed by many studios and financiers as being just that. "From a visual standpoint," she says, "from the production design to the camera-work, there were so many interesting choices. He finds a way to tell a very intimate story but put it against a big epic backdrop. And I thought he was ready to take this step to a bigger canvas."

When Hooper first saw the stage show, he was struck by the numerous challenges they faced in adapting the material for the screen. "One that hits you straightaway is you go from the prologue when you meet the convict and bishop, and then jump forward eight years, he's now mayor, grown into a successful entrepreneur, but he looks the same," Hooper tells me on the phone. "I was aware that Javert, the prison guard turned policeman, is reduced by his inability to see what's straight in front of him. Javert is just around for eight years and he's suspicious. How come he doesn't recognize Valjean?

"I also found it hard to believe that this ex-convict could become a successful mayor and entrepreneur in that society. When a fight breaks out in his factory, why was he distracted from dealing with it? There's no explanation. A number of challenges in this first transition are solved when you make him unrecognizable as the convict when see you him as mayor. So Hugh [Jackman] lost thirty pounds and went on a thirty-six-hour water fast."

Hooper was determined to make the idea of jumping through time utterly plausible: "Then we go to the moment when the two men meet again, and find a place where they come head to head. Javert is arriving into town as the new policeman; Valjean is changed. And in order to solve the problem of why Valjean is distracted from Fantine at a key moment, Javert is in the room to meet the mayor, suddenly the world drops out and we realize that he can think of nothing else, he's going through free fall. Thus the descent of Fantine is directly driven by the confrontation of Javert and Valjean, who has reason to feel guilt and talks about it, but we never quite understood before why he feels so responsible. This theme from his past carries his destruction."

One of the dividing lines between same-old and must-see is a filmmaker who is willing to take a huge risk in pursuit of the new new thing. In this case, Hooper was attempting to do what Peter

Bogdanovich had failed at so memorably with *At Long Last Love*—have his actors sing live on set. Both Universal and Working Title had to agree to let Hooper turn the movie into an all-singing musical, which is rare (*Tommy, Evita*), with the actors singing live. It was a huge risk. The studio was "very, very nervous," admits Langley, because very few sung-through musicals have been successful.

Most movie musicals cut back and forth between dialogue and song, and most don't feature live singing. Before Hooper came on board, the script of *Les Mis* was packed with dialogue. Mackintosh supported Hooper's belief that the movie version of the musical should be all-sung, says Langley: "The way to tell *Les Mis* was an expression of the music and all the soliloquies delivered musically; that's the power of the story."

Hooper told Langley: "My goal is to make a film where the audience is immediately okay with the fact that the characters are singing, rather than to create the scenario where I make them feel okay by having dialogue."

Hooper believed that by not going back and forth there would be less disjunction, less jarring between "real" dialogue and "fake" singing. Certainly Hooper had the benefit of newer technology to pipe live accompanying music into his actors' ears, as well as better singers. But he liked to run the songs in long takes, which exposed the live singing, with all its flaws, even more. This was not your standard polished movie musical. The question was whether audiences would be willing to embrace high-voltage heart-on-sleeve emotion in moist close-up. A lot of people tried to talk him out of it, Hooper says. And Working Title's Fellner admits that they were not sure if it would work until they saw the finished film.

Which is why Hooper had to work within a modest budget, by Hollywood standards, of just $62 million. (Universal wasn't going down the road of Weinstein's $90 million flop *Nine*.) Musical pro Hugh Jackman, Anne Hathaway (whose mother played Fantine on Broadway), and sometime rock singer Russell Crowe, who had to audition for the film along with everyone else, did not command their usual prices. Unusually, the studio did not chase Crowe, so he called them. "He fought for the role and won it," says Langley, adding that Mackintosh and original composers Claude-Michel Schönberg and Alain Boublil were integral to the casting process.

Just as Fred Astaire and Ginger Rogers danced and sang accompanied by a live RKO orchestra, Hooper had a pianist on his London set who was watching a video monitor, accompanying the singers live, and tuning in to their rhythm and cadence as they acted and sang. They could hear the piano in their molded earpieces, but to everyone else on set they sounded as if they were singing a cappella. Because the seventy-piece orchestra was added later, the singers did not have to sync to a prerecorded track. When Hooper recorded multiple vocal harmonies, the actors had to count to a marked tempo.

"Good acting is being in the moment," Hooper says after the film's first screening in L.A. for the Screen Actors Guild. "It's the pure language of the present. Arthur Miller said that if you sing to playback your choices are predecided, you don't have freedom in real time. Acting is generating the illusion that you are creating these lines from your soul, inventing them." This way, Hooper argues, his actors were allowed to become emotional, and control the tempo, which was "vital to the process."

Anyone who has seen this rigorously demanding show on stage recognizes the degree of difficulty this music would present for the actors, who would have to train their voices to last through multiple takes. That's why Hooper insisted on auditioning every actor for the film, including Jackman and Crowe. "No exceptions," he says. "They had to not just be able to sing but act and hold a close-up, they had to turn it into storytelling. It was exciting at early auditions to meet a man who showed me how it could be done. Hugh Jackman was on a short list of one for Valjean. Hugh sang around a piano at a three-hour audition. I realized he unleashed a huge power when acting through song. You allow an entire different, hidden self to emerge."

Jackman, who starved himself to play the prisoner Valjean, not drinking water for days to make his skin parchment thin, brought a spirituality to the role, says Hooper. "He'd go through tough times, tired, under pressure. He's kind of saintly, always gracious, never snaps. He's a great leader, has inner grace as a human being. To be a good man is a lot of hard work. To practice being good is a daily struggle. He fundamentally understood that inherent conflict and brought it to the role."

Hooper bored in on the actors with two cameras, one always close in on the faces, in long, often uninterrupted takes—Hathaway was an instant Oscar front-runner for her wrenching, uncut rendition of Fantine's tour-de-force "I Dreamed a Dream"—because he couldn't do the standard coverage. Even so, he tells me after the screening, some numbers went as long as fifteen and twenty-one takes: "We didn't do them all right away. Maybe we'd do a turn-around."

Hathaway nailed "I Dreamed a Dream" on the fourth take. Hooper knew he had it and told Hathaway they could move on to the next scene. But as Hathaway told Jon Stewart in an interview just before the Oscar nominations, she wasn't convinced. She worked herself to the bone (having already shed twenty-five pounds to play the impoverished factory worker forced into prostitution) doing a total of eight takes on the song. The one you see on screen, the no-doubter ticket to an Oscar? Take four.

Even onstage, a performer doesn't do the same song over and over. But they do sing many songs a night, eight performances a week. So not surprisingly the theater-trained actors fared best, especially Jackman, Hathaway, and Brit film rookie Samantha Barks, who traveled for four years with the show as Éponine. Hooper had seen her in the show two years earlier but made her go through the arduous process of beating out the intense competition for the role. "This girl is fearless," he says. Many among the supporting cast were drawn from the ranks of *Les Mis* vets.

Jackman's fine tenor was strained under these conditions, especially on the most challenging song, "Bring Him Home." His worst memory, he told me, was having to hold a perilously high G during that song—again and again—as Hooper's camera swooped away from a steep cliff in a trickily difficult move.

Mamma Mia! star Amanda Seyfried had to adjust to singing Cosette without days of prerecording and fixing to make her sound better. "This is completely me," she says. "I had to keep my voice in shape. It was so overwhelming and liberating, it's another level of emoting . . . It gets you to a place beyond the music." She prepared on her own for four months and had three to four weeks rehearsal. The actors went through their voice exercises en route to the set every day.

"They prepared like you wouldn't believe," says Hooper. "But you can't be perfectionist." Another tricky skill the actors had to master was to sing powerfully while keeping their faces relaxed and not contorting grotesquely in intimate close-up.

Hooper showed somewhat less confidence in the performance of Crowe as Valjean tormenter Javert, who is physically threatening and adequately expresses the songs in a rich baritone, but is not shown in as much extreme close-up. Crowe, who seems uneasy and vocally constricted in his songs, plays the obsessive gendarme almost too sympathetically, making his subsequent suicide less of a shock. So Hooper pulled the camera out and had him walk along various impossibly high parapets above Paris. Sacha Baron Cohen and Helena Bonham Carter offered welcome comic relief as shady innkeepers in sequences very similar in their bawdy tone to Bonham Carter's Mrs. Lovett in the Stephen Sondheim musical *Sweeney Todd.*

Thirty-year-old London theater vet Eddie Redmayne (*Red, Richard II*) had worked with Hooper seven years before on TV's *Elizabeth I,* in which the young actor had held his own against Helen Mirren, and learned to ride a horse—after insisting he already knew how. During his 2006 screen debut *The Good Shepherd,* he picked up acting tips from director Robert De Niro. And he romanced Michelle Williams as Marilyn Monroe in the 2011 drama *My Week with Marilyn*.

Hooper gave Redmayne the chance to prove himself by giving him time to improve his singing; he landed the role of Marius despite not having sung for twelve years, since his theater days. He borrowed something he learned from De Niro in order to better match the intensity of one take of the grieving survival-guilt song "Empty Chairs at Empty Tables" to the other—he'd perform it three times in a row without stopping. Hooper shot twenty-one takes.

Unlike the theater, where you can strive for perfection every night, fixing mistakes as you go, this kind of long-take filming was very exposing for the actors. After nine weeks of rehearsals—during which the writers added bits from Hugo's novel that were not in the stage musical in order to beef up the characters, and the actors tried to figure out how to enter a song believably without signaling the audience—the cast and crew arrived on set at London's Pinewood Studios. "It was a different type of fear," Redmayne tells me during an interview. "You haven't been able to sleep the night before, adrenaline is pumping, on a tiny set with three cameramen and the director behind them, with a piano playing in your ear. It creates a weird amalgam of things inside you to try to mold. You go home in the car at the end of that day, that was it, it was out of your control."

Hooper filmed on location in France as well as on Pinewood soundstages. One day on the 350-foot-high elaborately detailed Parisian street set, he dressed five cameramen as peasants in order to shoot live as fifty peasants and students scrambled to build the Paris barricades using pianos and furniture thrown out of windows.

"We had ten minutes of stock in the cameras," recalls Redmayne. "'Build a barricade! Action!' It was anarchy. We didn't know where the cameras were. Complete fear. It was makeshift, we pieced together what we could. It was wonderful and terrifying." Hooper used what they built, pinning it together with nails, but shooting on it for another month, adds Redmayne, "was still a boobytrap."

Universal's marketing department was more frightened than anyone of this all-singing feature, because unlike *Sweeney Todd* and other musicals, they wouldn't be able to disguise its true nature. The international marketing people embraced what the film was, while the domestic people tried to hide the singing. After the April CinemaCon unveiling of the one-take clip of Hathaway's "I Dreamed a Dream" wowed exhibitors, the marketers suddenly recognized that the film had the potential to move people. "It emboldened them to embrace the movie," says Langley, "to sell the movie as the movie actually is."

While Langley would have happily booked the film into festivals had it been done in time—the studio pushed back the release by a few weeks to accommodate the filmmakers—the no-holds-barred tearjerker of a dramatic musical was an instant huge Christmas hit all over the world, despite its two-and-a-half-hour running time. Hooper's goal was to pull every audience member into every tic of feeling. It's too claustrophobic for some folks—including film critics, who have both embraced and resisted the film. They sang the praises of the film's strong performances (especially Hathaway's and Jackman's), and admired the successful hybridizing of the musical with the Victor Hugo source material, but the emotional intensity of *Les Misérables* didn't work for everybody; for some the film is grandiose and sags under its own bombast. But luckily for the filmmakers, Universal and Working Title, critics represent neither worldwide moviegoers nor Academy voters, who were more likely to recognize the film's degree of difficulty and sheer audacity. And musicals have historically done well with the Academy, from *Oliver!* to *Chicago*. The movie scored at the box office with $441 million worldwide.

What made the film work? "I think there's a hunger for quality and a hunger for authenticity," says Langley. "*Les Mis* is about very archetypical themes, writ large, and it is about people expressing their emotions. We've experienced that people really do love it, even if they don't love musicals. There is something about the experience of *Les Mis*, from the story themes and the music, that is moving to people."

DJANGO UNCHAINED

Also a late arrival in the holiday season is Quentin Tarantino's latest opus, which from the start was a long shot to get finished in time for its December 25 release date. Tarantino went over on shooting, negotiating for three extra weeks on the final sequence by agreeing to let the company recoup the extra money he spent before he would receive his share of the profits.

Tarantino takes his time between movies. Unusually among writer-directors in Hollywood, he enjoys a patron relationship with indie mogul Harvey Weinstein that goes back to 1994's *Pulp Fiction*. When Tarantino pulls back from hanging out with pals—I'll never forget one exhilarating marathon session at the Hotel du Cap at Cannes with actor-director Tim Robbins, documentarian Marina Zenovich, and photographer Jeff Vespa—the fast-talking Luddite gets down to business. While he used to retire to the seclusion of a city like Amsterdam to write out his genre-inspired, character-rich, intensely violent scripts on yellow legal pads, followed by lengthy hunt-and-peck sessions on the old Smith Corona he's used since *Reservoir Dogs,* he now actually goes out to scribble in a notebook on the balcony of his home in the Hollywood Hills, followed by a swim during which he asks himself, Hemingway-style, "How can I make it better?"

Tarantino is a rare bird: he has refused to succumb to the temptations of the Hollywood studios, which tend to wave around large sums of cash to try to lure away the best writer-directors from the painful act of summoning original screenplays. Tarantino has turned down, among other things, *Men in Black, Speed,* and the James Bond film *Casino Royale.* He creates his movies out of his own head. At a time when knock-offs are the rule, Tarantino is an original.

That's because the filmmaker, who turned fifty in 2012, cares deeply about his legacy, about having his films—*Django Unchained* is his eighth feature—stand the test of time. Since he wrote the 1993 film *True Romance,* directed and changed considerably by Tony Scott, and *Natural Born Killers,* helmed by Oliver Stone, he has directed his own scripts. Indie hits followed, including *Reservoir Dogs;* Palme d'Or winner *Pulp Fiction,* which also earned Tarantino an Oscar for cowriting the screenplay with Roger Avary; bounty hunter drama *Jackie Brown,* starring Robert De Niro and Pam Grier; *Kill Bill* volumes I and II, starring Uma Thurman as a sword-wielding samurai; the uber-violent car-screeching actioner *Death Proof,* which, while well reviewed, upset him greatly when it did not fare well at the box office; and his homage to World War II movies and fifth Cannes entry, *Inglourious Basterds,* which grossed $120.5 million domestically—his biggest hit until *Django Unchained.*

Always reliant on flamboyant, distinctive dialogue (except for the almost-silent *Kill Bill* films), Tarantino builds his projects around novelistic rather than cinematic structures. The $70 million *Inglourious Basterds* was broken into five separate chapters, each shot in a different film style. "I create mosaics, following this story and that story, and eventually they all converge," he tells me on the phone after *Inglourious Basterds'* debut in Cannes, "unless you're dealing with *Reservoir Dogs* or *Death Proof,* which have straightforward storytelling."

The opening sequence of *Inglourious Basterds,* an intense face-off between Jew hunter Colonel Landa (multilingual Austrian actor Christoph Waltz won his first Oscar for the role) and a French farmer (Denis Ménochet) seeking to protect his three lovely daughters, was inspired by Sergio Leone westerns as well as the opening sequence of *Heaven's Gate*. (Tarantino thinks his writing in this scene tops his personal best: the Sicilian speech in *True Romance*.)

Tarantino tells me that the trick to keeping his movies modern and, yes, hip, so that they hold up well into the future, is to play it risky, not safe. On *Inglourious Basterds,* he got away with the reflexive use of titles, musical cues from iconic octogenarian Ennio Morricone, an unidentified narrator (Samuel L. Jackson), and multiple film references. There's no knowing what he's going to do, from charming us with heroic, charismatic World War II–era Germans, like the one actor Daniel Brühl plays in *Inglourious Basterds,* to killing off the characters we like. "I want to do a movie that pushes you in, and pulls you out," he says.

With *Django Unchained,* which throws the revenge theme of *Inglourious Basterds* into a provocative pre–Civil War Southern setting, when the slave economy was in full swing, Tarantino offers up a meaty dish to be savored and interpreted, crammed with movie references and rich performances from a wide range of great character actors. He deepens his homage to the 1960s spaghetti westerns of Italy's two Sergios, Leone (*The Good, the Bad and the Ugly*) and Corbucci (*Django*). In fact, the world of Corbucci helped Tarantino figure out how to do *Django Unchained*. While writing a critical essay on the filmmaker and listening to spaghetti western music the first scene came to him: a man riding up to buy a slave off a Texas chain gang.

"His was the most pitiless west that a character could walk through," Tarantino tells Taylor Hackford after the film's first L.A. screening at the Directors Guild of America (DGA) on December 2. "They're cruel movies; their characters are capable of cruel actions; they were comments on Fascism left over from World War II. And exciting stories can happen inside of that landscape. I was trying to find an equivalent of Sergio Corbucci no-man's land, where life is cheap and people are pitiless. Being a slave in the antebellum South, that would be life is a dime. I always wanted to tell that story anyway, and from that moment on everything fell into place."

As with many of Tarantino's projects, *Django* had been bubbling on the back burner for a while, thirteen years, he tells a packed, cavernous Hall H at Comic-Con in July. "I've always wanted to do a western," he says. "Spaghetti westerns have always been my favorite. The violence, the surrealism, the cool music, and all that stuff. The initial germ of the whole idea was a slave who becomes a bounty hunter and then goes after overseers who are hiding out on plantations."

Tarantino says that adding the long-missing ingredient—slavery—to the familiar western tropes makes it fresh, finally. The crowd loves it when Tarantino describes the movie as a prequel to *Shaft*: "Broomhilda and Django will eventually have a baby and then that baby will have a baby and that baby will have a baby and one of these days, John Shaft will be born. John Shaft started with this lady here. They're the great-great-great-great-grandparents of 'Shut your mouth!'"

Eight years ago one of the film's producers, Reggie Hudlin, was explaining to Tarantino what he didn't like about a particular movie about slavery: it wasn't as empowering as he had hoped it would be. He told Tarantino, "Look, this is a movie obviously made with the best intentions, yet at the end of the day, for black folks watching it, it's not half as empowering as *The Legend of Nigger Charley*."

"I understood exactly what he meant," Tarantino says to Harvard historian Henry Louis Gates Jr. during an in-depth interview in *The Root*. "It was a diamond bullet of reality. I took it in, and then I said, 'I have to make that movie one day.' *The Legend of Nigger Charley* is an empowering movie. And it stands alone."

Antebellum slave dramas have not been turned into many movies at all. Tarantino was pouring an 1858 slave drama into the western genre mold; that required research. "I can understand people being uncomfortable with slave narratives," he says to Hackford.

"It's the ugliest time of this country, and we haven't gotten over it yet. Nevertheless, everyone talks about: there's no stories, there's nothing left to tell, especially westerns, I've seen every type of western. There's all kinds of stories that could be told in a slave narrative that have never ever been touched. Let this be the first rock through the window!"

While Tarantino was writing the script, his *Inglourious Basterds* Oscar winner Christoph Waltz came into town and read what the director had completed thus far. One night, before Waltz took Tarantino to see the second installment of the L.A. Opera production of Wagner's Ring Cycle, he took him out to dinner and told him the story of the opera. "There was nothing like Christoph telling you the story of Siegfried and Brunhilde, he was born to do that, he was terrific," recalls Tarantino, who had already named Django's wife Broomhilda. "While I was watching the second opera, I realized the stories were parallel. The daughter of Wotan is the daughter of all the gods—that's Bruce Dern—the mountain is Candieland, Candie is the dragon, the circle of hellfire is around her, and Django is Siegfried. It would be wonderful to see Christoph telling the story. I like bringing a fairy-tale aspect to the story, anyway."

Tarantino finished the script on April 26, 2011. This time he adopted a straightforward narrative centered on one through-character for us to follow from beginning to end, a superhero origin story about the freed slave Django, an angel of vengeance who learns to "kill white people and get paid for it," Tarantino tells *LA Weekly* critic Karina Longworth. "Fastest gun in the South."

Waltz tells me a Tarantino movie is "a living organism. The script is a point of departure. Shooting takes care of collecting material for the edit. We had sixty-four days to shoot. In Germany on *Inglourious Basterds* the schedule was tighter and the budget smaller. Here we were on home turf, emboldened by the experience and success of *Basterds*. This was a little more expensive [$83 million], the leeway was broader, here a lot of things changed, according to necessity. He sees stuff long before they really make their presence felt. He thinks ahead. He's the author, not so much the director. He started out in his head, and it will end in his head. The thing is to transpose what's in his head via the material he's shot through the edit, through the film."

While Waltz was on board from the start to play German bounty hunter King Schultz, speculation about casting dogged Tarantino, as various actors were in and out of the eighteen-week production, from Kevin Costner, Joseph Gordon-Levitt, Anthony LaPaglia, and Kurt Russell to Sacha Baron Cohen and Idris Elba. Will Smith turned down the title role, he later told *Entertainment Weekly*, because it wasn't the lead. He saw Waltz's sophisticated European, who trains Django, as the leading role. And while Smith admired the script, he didn't want to hold up Tarantino by trying to fix it.

So Tarantino turned to Jamie Foxx, the respected Oscar-winning star of *Ray*, who boasts considerable range, from action and comedy to drama. Foxx sold Tarantino, the actor tells me at Comic-Con, partly by promoting his skills as a horseman. The actor had grown up playing cowboys and Indians in Texas, complete with a green *Bonanza* jacket. "I got a couple horses," he told Tarantino. "Let me ride my own horse. She's able to handle the stunts."

As Foxx dealt with the dramatic evolution of his character, the slave who goes from being number six on a chain gang to sitting on top of a horse as a free man, so his horse Cheetah learned to handle a noisy film set. When they visit the plantation run by Big Daddy (Don Johnson), Schultz has Django ride up wearing a frilly Blue Boy costume. "I wrote that scene in the script," says Tarantino. "And Jamie said Django should choose that outfit: 'I want that fly shit. That should be Django's choice.' Sounds like a good idea.

"I couldn't have made this movie with a Django who didn't see eye to eye with me, who didn't understand the story we wanted to tell, why we were doing what we were doing, how to nail the humor. And Jamie in this movie was a true lead, and a lead actor leads by example. That's what he did, for the whole cast and the crew, he was just wonderful. But he had that extra little ingredient: he trusted me. There were moments, like, 'Wow do we need to do this?' and I'd say 'Well, it really is the trick,' and we'd talk about it. And, 'Okay, we'll do it.'"

Tarantino was open to letting characters develop in extensive rehearsals and on set, according to Foxx: "He'd change this over here, he was open to things. He'd rewrite the script on a dime; sometimes the changes would be fantastic. He goes to lunch and comes back with four pages. We'd shoot it."

On-set rewriting is usually about "massaging," Tarantino says. "You write a scene in your bedroom six months earlier, then getting ready to do it on the day, you realize things have changed. On an epic movie like this, yeah, you have the script, you've done the first half, you know what you have, what you need, what you don't need to spend time on anymore, so it's adjusting and massaging like that. I try not to come up with too many pseudo-fabulous ideas in rehearsal, that we all think are great, and I end up shooting, but they never make the movie. I love all those fun times exploring it, but it never makes the movie. Every once in a while they do."

Tarantino was afraid that Foxx wouldn't be able to dig down below his entitled celebrity veneer to feeling like the lowly slave he is at the beginning of the film. At the very start Foxx offered too much self-confidence, and Tarantino told him to go back and imagine what being a slave was like. "I got together with Jamie, by ourselves, and I said, 'You know, we don't have a story if Django is already this magnificent heroic figure who just happens to be in chains,'" Tarantino says to Gates. "It's like, look, the stuff that we show is really harsh, and it's supposed to be harsh, but it was [actually] a lot worse."

"The most important thing was letting everything go because we all have egos," Foxx informs Hall H. "That was what was unique for me, to actually do homework, to listen to what he says, strip yourself down, and start all over again."

Needless to say, the portrayal of poor slave conditions and violent treatment carried a considerable charge for the African Americans on set. "There were a lot of tough days," Foxx admits. "To watch men is one thing, or to have something happening to me, but to watch Kerry Washington be whipped—she said, 'I want to be hit with the lash,' it was the nylon version—was one of the toughest things, how she embodied that. Quentin went to every person on that set, the extras, made sure they were okay between each scene. He'd crack a joke, play music to get our mind off things."

Washington was appalled to realize how little she knew about the details of what was done to African Americans during slavery. She thought iron masks put on slaves was a Tarantino exaggeration, not something discovered in painstaking research. "The face of the hero is one we don't often get to see as the hero of this kind of film, the African American in the antebellum South," she says. "Quentin has never been intimidated by evil or gore or blood, the dark side of humanity. In some ways that's why he's a powerful storyteller in the context of slavery. For a long time we've been afraid of portraying the ugliness of this history." The actress found that out the hard way, not only by experiencing being whipped, but by spending hours in a tiny metal "hot box" buried in the ground, full of biting spiders, worms, and centipedes.

They wound up filming on location at a historic New Orleans plantation for Candieland, which is ruled by Calvin Candie, played with an evil sneer by greasy-haired Leonardo DiCaprio. The star approached Tarantino about playing the character, who was written as a sixtyish older man. "The pretext we're selling is this southern aristocratic society, what they consider to be European aristocracy," he says to Hackford. "They took what they liked, and what they didn't like, they threw out, and they made it up. They lived a life of barons and burgermeisters. Candie has sixty-five miles of land, not uncommon in an industrial plantation with an army of slaves. They were your subjects, and you had a whole army of poor white workers who were paid slave wages to keep the slaves in line. You were a king. What you say goes."

The director worked closely with DiCaprio on refining his character, says Tarantino: "Calvin Candie would be the perpetual boy emperor, his daddy's daddy was a cotton man, he's sick of it, the farm goes on for so long it takes care of itself. He's the bored and petulant emperor, he comes up with hobbies to keep himself interested, like Mandingos."

DiCaprio added the notion that Candie was a student of the pseudoscience of phrenology. "That gave the white class a scientific proof and reason to be as racist as they were," says Tarantino. "He gave me some phrenology books. This shit writes itself, it was so fucking crazy, what they're saying." During the filming, DiCaprio cracked open a glass and cut himself; as his blood flowed, Tarantino kept rolling. The crew applauded when he stopped. "My hand started really pouring blood all over the table," DiCaprio recounts to the *Hollywood Reporter*. "Maybe they thought it was done with special effects. I wanted to keep going. It was more interesting to watch Quentin's and Jamie's reaction off camera than to look at my hand." They bandaged his hand in later scenes in case Tarantino used that take. He did.

The Ku Klux Klan sequence was among the most daring, in that it was not only intended to be hilarious, but to make direct reference to the infamous silent film *The Birth of a Nation*." "It was my 'fuck you' to D. W. Griffith," Tarantino says at the DGA. "I had a trepidation about doing the bag scene. I thought it was one of the funniest scenes in the script, but it played so funny on the page that I was positive I'd fuck it up, it was too funny. I did it, felt okay about it, was scared about editing it."

So he elected to film the KKK charge first, "to get our feet wet. So we did the charge, so fun to shoot. So I did that, and they're actually scary." The director realized that if he "showed that they're fucking idiots right at the beginning, I'm going to kick the whole sequence in the shins." So he decided to use a flashback. "I wasn't sure if it worked. We had a research screening, and we showed it. And everyone laughed more than they did throughout the film, and it's everyone's favorite scene."

The director invited his cast and crew to Sunday screenings at the Sergio Corbucci Theater every week. "You get a film history class through his telling of the story behind one movie," says Walton Goggins (*Justified*), who plays a ruthless Mandingo fight trainer on Candie's plantation. "There's realism and absurdity inherent in all of Quentin's characters. It seems real to me."

Working with a more relaxed production schedule, with Oscar-winning cinematographer Robert Richardson shooting in 35 millimeter, Tarantino loosened up on figuring out his shots in advance and was open to experimentation and a more rock-and-roll approach. "Good-looking for Quentin is a different aesthetic," Richardson told *Thompson on Hollywood*'s Bill Desowitz. "The beauty of a Tarantino film is that the visuals match the rhythm of the words. That's his goal. And that's my goal."

They shot in Lone Pine, California, and Louisiana from late November 2011 to July 25, 2012. Various things set the production behind by three weeks. During a *Hollywood Reporter* Q&A, producer Stacey Sher said she was ready to shoot the winter scenes of *Django Unchained* in a Mammoth, California, ski resort location, but no snow was falling—for the first time in one hundred years. After several days of anxiously tracking weather reports, the production had to pick up and move the set to Jackson Hole, Wyoming.

All the actors are excellent: Waltz's charming but ruthless German bounty hunter; Foxx as the slave who comes into his own and will move mountains to rescue his lovely lost wife, Broomhilda (Washington), who is owned by DiCaprio's entertainingly debauched Candie; and Samuel L. Jackson, who gives a brilliant, layered performance as the head house slave. It's Jackson who comments on an entire history of actors playing Uncle Tom. "His character, Stephen, makes Stepin Fetchit look like Malcolm X," marvels Henry Louis Gates.

"Sam is a good writer," Tarantino responds. "Some actors try to improvise and everything, but you know, frankly, if they're not just adding 'mmms' and 'ahs' or cusswords, that's actually called writing, and that's usually not what you hire actors to do. Having said that, he sprinkles the dialogue with his own little bit of Sam Jackson seasoning. But that character is on the page."

Tarantino worked on a relatively intense delivery schedule between 2009's *Inglourious Basterds* and 2012's *Django Unchained,* partly because the Weinsteins needed him to deliver to have a commercially lucrative release over the holiday season.

Thus Tarantino had to complete the movie in time for a December 25 wide release. The film officially wrapped around July 7, which meant that *Django* would not have the benefit of the fall film festival circuit. A provocative movie like this could have used careful handling and set-up from critics and media to educate audiences on what to expect. While *Django Unchained* is not sensationally exploitative like Richard Fleischer's 1975 *Mandingo,* Tarantino's movie was clearly designed to blow people's gaskets.

Tarantino finally relinquished the film to the Weinstein Company weeks late, after a long battle in the editing room to get it down to two hours and forty-five minutes. This is nothing new for the slow and deliberate writer-director. But Tarantino had been accustomed to working closely with longtime editor Sally Menke, who sadly died at age fifty-six in September 2010 while hiking in L.A.'s Griffith Park on one of the hottest days in the city's recorded history. Tarantino called Menke, who was nominated for Oscars for both *Pulp Fiction* and *Inglourious Basterds,* "my only true genuine collaborator," like a cowriter in the editing room. She and Tarantino had established a working pace. She'd get started early every morning; he'd come in noonish to work with her for the rest of the day. He trusted her, and she could argue with him; she knew his rhythms, the pace of the long shots, dialogue, and action, how to adapt to changes in tone, sequence by sequence. On *Inglourious Basterds,* she convinced him to try to structure the narrative without the separate chapters, she told me. It didn't work, and they returned to the way he wrote it.

Tarantino writes each script so that it can stand alone as a piece of writing, whether or not he winds up directing it, and he doesn't necessarily intend to shoot or include everything. He knows he'll lose things in the editing room. *Django* editor Fred Raskin had worked as assistant editor with Menke on *Kill Bill* volumes I and II. Arguably, *Django Unchained* could have used more time to find its proper pace, length, and tone. There are ways this story could have reached beyond the genre of an entertaining, sometimes shocking spaghetti western to find real comedy and pathos; it often feels flat, constrained, and stuck. Finally, Tarantino admitted to Longworth, without Menke he had to be more responsible for his own movie.

And the score is noisy and intrusive. Tarantino had been using spaghetti western music in his past five films; on *Django Unchained* he went all-out and, for the first time, collaborated with artists to create original film music. The score, packed with anachronistic spaghetti-western-style songs (new ones from Rick Ross and John Legend, along with vinyl recordings from his collection) and some fabulous original music from Ennio Morricone, doesn't help to build emotion; it feels cluttered, attention-grabbing, and disjunctive.

In the preview process, Tarantino realized that what was fine for him in the more violent scenes was too upsetting for audiences. Both the Mandingo male slaves fighting to the death for sport and the gruesome dog-mauling scene were cut back. "This movie has to work on a bunch of different levels," he told Gates. "The comedy, the horrific serious scenes had to be able to work, I have to be able to get you to laugh a sequence after that to bring you back from [the horror]. When the Mandingo scene and the dog scene were rougher, I traumatized [the audience] too much, because they actually had been enjoying the movie before then. And the thing is, I actually got them back."

The black community reacted in a range of ways. Historian Gates, to his credit, engages Tarantino in a serious and provocative debate in which they dig into what was real and what was exaggerated in the film, as well as the use of violence, the N-word, and Foxx's discomfort with playing a slave. Tarantino also expresses his hatred for western master John Ford, partly because he was willing to play a klansman in *The Birth of a Nation*. Both men know their history, give each other respect. And Tarantino holds his own.

When Gates asks about the use of the N-word in the film, Tarantino replies, "Well, you know, if you're going to make a movie about slavery and are taking a twenty-first-century viewer and putting them in that time period, you're going to hear some things that are going to be ugly, and you're going to see some things that are going to be ugly. That's just part and parcel of dealing truthfully with this story, with this environment, with this land.

"Personally, I find [the criticism] ridiculous. Because it would be one thing if people are out there saying, 'You use it much more excessively in this movie than it was used in 1858 in Mississippi.' Well, nobody's saying that. And if you're not saying that, you're simply saying I should be lying. I should be watering it down. I should be making it more easy to digest. No, I don't want it to be easy to digest. I want it to be a big, gigantic boulder, a jagged pill and you have no water."

On the other hand, on Twitter @SpikeLee engaged with his fans by explaining why he refused to see the film: "American Slavery Was Not a Sergio Leone Spaghetti Western. It Was A Holocaust. My Ancestors Are Slaves. Stolen From Africa. I Will Honor Them."

And filmmaker Ava DuVernay writes me an explanation of why she, Lee, and others are reluctant to check out the movie themselves (Lee does not tell anyone not to go see it): they don't want to deal with this subject in this manner. I still think that Lee could have engaged meaningfully if he had actually seen the movie. I'm not the only one who is eager to know what his reaction would be. In some ways, Tarantino makes the dicey and horrific subject matter easier to handle via the genre. He's providing a distancing device. A realm of safety. But he also backs off of some of the emotion that way.

When Tarantino's bloody western-down-South opened Christmas Day, many critics raved (89 percent on Rotten Tomatoes, 80 percent on MetaCritic), singing the praises of the film's stellar cast and its fierce yet disturbingly funny confrontation with the most shameful chapter of American history. More divisive was the film's length, with some enjoying the epic 165-minute run time, and others finding it an overbloated self-indulgence. While many thought this violent western was too gory for Christmas audiences—it certainly wasn't PG family fare—adults flocked to see it. That's why Harvey Weinstein rushed the film into holiday release, convincing Tarantino not to wait until March. He wanted that heightened vacation playing time, when hordes of moviegoers flock to theaters. The movie grossed $424 million worldwide.

And Weinstein knew that a late release could pay off in award season—it's the freshest thing on voters' minds. But attendance at movie wickets got off to a slow start; and Weinstein had held off from sending the special "for your consideration" DVD screeners to the homes of Academy voters, a routine promotion for awards-seekers.

DVD screeners take weeks to prepare and ship. While *Django Unchained,* with its stellar cast, landed five Golden Globe nominations, it lost out on any mentions from the Screen Actors Guild. Later, Weinstein admitted that he had stalled on shipping screeners because he wanted voters to see it on the big screen. Would this move hurt its Oscar chances?

CHAPTER 9

TEN THINGS THAT CHANGED THE OSCAR RACE

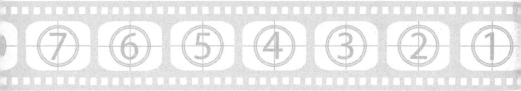

The Oscar race starts slowly with a couple of indie candidates introduced at Sundance, picks up speed at Cannes, takes off at the fall film festivals, and goes full throttle over the Christmas holidays, when critics groups build momentum with their awards. This is followed in the New Year by awards from the writers, actors, producers, directors, and craft guilds; the Golden Globes; the Oscar nominations; and finally the Oscar telecast, which is beamed live to some hundreds of millions of viewers in 250 countries around the world.

The 2012 Oscar derby is less predictable than usual because various rule changes and calendar idiosyncrasies have been thrown into the mix. There's been grumbling ever since the Academy elected to increase the number of Best Picture nominees from five to ten in an attempt to open the door to more mainstream movies such as Christopher Nolan's *The Dark Knight,* which missed being among the top five 2009 films, passed over in favor of *The Reader,*

Milk, Frost/Nixon, The Curious Case of Benjamin Button, and ultimate winner *Slumdog Millionaire.* No question, the 2010 show could have used a major ratings boost. It was among the lowest rated. (The best-watched shows are the ones featuring the biggest blockbusters, such as James Cameron's *Titanic* and *Avatar,* and Peter Jackson's *The Lord of the Rings: The Return of the King.)*

However, inviting voters to choose ten films effectively added more indies to the Best Picture nominees, among them *Precious, An Education, A Serious Man,* Pixar's *Up* and *Toy Story 3,* and, yes, Nolan's *Inception.* So the Academy tweaked the rules once more for the 2012 Oscar show, allowing for as few as five nominees if the top candidates don't earn enough votes. The goal: voters won't feel like they're stretching to include lesser films as the year's best.

No question, the preferential balloting system is mathematically arcane. Voters fill out a ballot with a list of films they rank from one to five. Basically, movies that don't earn a substantial number of first-place votes get thrown out, and a movie that gets many first-place votes also needs to accrue second- and third-place votes to stay in play. Eight popular 2011 films were nominated for Best Picture, and nine 2012 films will vie for the top spot.

For the 2012 Oscar-year voting, led by new CEO Dawn Hudson—the ex-head of successful nonprofit Film Independent, which mounts the Independent Spirit Awards—the Academy gets over its fears of potential security breaches and provides online electronic balloting for its members. Unfortunately, such elaborate hurdles are erected to keep hackers at bay that the first-ever online voting for the nominations is frustrating even for the computer literate—at first, Mac users with Safari browsers are shut out. Many voters give up and either drive to Academy offices in New York, London, or Beverly Hills to vote in a kiosk in the lobby under supervision, or ask for old-fashioned paper ballots. Academy of Motion Picture Arts and Sciences (AMPAS) president Hawk Koch insists that with heaps of e-mail reminders and trade ads, more members wind up voting than ever before. At a May 2013 Beverly Hills town hall membership gathering at the Academy in Beverly Hills, Koch states that 90 percent of the membership voted for the 2012 Oscars.

As with any political campaign, pressing the flesh, charming the voters, and reminding them why they like you makes a huge difference. So do any perceived changes in direction, outright mistakes, or even the subtlest of miscues, which can lead to significant wins and losses in any awards derby. Awards year 2012 is no exception.

In the end, the Academy deems 282 movies released in 2012 eligible for the Best Picture Oscar. But even for studio pictures backed by massive marketing campaigns, landing an actual Oscar nomination is a tricky and expensive dance that requires first and foremost getting the attention of the sixteen AMPAS branches that nominate a total of twenty-five categories in the Oscar race. (In 2013, a seventeenth branch, casting directors, will be added.) A movie must be seen to be admired.

There's never been more noise and clatter in the awards media space. Special awards campaign publicists are hired to navigate the people and movies through their paces. That's because the press is an active participant in the process of selecting the candidates who nab the awards from critics groups and guilds necessary to build momentum. Especially in a year like 2012, with so many strong contenders vying for prizes, every single acceptance speech counts. If a contender lets the winning story arc pass to another film, it can wind up being ignored.

Front and center within the industrial-awards complex are the trade publications, especially ancient rivals *Variety* and the *Hollywood Reporter* (I've worked for both), which now print weekly editions crammed with ads, plus dozens of special awards supplements. Then there are the websites such as *Deadline, The Wrap, Awards Daily, In Contention, Movie City News, Hollywood Elsewhere, GoldDerby,* and my home base, *Indiewire.* Even the major metropolitan dailies, the *Los Angeles Times* and the *New York Times,* rely heavily on Oscar "for your consideration" advertising—aimed squarely at guild and Academy members—and the endless interest (valuable eyeballs and traffic) that this glitzy race engenders.

And thus distributors and publicists put their candidates through endless rounds of festival, guild, screening, and party appearances; Q&As; and interviews, leading, they hope, to many rounds of award ceremonies and wins. The cost for someone actually in the running is astronomical—for *Silver Linings Playbook,* the Weinstein Company spent hundreds of thousands of dollars jetting Jennifer Lawrence and her costly crew of stylists from one festival and award ceremony to another. The global promo blitz keeps her in contention on the awards circuit and is picked up by the likes of *People* and *Us* and fanzines that reach actual movie ticket buyers. It helps to sell the film at the box office.

Sony Pictures Classics spends far less on Lawrence's biggest Best Actress rival, eighty-five-year-old French *Amour* star Emmanuelle Riva, who with limited stamina travels only twice to the United States from her Paris apartment and attends select events, doing most of her interviews via phone or, in my case, by answering e-mail queries that are then translated by the film's bilingual New York publicist, Sophie Gluck. Nonetheless, Riva becomes Lawrence's biggest rival for the Oscar gold.

Given the idiosyncratic nature of the Academy, inside Oscar prognosticators bring more to the race than the mathematical tools used by statisticians like the *New York Times*' Nate Silver, who tries to apply his statistical election strategy to predicting the Oscars, but will only accurately guess four out of the six major categories. Experience and intuition—and listening to Academy voters—goes a long way toward figuring out which way the wind blows.

Moderating multiple industry Q&A panels, which is *Deadline* Oscar columnist Pete Hammond's stock in trade, can throw off your picks, because you tend to unconsciously favor the folks who zap you with their star wattage. In 2011, I rooted far too long for

George Clooney and *The Descendants* before bowing to the inevitable *Artist* sweep. Over the years you get to know these folks, and they get to know you. Clooney's one of the good ones. Does he work me like a politician? Yes. And I love it. That self-deprecating charm and savoir faire—along with his taste for quality material with no paycheck in mind—is why he's an Oscar perennial.

Back in the eighties, when I filed an annual "Oscar Predicts" column for *Film Comment* right after the nominations, I learned to figure out how to forecast the future based on the past, and to judge Academy tastes and behavior. Over the next years I shared my hard-won insight with my readers at *LA Weekly, Entertainment Weekly,* monthly magazine *Premiere,* and dailies the *Hollywood Reporter* and *Variety.* After I left the publication in 2009, I figured that if *Variety* could sell online Oscar ads at a premium on the daily blog *Thompson on Hollywood,* based on a large readership of Academy voters, so could rising *Indiewire,* which functions as both an industry trade catering to the independent film community and a consumer site for smart film and television fans.

And so I still track the Oscar race online 24/7 during the full-tilt awards campaign season, from November 1 through the date that the final ballots are due. With the 2012 films, active Academy members can begin submitting their nomination ballots on December 17. They are due back to PricewaterhouseCoopers, an international accounting firm, on January 3, 2013. On Thursday, January 10, the nominations are announced at 5:30 a.m. Pacific time at the Academy building on Wilshire Boulevard in Beverly Hills. A celebratory nominees luncheon follows at the Beverly Hilton on February 4. On Friday, February 8, the final voting begins, with ballots due by February 19 at 5 p.m. And the winners are declared Sunday, February 24, during the 85th Academy Awards at the Dolby Theatre in Hollywood.

Things get particularly intense during the months of December and January, as the New York, Los Angeles, and other film critics hand out their awards, and the Golden Globes and Critics' Choice Awards take place. Honors are also bestowed at this time by the Screen Actors, Directors, Writers, and Producers Guilds. The die is cast over the course of the long campaign as key events—anomalies, omissions, and surprises—irrevocably change the course of the Oscar race. All of these political machinations—and more—are in play during the uniquely competitive Oscar race of 2012.

Here are ten things that change the course of the 2012 Oscars, in chronological order:

January 28:
BEASTS OF THE SOUTHERN WILD TAKES THE GRAND JURY PRIZE AT THE SUNDANCE FILM FESTIVAL

The instant that the Sundance Grand Jury Prize is awarded to Benh Zeitlin's *Beasts of the Southern Wild,* along with a cinematography award for Ben Richardson, Fox Searchlight has a shot at some award season wins. The distributor can boast of these prizes on every subsequent ad as it chases more awards down the line, just as it did with its 2006 Sundance labor of love *Once,* another must-see film created from scratch with a cast of unknowns and an unconventional narrative. After *Beasts* plays Un Certain Regard at Cannes and wins the Camera d'Or for best first film, Searchlight counterprograms the $1.8 million film against the summer behemoths in late June, looking to establish it as an indie hit going into award season.

Searchlight's canny marketers also make moviegoers aware of the film's undeniable emotional impact with an online video campaign. The picture easily outgrosses the two top-grossing Sundance winners to date (*The Brothers McMullen* and *Precious*), which each passed $10 million; *Beasts* grosses $12.8 million despite never playing in more than 318 theaters, hardly an expected outcome.

And Searchlight manages to take long-shot *Beasts* rookie Quvenzhané Wallis, age nine, from breakthrough actress at the National

Board of Review on December 5 all the way to the youngest-ever Best Actress nomination. This was by no means a given, nor is a total of four Oscar nominations for the indie, including Picture, Adapted Screenplay, and Director.

Searchlight's other Sundance pickup is Ben Lewin's delicate drama *The Surrogate,* later retitled *The Sessions,* which also won two Sundance prizes, the Dramatic Audience Award and a special jury prize for its ensemble acting, led by Helen Hunt and John Hawkes. They hold this one for the fall fests, as the challenging drama needs more branding and attention for Hunt and Hawkes's literally naked performances. Despite some stellar reviews, the movie never takes off with audiences, topping out at $6 million domestic. Searchlight opts to place former Best Actress Oscar winner Hunt (*As Good As It Gets*) in the category of Supporting Actress rather than Lead Actress, both because they don't want her to compete with Wallis and because they feel she has a better shot there.

Actors assessing each other's performances tend to respond to vulnerability, disability, and degree of difficulty, all in ample evidence in *The Sessions.* But sex—as well as disability—can make people uncomfortable, so the intimate true story written and directed by unknown Australian Lewin doesn't make it to the top of many screener piles. In the end, Hawkes and Hunt do score Golden Globe and Screen Actors Guild nominations. On Oscar nominations morning, Hunt lands a Supporting Actress nod, but the Best Actor race is so tight this time that *Winter's Bone* nominee Hawkes doesn't make the cut.

January 28:
DOCUMENTARY *SEARCHING FOR SUGAR MAN* NABS
TWO SUNDANCE PRIZES

Swedish music docmaker Malik Bendjelloul's moving biodoc *Searching for Sugar Man,* which Sony Pictures Classics picked up on opening night of the Sundance Film Festival, takes home two significant prizes on closing night: the World Cinema Documentary Audience Award and a special world cinema doc jury prize, the first of many more to come on the road to the Oscars.

In a year packed with superior documentaries, both well made and compelling, *Sugar Man* slowly becomes the leading contender, popping at March's SXSW Film Festival, winning best doc at the National Board of Review on December 5, and earning numerous critics' awards. It never loses that spot, and by the end grosses a respectable $3.7 million domestic. The heartrending rediscovery of long-lost folk musician Rodriguez has legs—I see the sixty-nine-year-old play, rustily, at SXSW, but then he starts touring again, his songs return to airplay, and his career takes off. By the time *60 Minutes* catches up with Rodriguez's story on October 6, 2012, it seems that no other documentary has a chance.

On the other hand, music docs don't tend to do that well with the insular Academy documentary branch (then numbering 176 members), which new Academy governor Michael Moore has been trying to shake up. They tend to steer toward gravitas and away from show business. And thus intense competition comes from other Sundance titles with legs, including Kirby Dick's muckraking military rape agitprop *The Invisible War,* Heidi Ewing and Rachel Grady's dystopian cityscape *Detropia,* and Lauren Greenfield's recession-era riches-to-rags saga *The Queen of Versailles.*

Oddly, even though the high-profile winner of the Sundance doc Grand Jury Prize, Eugene Jarecki's brainy antidrug war polemic *The House I Live In,* is pushed by executive producer Brad Pitt and lands plenty of media attention, it never gains traction with critics groups, audiences . . . or documentarians.

But the Oscar documentary race is harder to call than usual because in January 2012 Moore manages to push through radical new rules—meeting with some resistance and grumbling from the membership. Previously, small groups divided up the submissions, with each watching only a smattering of the films, which led to acclaimed docs such as Werner Herzog's *Grizzly Man* and *Cave of Forgotten Dreams,* Jennie Livingston's *Paris Is Burning,* Steve James's *Hoop Dreams,* and Errol Morris's *The Thin Blue Line* not being nominated. Under Moore's new rules, all the members over the course of the year try to watch all eligible films on screeners—which does not mean they succeed.

The problem had been that branch members' well-intentioned zeal to make sure that every qualifying low-budget doc was screened to give it a chance at an Oscar (with or without a distributor) via small committees meant that if just one or two distempered voters didn't like the movie, it was toast. That's how the likes of Michael Apted's *Up* series were overlooked over the years. "That's over," Moore tells me. "We have to stop the madness. Let's open it up, start a democracy movement, stop the committees' private voting. The editors vote for editors. Let the entire documentary branch pick the five nominees, and then let the entire Academy see all five films and vote."

The Academy also changes the rules to favor theatrically released films over TV fare from the likes of HBO. Now a film has to be shown in Los Angeles and New York and reviewed by the *Los Angeles Times* or *New York Times* in order to be eligible. "Oscars are for real movies distributed in theaters," says Moore. "*Senna* and *Into the Abyss* and *The Interrupters* were made to be in movie theaters. Their slots were taken away by films intended as TV movies."

The downside of asking the Academy doc branch to view all Oscar-qualifying docs is that now there is a screener pile. The same forces that come into play on the feature side—marketing, publicity, for your consideration ads, dog-and-pony shows—bring to voters' attention the films that have been lauded and feted and bought and paid for. "Our branch is not swayed by Harvey," insists Moore. "We're a different breed."

Obviously, the likes of Oscar winners Moore (*Bowling for Col-*

umbine) and Alex Gibney (*Taxi to the Dark Side*) are already name brands whose films will get released and moved to the top of the pile. At the bottom will be all the little movies from nowhere with no marketing budget that no one has ever heard of. That's what documentary voter Lynne Littman was afraid would be lost with the new rules: at least with the old committee system, everything got screened.

Now smaller filmmakers without distributors, who maybe don't have fest awards to tout, will have to use their limited means and moxie to gain some traction, lest their films remain buried. This is one area where Moore, for all his populism, acts more like a Republican: Let the market rule. Moore's argument: We should be like the rest of the Academy.

The doc branch has always pushed for making docs available on screeners, and now they will do the same with the final voting. No longer do voters have to sign into a screening in New York or Los Angeles to vote. This instantly removes one favorite vote-rigging strategy for smaller films. Once nominated, filmmakers could rigorously control the number of screenings so that only the films' passionate supporters would see them and therefore be part of a critical voting block. (Members like Moore, who lives in Michigan and hadn't seen all films in a theatrical setting, couldn't vote.) Moore's move brings documentaries closer to being on the same footing as feature films. And Academy CEO Dawn Hudson has long pointed out that the advent of screeners opened up the Oscars to the indies.

There's still the question of how the Academy will handle small features in an increasingly digital universe that is no longer defined by theatrical release. "Five years from now (with the possible exception of superhero blockbusters) the theatrical market for not just docs but fiction films may be in peril," Alex Gibney tells me after the 2013 Oscars. "My biggest concern comes for innovative theatrical releases on VOD and online streaming which will be more and more prevalent. If the Academy doesn't account for those, this will become the blockbuster rule. I would still like the doc branch to tinker with this current formula to preserve the importance of theatrical films but in a much broader context."

Thus while Moore is still fighting for films to be seen in theaters, market forces are taking them online. How will the Academy handle that going forward? The twenty-five-member exec committee of the Academy doc branch, at least, has built in a review policy, so it can poll its members and see how the new process works. "We will not leave any stone unturned," says Moore. "We want to be fair and just, egalitarian and transparent."

While the members have a tough time watching some 132 documentary films, and naturally tend to see the ones that grab the most attention via film festival and critics and doc group wins, the final shortlist of fifteen is the strongest in years—it includes *Searching for Sugar Man* and several of its Sundance competitors, even self-distributed *Detropia*. All are sent to the members to watch, and screeners of the final five—*Searching for Sugar Man, The Invisible War,* AIDS history *How to Survive a Plague,* and Mideast films *The Gatekeepers* and *5 Broken Cameras*—are sent to the entire Academy.

Sony Pictures Classics is in the happy position of having two front-runners in the doc category. *Searching for Sugar Man* keeps winning awards, and their year-end release, Dror Moreh's *The Gatekeepers,* featuring interviews with the five heads of Israel's security arm Shin Bet, is also knocking out audiences and Academy voters.

Why are so many docs so good these days? "There are two things going on," SPC's Michael Barker tells me at the Academy nominees lunch. "On a technical level documentarians like Dror and Malik are making docs for movie theaters, that work in theaters best, and also work on TV and DVD. These five docs are made to be seen in movie theaters, which elevates them. And due to current events and global politics, documentaries are becoming so much more important to the public."

April 22:

ANNE HATHAWAY'S "I DREAMED A DREAM"

FROM *LES MISÉRABLES* WOWS AT CINEMACON

As soon as Universal's marketing department, which had been so nervous about all the singing in *Les Misérables,* made the call to unveil footage of the tear-flooded Anne Hathaway's heartbreaking rendition of "I Dreamed a Dream" to exhibitors and media at CinemaCon in April, she became the front-runner for Best Supporting Actress. Hunt and her fellow nominees never had a chance. In fact, the studio anchored much of its marketing campaign on that song; it was undeniably moving and showed people what the movie was about: raw emotion.

It became an accepted truth that Hathaway had a gold statue in the bag and could not lose, short of some major PR catastrophe. Indeed, Hathaway was forced to dodge some bullets. After a photograph of her leaving a limo wearing an edgy sleek black dress with a revealing deep slit but no underwear was plastered all over the Internet, she deftly responded to Matt Lauer on *The Today Show*:

> It kind of made me sad on two accounts. One, I was very sad that we live in an age when someone takes a picture of another person in a vulnerable moment and rather than delete it and do the decent thing, sells it. And I'm sorry that we live in a culture that commodifies sexuality of unwilling participants. Which brings us back to *Les Mis*, because that is what my character is. She is someone forced to sell sex . . . So, yeah, let's get back to *Les Mis*.

Academy voters historically approve of drastic weight gain or loss (see: *Raging Bull*) and degree of difficulty (singing live in one take with a camera staring down your gullet). But even so, toward the end of an endless awards campaign, folks are getting tired of hearing about Hathaway's obsessive twenty-five-pound weight loss—she lived on two oatmeal pellets a day—and her Fantine-playing stage mother. Near the end of the Oscar voting, she is named the celebrity people most love to hate.

And yet she survives that, as well as a hilarious "I Dreamed a Dream" parody video takedown by actress Emma Fitzpatrick (*The Collection*): "I sang a song about my woes / My hopes and fears, my dreams and wishes / And though I had to blow my nose / I did it all in one take, bitches."

May 27:
AMOUR GRABS THE CANNES PALME D'OR

At the Cannes closing awards ceremony, writer-director Michael Haneke brought his two stars, Jean-Louis Trintignant and Emmanuelle Riva, up to the stage to accept the Palme d'Or for *Amour*. From there, Sony Pictures Classics expertly shepherded the film through the fall film festivals ahead of its stateside opening at the height of award season on December 19.

The film steadily built a string of foreign language film wins at the New York Film Critics Circle, National Board of Review, Critics' Choice, Golden Globes, and BAFTAs, which also honored Riva with Best Actress, as did the Los Angeles Film Critics, the National Society of Film Critics, and the European Film Awards. The L.A. critics went so far as to award the film Best Picture.

On Oscar nominations morning, *Amour* scores an astonishing five nods, landing on the Best Picture list of nine and earning surprise writing and directing nominations for Haneke. The Foreign Language nomination is expected, but *Amour* marks the first time since *The Emigrants* in 1973 that a foreign Best Picture nominee also lands a Best Actress nomination. Films that have nabbed both Best Actress and Foreign Language nominations belong to an elite club indeed: *Life Is Beautiful, Z,* and *Crouching Tiger, Hidden Dragon.*

Sony Pictures Classics, which always releases more than a few foreign films in Oscar contention, faces the not unwelcome potential challenge of dueling Best Actress nominees, both glories of the French cinema: previous Oscar winner Marion Cotillard, for her mesmerizing turn as a gravely injured woman who finds love, self-respect, and a second career as a rough and tumble boxing manager in Jacques Audiard's *Rust and Bone,* and the unforgettable Riva. Trintignant, who still has a sexy glint in his eye as he flirts with Riva, is equally deserving of a statuette. Neither he nor Cotillard score nominations.

But eighty-five-year-old Riva, who starred in *Hiroshima Mon Amour,* a movie that many Academy seniors remember, reaches into voters' hearts and becomes the oldest Best Actress nominee to walk the red carpet—on her eighty-sixth birthday. As it turns out, Riva has the best shot at unseating Lawrence. Even though it's a tough, wrenching look at the end of life, *Amour* plays well with many older Academy members. "It's my life," director Paul Mazursky, eighty-two, tells me.

But Riva has limited stamina for awards campaigning. So Sony puts her on the phone with press. They send Haneke to the L.A. Film Critics awards and Golden Globes, and put Riva in the limelight at the New York Film Critics Circle and National Board of Review awards. It's her first trip to America. She asks Barker for a car so that she can drive to lower Manhattan and see the Statue of Liberty. The day after accepting the César for Best Actress in Paris, Riva takes the grueling long flight to L.A. for the Oscars.

DECEMBER 19:
ON THE OPENING DAY OF *ZERO DARK THIRTY,* THREE
U.S. SENATORS ACCUSE THE FILMMAKERS OF INACCURACY

Kathryn Bigelow's *Zero Dark Thirty* takes off like a shot with film critics, winning New York Film Critics Circle awards for Best Film and Director on December 3, followed by National Board of Review awards for Best Film, Director, and Actress (Jessica Chastain) on December 5. And Bigelow is runner-up for Best Director at the Los Angeles Film Critics Association vote on December 9.

The filmmakers studiously avoid politics by not revealing the movie's content until after the November presidential election, but that strategy goes out the window when the movie opens. On that very day, December 19, 2012, after having viewed the film, Senate Intelligence Committee chairman Dianne Feinstein, Senate Armed Services Committee chairman Carl Levin, and Senate Armed Services Committee ranking member John McCain send a scathing letter of complaint to Sony Pictures Entertainment chairman and CEO Michael Lynton about the reported but fictionalized film account of the CIA's ten-year hunt for Osama bin Laden.

The senators describe the movie as "grossly inaccurate and misleading," and focus their ire on footage depicting CIA officers torturing prisoners that "credits these detainees with providing critical lead information" on the courier who eventually led the CIA to the bin Laden compound in Pakistan: "*Zero Dark Thirty* is factually inaccurate, and we believe that you have an obligation to state that the role of torture in the hunt for Osama Bin Laden is not based on the facts, but rather part of the film's fictional narrative."

While the resulting controversy and debate drives moviegoers to the box office and fuels the $45 million film's strong stateside numbers (it totals $95.7 million domestic, $42 million foreign), the awards campaign never recovers. At the BAFTA tea party on Golden Globes weekend, I ask Bigelow if the studio presented *Zero Dark Thirty* as too much true story and too little fiction. She looks me in the eye and says, "I would not change a thing."

Though the movie gets five Oscar nominations, including Best Picture, Bigelow is not nominated for Best Director. Producer-writer Mark Boal lands a nomination for Original Screenplay, and rising star Jessica Chastain for Best Actress in a Leading Role. (The other two nominations are for film and sound editing.) Chastain remains a strong contender in her category, but perhaps because she identifies with her role as CIA agent Maya, the smartest person in the room, her interviews and acceptance speech at the Critics' Choice Awards—her first Best Actress win on the road to the Oscars—take on a feminist slant. She says, "It was a great honor to play a woman defined by herself and not her male counterpart."

Chastain is expected to go on to win the dramatic actress prize at the Golden Globes, and does, saying, "Bigelow has done more for women and cinema than she takes credit for." But it is impossible not to notice some of the male blowback online. No one looked snazzier on the red carpet, but Chastain's Jessica Rabbit curves belie her assertive intelligence.

At the Academy luncheon on February 4, Bigelow exudes nothing but confidence, enjoying her biggest box-office hit to date and being the subject of a *Time* magazine cover story. "It was sort of surreal," she admits, "but it was great."

At the Directors Guild Awards some weeks later, nominee and presenter Bigelow, who accepted the DGA award for *The Hurt Locker* two years before, thanks Sony's Amy Pascal, saying, "To support a movie that has a few sharp edges is no small feat."

However, while critics recognize and admire the advances Bigelow has made by breaking Hollywood narrative genre and gender conventions, the Academy is largely made up of older white males. (That 2013 *Los Angeles Times* study showed that Oscar voters are nearly 94 percent Caucasian and 77 percent male.) Perceived as an early leader, *Zero Dark Thirty* swiftly became the focus of a fierce negative campaign. But its lack of support came from within the Academy.

The Academy knows it needs to deal with the lack of diversity in it ranks. Ever since Dawn Hudson came on board as CEO in 2011, the Academy has made a point of inviting more young members and people of color, including, in 2012, Berenice Bejo, Jonah Hill, Diego Luna, Demián Bichir, and Octavia Spencer. In 2013, the

Academy sent membership invites to a whopping 276 people, 100 more than the year before, many of them young, gifted, female, or ethnic, including actors Joseph Gordon-Levitt and Michael Peña; actresses Kimberly Elise, Milla Jovovich, Lucy Liu, Jennifer Lopez, and Emmanuelle Riva; writer-director Ava DuVernay; writers Lena Dunham, Sarah Polley, and Julie Delpy (whose Oscar-nominated *Before Sunset* cowriters Richard Linklater and Ethan Hawke had been invited years before); octogenarian documentarian Agnès Varda; Brit director Steve McQueen; Warner Bros. executive Kevin Tsujihara; and the rock star/composer known as Prince.

January 10, 2013:
IN A STUNNER, THE OSCAR DIRECTORS FAIL
TO NOMINATE BEN AFFLECK

Only members of the Academy directors' branch are eligible to nominate in the Best Director category. Three of the five slots go to Spielberg (*Lincoln*), Ang Lee (*Life of Pi*), and David O. Russell (*Silver Linings Playbook*). When Michael Haneke (*Amour*) and Behn Zeitlin (*Beasts of the Southern Wild*) unpredictably snag the other two slots, this throws the Oscar race into a tailspin. Many observers (this one included) expected the directors to nominate Bigelow (whose film *Zero Dark Thirty* nabs five nominations), Ben Affleck (*Argo,* seven), Tom Hooper (*Les Misérables,* eight), or Quentin Tarantino (*Django Unchained,* five), all of whom have films among the top nine Best Picture nominees. The directors branch is known for making idiosyncratic choices, but rarely have the DGA (which the next week nominates Spielberg, Lee, Bigelow, Affleck, and Hooper) and Academy lists been so different.

The stats are unforgiving. It's so rare for a film to win Best Picture without a director nomination or DGA win that Spielberg, who directed *Lincoln,* which led the pack with a total twelve nominations, and Lee, whose *Life of Pi* scored eleven, are instantly placed in the lead to win Best Director and Picture, followed by writer-director Russell, whose *Silver Linings Playbook* scores eight nods. The last movie to make it to Best Picture without a director nomination was *Driving Miss Daisy,* which won the Oscar without a nomination for Bruce Beresford back in 1990; you have to go back to 1929 silent classic *Wings* and 1932 *Grand Hotel* for the only two other examples.

Clearly, the brainy Academy directors' branch chose to support two perceived underdogs. Perhaps a young indie and a senior Austrian made less threatening competitors. The Academy directors, who count quite a few foreign filmmakers among their 371 members, make up just 6 percent of the Academy's entire membership. Their choices hardly represent the entire voting group; they always throw a few surprises into the mix, from Brit Mike Leigh to Spain's Pedro Almodóvar. But post-nominations, the conventional wisdom was to question whether *Argo, Zero Dark Thirty, Django Unchained*, or *Les Misérables* had even a prayer of beating *Lincoln* over the next voting phase . . . and beyond.

Within twelve hours of the Oscar nominations, major players assemble at the first broadcast awards ceremony of the year, the annual Critics' Choice Awards. Voted on by some 250 broadcast and online members of the Broadcast Film Critics Association (including me), many Critics' Choice winners match up with the Oscars. This year the show is being broadcast live on the CW, three days ahead of the Golden Globes, from a chilly hangar at the Santa Monica Airport. The morning's nominations are the hot topic as studio execs, publicists, agents, and talent sip fizzy champagne at crowded round dinner tables and debate the reasons why directors Bigelow, Affleck, Hooper, and Tarantino were robbed by the Academy directors' branch, as well as why little-indies-that-could *Beasts of the Southern Wild* and *Amour* did so surprisingly well.

One problem for *Django Unchained* is that it came out of the gate so late, and the Weinstein Company didn't send screeners to the voters until the week before the nomination ballots were due. (Harvey Weinstein later takes the rap for Tarantino not doing better on nominations morning. The mogul admits to *Deadline*'s Mike Fleming that he felt so strongly that Academy members should see the film on screen that he refused to send them DVDs until the last minute.) As for Bigelow, everyone agrees that she suffered from the controversy about torture. And the consensus on Hooper is that while the past winner is respected for his directing chops, he may have pushed too far with the live-action singing and alienated many of his peers.

But clearly the most shocking omission is Affleck, who was considered a shoo-in. Theories abound as to why he was overlooked. I never buy forty-year-old Affleck's own notion that his director colleagues consider him to be too young and callow. Historically, when actors are nominated for Best Director they become the instant favorite because they are in effect winning a popularity contest. In the past, actor-directors George Clooney, Kevin Costner, Robert Redford, Kenneth Branagh, Mel Gibson, and Warren Beatty were all rewarded with directing nominations—back when there were just five Best Picture contenders. The math of nine slots vs. five directors is unforgiving. Someone is going to be left out. But the truth is if Affleck *had* been nominated, he would have been the clear favorite among the Academy at large.

So it's a huge surprise when *Argo* wins the Critics' Choice Awards for both Best Director and Best Film. Producers Clooney and Grant Heslov stand onstage with the Oscar-snubbed Affleck, who quips, "I want to thank the Academy . . ."

The next day at the classy and intimate American Film Institute's Best of 2012 lunch at the Four Seasons, studio heads and many of the same players continue the conversation. Affleck and Bigelow commiserate in one corner of the crowded white room jammed with round lunch tables, as grinning nominee Zeitlin talks to two other directors left out of the running, Hooper and Chris Nolan. One veteran *Lincoln* Oscar campaigner suggests that Affleck has been too available to the press, even overexposed. True, Affleck was front and center as director and star while promoting his film. And, he tells me, he plans to continue to work for the film.

Thus, while they were once considered solid contenders, Affleck and *Argo* are now shunted to the back of the pack by Hollywood and the Oscar pundits. Crucially, Affleck pays no attention to the stats. He knows the movie plays well for his friends, fans, and followers. He actually earns sympathy for being passed over. And the actor, who is nothing if not charming, earns more good will as a horse coming up on the outside than he would as a front-runner. The outside, in this case, is actually a preferable place to be. The loss drives him to work his wiles on every potential voter he can, armed with sage advice from producer Clooney on how to be appropriately deferential but confident, eager but not hungry, adorable but not cloying. It's the Oscar tap dance.

Finally, *Argo* has more going for it than Affleck. It's the populist crowd pleaser of the bunch, the consensus movie everyone likes, the smart but unpretentious and entertaining thrill-ride that keeps audiences on the edge of their seats and allows Hollywood to cheer for itself.

January 10:
SILVER LININGS PLAYBOOK WALKS INTO HISTORY
WITH FOUR ACTING NODS

On Oscar nominations morning, for the first time in thirty-one years (since Warren Beatty's epic *Reds*), *Silver Linings Playbook* scores in all four acting categories, putting the comedy drama in a league with Oscar winners *Sunset Boulevard* and *Streetcar Named Desire*. First-time nominee Bradley Cooper, second-timers Lawrence and Australian actress Jacki Weaver (*Animal Kingdom*), and Oscar winner Robert De Niro (*Raging Bull*), who has not been included in an Oscar race since 1991's *Cape Fear*, all score nominations. It's a sign of considerable strength, even for a modest indie talkie lacking the visual bells and whistles of larger-scale contenders.

The fact that Russell scores Writer and Director nominations and that the film is a Best Picture candidate is all to the good, but the four acting slots gives the film a strong push because the actors' branch is by far the biggest in the Academy, some twelve hundred strong. The next biggest branches (in the four hundreds) are executives, producers, and publicists.

Though Jessica Chastain won Best Actress at the National Board of Review, four days later Lawrence took the far more prestigious Los Angeles Film Critics Association Award—sharing the prize with *Amour* star Riva.

Oddly, at the Critics' Choice Awards, *Silver Linings* star Lawrence is competing in three categories, not only Best Actress, but also Actress in a Comedy and Actress in an Action Film. She charmingly accepts awards in the latter two categories for *Silver Linings* and *Hunger Games,* respectively. "I love critics," she says, grinning at the room. "I am the happiest I've ever been in my life."

That night, *Silver Linings Playbook* gets another boost for its Oscar campaign by winning Best Acting Ensemble and Best Actor in a Comedy for Cooper, who thanks David O. Russell for "a real script. He got all of us to be real." The film also wins Best Comedy; Russell clarifies: "It's a comedy and a drama," and thanks his son, who inspired him in making the film.

Weinstein hired a consultant specifically to target the film's mental health issues with the press. At the Academy luncheon nine days later, Russell stays on Weinstein campaign message to position entertaining romantic comedy *Silver Linings* as a more serious movie. Comedies don't do well at the Oscars, so the stress is on serious topic mental illness. Russell and his cast are all on point as they make their last-ditch press rounds to Katie Couric (where De Niro cries) and more. "We stigmatize mental illness," Russell tells me earnestly at the lunch. "Having that posture toward it is wrong. Why treat it like that?"

Lawrence works the TV press circuit poolside at the Beverly Hilton after the lunch, along with her costar Jacki Weaver and *Flight* star Denzel Washington. Meanwhile, De Niro submits to the hands-and-feet ceremony in front of Grauman's Chinese Theatre on Hollywood Boulevard and attends an Aero Theatre tribute and Q&A in Santa Monica for West Siders. De Niro looks to have a good shot at a Supporting Actor award in a wide-open field led by *Lincoln* SAG-winner Tommy Lee Jones. But with five strong Oscar winners in Supporting, anything can happen.

The Weinstein Company plays out a risky distribution and marketing plan as the movie's wide release keeps being pushed back. When a movie is platformed in select cities and theaters and slowly broadens, the question is when to go wide. *Silver Linings* builds strong word-of-mouth with audiences, but the company is trying to maximize its expenditures while taking full advantage of all the awards buzz for a movie that lacks strong audience awareness going in, says Weinstein Company COO David Glasser, who supervises distribution and marketing. In the end, TWC waits until the week before the nominations to go wide.

January 13:
BILL CLINTON INTRODUCES *LINCOLN* AT
THE GOLDEN GLOBES

From the start, it's received wisdom in Hollywood that Steven Spielberg's *Lincoln,* the highest-grossing film of the Best Picture nominees ($178 million as of January 25) with the most nominations (twelve) has the right stuff to win Best Picture. But dynamics change.

While the New York Film Critics Circle goes for Daniel Day-Lewis and Tony Kushner, the National Board of Review and the Los Angeles Film Critics ignore *Lincoln* altogether.

On the night of the televised Critics' Choice Awards, which offer Oscar contenders a chance to practice their acceptance speeches, Best Actor winner Daniel Day-Lewis basks in a standing ovation and then lays his plummy British charms on the crowd, calling Spielberg and Kushner "fearless Sherpas." He adds that making *Lincoln* was "one of the greatest unforeseen privileges of my life."

But Adapted Screenplay winner Kushner—considered the Oscar favorite—is discomfited that his eloquent acceptance speech is not televised. And eighty-year-old winning composer John Williams, seated with Team Lincoln, doesn't get to make one at all, to the dismay of the group. Over the Golden Globes weekend, at Saturday's annual BAFTA tea at the Four Seasons, *Lincoln* producer Kathleen Kennedy jokes with *Silver Linings Playbook* producer Bruce Cohen about the times they've gone up against each other, from *The Curious Case of Benjamin Button* vs. *Milk* to *The Sixth Sense* vs. *American Beauty*. The veteran campaigners both know better than to believe that anything is in the bag.

On Sunday, at the Hollywood Foreign Press Association's Golden Globe Awards, DreamWorks reveals their anxiety. They surprise everyone seated at the glittering studio tables at the Beverly Hilton, as well as the global audience, by playing the Bill Clinton card. The ex-president unexpectedly pops in to introduce big-league Democratic donor Spielberg's film about the world's most famous president. But that unexpected power move—bringing in the Washington Beltway heavy-hitter and Hollywood outsider to remind everyone that Spielberg is a friend of Bill's—doesn't have the effect DreamWorks has in mind. It carries a whiff of condescension. It seems to say, "You may not realize the historic significance, the sheer gravitas of what we have accomplished. This U.S. president gets it. What's your problem?"

By overplaying its hand, Team Lincoln shows weakness, not strength. The *Lincoln* Oscar campaign reeks of entitlement from Hollywood's top-ranked, most powerful director. Even the press materials stand out, from an elaborate white box lined with tissue paper and ornate printing containing the screener and press notes, to an overscale white hardcover of the screenplay. Everyone else sends out standardized slim paperback scripts.

Like *Zero Dark Thirty*, *Lincoln* is hit by a poison dart in the form of a well-timed revelation—two weeks before the final ballots are due on February 19—from Connecticut Representative Joe Courtney, who figures out that Kushner's script misrepresents the 1865 House roll call vote. In the movie, Connecticut votes against the Thirteenth Amendment abolishing slavery, but in real life, the state voted for it. The congressman sends out a press release of his letter to Spielberg with the headline "Ahead of Oscars, Courtney asks Spielberg, DreamWorks to correct Lincoln inaccuracy that places Connecticut on wrong side of slavery debate."

Meanwhile Kushner admits that he took some dramatic license with this fifteen-second moment: "The closeness of that vote and the means by which it came about was the story we wanted to tell. In making changes to the voting sequence, we adhered to time-honored and completely legitimate standards for the creation of historical drama, which is what *Lincoln* is."

A growing sense takes hold in Hollywood that what really makes the movie stand out is not so much the writer or director but the perfectionist star who insisted that the set be pure and historic and real—and whose performance makes the movie a must-see.

Everyone sees that nothing is going to stop Daniel Day-Lewis, who also accepts Best Actor at the Globes. He's not about to lose the gold man.

February 6:
ANG LEE WINS THE APPLAUSE METER AT THE ACADEMY NOMINEES LUNCH

On the other hand, *Life of Pi*, which is comparable to a *Lord of the Rings* or *Avatar* as a tour-de-force epic without any acting nominations, is starting to look like a stronger contender after all. Fox has to overcome early preconceptions that the movie is a family flick based on a heart-tugging bestseller, and that it was too expensive to be successful. Eventually, *Life of Pi* turns into a word-of-mouth hit overseas and stateside, and Academy members get a chance to see all the feats of cinematic derring-do from Lee and his visual effects (VFX) team at Rhythm & Hues. I sit with Lee at the Critics' Choice Awards; he asks me if the movie's up for VFX. It is. And that's exactly what it wins.

As the weeks progress, *Life of Pi* keeps winning craft awards—from the Visual Effects Society, from the American Society of Cinematographers. And eventually it becomes clear that Spielberg is no longer a slam dunk to win best director. Lee has a shot.

First, he has pushed a seemingly unfilmable film adaptation into existence, via not only David Magee's script, but the believable actualization of CG tiger Richard Parker on a boat in the ocean. Inside the movie industry, people understand the obstacles Lee has surmounted. He has achieved that impossible merger of art, spirituality, and technology.

The annual Academy lunch, midway between the nominations and the final ballot deadline, brings together at the Beverly Hilton Hotel all the nominees, not only to celebrate their rarefied status and pose for a historic photograph, but to do some last-minute campaigning. During the cocktail hour they work the ballroom with drinks in hand and then settle into their assigned round tables with a mix of nominees, governors, and press scattered around the room. Sony's Michael Barker hangs out with *Les Misérables* director Tom Hooper; Kathryn Bigelow sits next to Robert De Niro; Fox's Jim Gianopulos is paired with Bradley Cooper.

The nominees submit to the usual begging to keep their acceptance speeches short if they take the stage at the Oscar event in ten days. "Get to the stage quickly," exhorts Oscar show producer Craig Zadan. "You have forty-five seconds. Winning groups should select a speaker who will begin immediately and give a heartfelt funny speech. Speak from the heart, not a piece of paper. You are talking to over a billion people in two hundred twenty-five countries." (Not. It's hundreds of thousands.)

At that moment, the room rustles with discomfort. "Piece of cake!" cracks my tablemate Mark Andrews, codirector of *Brave.* "Inspire billions! Be funny! Speak from the heart!"

The Academy lunch applause meter is always revealing. Producer Frank Marshall is the event DJ, spinning discs as his wife, Kathleen Kennedy, new CEO of Lucasfilm and producer of *Lincoln,* is the first one called by AMPAS president Hawk Koch to line up in a semicircular set of four tiers for the annual nominees group photo—Spielberg is the last to squeeze into the end of a row. Among the names generating enthusiastic applause while heading up to accept their nomination certificates from Koch: directors Spielberg, Russell, Bigelow, Burton, and Bendjelloul; writer Kushner; *Argo* and *Zero Dark Thirty* editor William Goldenberg; and *Anna Karenina* production designer Sarah Greenwood. The actors always get the biggest hands, from Affleck (nominated as producer for *Argo*), Denzel Washington, Tommy Lee Jones, and Jacki Weaver to Naomi Watts, Joaquin Phoenix, and sprite Quvenzhané Wallis, who earns a big laugh by sitting on the Oscar statue in the middle of the photo.

At that moment, Spielberg's blockbuster *Lincoln,* with twelve nominations, is regarded as the establishment contender. Rivals portray it as dull and educational. Day-Lewis, who was felled by flu and didn't make the lunch, and Kushner are seen as locks for Best Actor and Adapted Screenplay. But Picture and Director? Lionsgate motion picture executive Rob Friedman—one of the two leading contenders to take over the AMPAS presidency after Koch's one-year tenure—warns a group of us that the Oscars are still "wide open." (Although Koch lobbies the Board of Governors for Friedman to take over after his term, entrenched Academy insider Cheryl Boone-Isaacs wins the vote on July 31, 2013, becoming the first African American to hold the AMPAS presidency, and the third woman—Bette Davis only lasted for two months in 1941, while respected screenwriter Fay Kanin ran the Academy from 1979 to 1983.)

Of all the people going to the front of the room, Ang Lee garners by far the most enthusiastic round of applause. Visually glorious and spiritually uplifting, *Life of Pi* picks up steam as it cleans up the pre-Oscar tech awards and passes the $500 million mark worldwide. It's tough for Fox to campaign without name actors—but well-respected Lee and Visual Effects Society winner Rhythm & Hues are the film's real stars. Lee's riding high, as one actor after another through the lunch goes over to him to pay their respects. Can he beat Spielberg?

January 13:
BRAVE WINS THE GOLDEN GLOBE

In the animated category, Disney boasts a surprising three Oscar nominations, for Tim Burton's artful stop-motion expansion of a 1984 Disney short, *Frankenweenie*; Pixar's gorgeous first princess film, *Brave*; and an homage to video arcade games, *Wreck-It Ralph*. Sony/Aardman's domestic box-office flop *The Pirates! Band of Misfits* ($31 million), which did three times better overseas, is a surprise inclusion, coming at the expense of DreamWorks' would-be franchise *Rise of the Guardians*, which barely recouped its $145 million budget with $370 million worldwide (remember, only half goes back to the studio). Also nominated is Laika animators Sam Fell and Chris Butler's CG-enhanced stop-motion *ParaNorman*, which became the family horror hit that similar *Frankenweenie* wanted to be.

Disappointing box office can negatively impact an awards race. For *Frankenweenie*, his most personal movie since *Edward Scissorhands*, Burton returned to his home turf of the Burbank suburbs and shot his film in black-and-white. Though the modestly budgeted $39 million feature is a welcome reminder of what an artist can do when he's not playing to the marketplace, its lack of success taints the movie with Academy voters. The grosses top out at $35 million domestic and $46 million foreign.

Since its first film in 1995, *Toy Story,* Pixar has been on an Academy roll, winning seven Best Animated Feature Oscars, most recently for *Wall-E, Up,* and *Toy Story 3.* But *Brave* is tarnished by creative conflict. Long a boys' club distinguished by groupthink and replaceable directors, Pixar attracted rare slings and arrows from the press when its studio head (and Disney animation czar) John Lasseter hauled in Mark Andrews to fix what wasn't working in this Scottish mother-daughter story. The film's original writer-director, Brenda Chapman, who would have been the first solo woman director on a Pixar or Disney animated feature, was understandably upset.

Andrews overhauled the story (with help from Steve Purcell, Irene Mecchi, and Michael Arndt) and added more male characters and comedic action among princess Merida's younger siblings. Pixar knows how to reach the widest possible audience for animated storytelling. The movie survived the tinkering; it's one of Pixar's most stunningly beautiful films. But Chapman isn't able to harmoniously take one for the team. She publicly complains. And Lasseter stays angry.

No matter. Disney savvy marketers shrug off the bad vibes on their box-office hit ($539 million worldwide) and have the sense to send Andrews and Chapman, who are friendly, on the promo trail as a happy team.

Highly amusing even for adults, *Wreck-It Ralph,* starring the indispensable John C. Reilly, is one of the strongest Disney titles in many years, one that Lasseter is enthusiastically behind. But Disney sells it as an eighties retro gaming movie with male appeal. And the Academy tends to favor live action. Many members don't get around to discovering the film's strong female character (a princess!) or its emotional depth. Critics apportion their awards among all three films. The top animated feature awards, known as the Annies, go to *Wreck-It Ralph,* while the Visual Effects Society awards *Brave.*

The race is on.

January 27:

ARGO WINS SCREEN ACTORS GUILD FOR OUTSTANDING PERFORMANCE BY A CAST

After its Critics' Choice and Golden Globe wins, *Argo* keeps winning the guilds—by far the most predictive bellwethers of Academy popularity. The film wins the Producers Guild award on January 26 and, on January 27, the Screen Actors Guild's equivalent of Best Picture, the cast award. On February 2 come the announcements of the top awards from the Directors Guild.

Half-hour TV show winner Lena Dunham (*Girls*) accepts her award by saying, "Steven Spielberg, I'm coming for you. Ben Affleck, I already came for you." She forecasts the heat that attends *Argo,* which by evening's end has continued its awards surge by taking home the DGA's top honor for Best Feature. When Chris Terrio wins the Writers Guild of America award for Best Adapted Screenplay on February 17—two days before the Oscar final ballots are due—it's a sign that *Argo* can't lose.

Affleck joins other actor-directors who have won the DGA: Woody Allen, Robert Redford, Warren Beatty, Ron Howard, Kevin Costner, and Clint Eastwood. His win marks only the third time a director has won the DGA without an Oscar nomination. And on both of the other occasions it was a sign of weakness: neither Spielberg's *The Color Purple* (1985) nor Ron Howard's *Apollo 13* (1995) went on to win the Best Picture Oscar. Only seven DGA winners have not gone on to win the directing Oscar—obviously something Affleck can't do since he isn't a nominee.

But Affleck has reasons to be cheerful. *Apollo 13* was the only film to ever sweep the top Guild awards—PGA, SAG, and DGA—and not win the Best Picture Oscar the same year. And only thirteen times in the past sixty-four years has the film directed by the DGA winner not been named Best Picture by the Academy.

First-time nominee Affleck has beaten three-time DGA winner

Spielberg, who earned a standing ovation, and two-time DGA winner Lee, the only two DGA nominees who are also in the running for the Best Director Oscar. (The others are Oscar-snubbed Bigelow and Hooper.)

The DGA is considered a more mainstream group than the nominating Oscar directors or the Academy at large. Thus *Lincoln* is revealed as tellingly vulnerable in the Oscar race for Best Picture.

February 24:

THE OSCAR SHOW—WINNERS AND LOSERS

And so *Argo* rolls into the big night with all the signs of a winner. That, combined with the charming Affleck's undeniable appeal and humble-brag brilliance as a campaigner, fuels the movie's Best Picture triumph. As producer George Clooney reminds me later, the winning *Argo* votes were already in for the Critics' Choice and Golden Globes before the Academy directors' "snub." In other words, the film was a strong competitor from the start.

There are other factors pushing *Argo*'s Best Picture win. After playing to enthusiastic crowds at Telluride and Toronto, *Argo* rocked its L.A. premiere at the Academy. I saw the way the Hollywood crowd responded to this hugely satisfying movie about American heroes. It was a thrilling true story, and when ex-CIA agent Tony Mendez stood to take a bow, the crowd went wild. They could cheer for America for once. And for Hollywood.

That uplift is an unbeatable combination. It also marks Affleck's own redemption, from *Gigli* to Best Picture Oscar winner. "Fifteen years ago I had no idea what I was doing," Affleck says onstage of his first Oscar win, for cowriting *Good Will Hunting.* "I never thought I'd be back here. So many people helped me . . . It doesn't matter how you get knocked down in life. All that matters is that you get up."

So what happens to *Lincoln*? The older Academy usually goes for its level of quality, heart, and period seriousness. Why does this widely admired Spielberg movie run out of gas? Partly it is front-runner syndrome—on top is a precarious place to be. Like another early leader of the pack, Clint Eastwood's 2006 *Letters from Iwo Jima, Lincoln* is seen as a stuffy but honorable history lesson. On top of the self-important marketing campaign, the poisonous anti-*Lincoln* campaign is sticky. Widely repeated everywhere: *Lincoln* is "boring."

Far from the truth, but in the absence of eager campaigners—Spielberg, Tommy Lee Jones, and eventual winner Daniel Day-Lewis have to be pushed into doing the minimum of public appearances—Kennedy, Kushner, and Field can't carry the day. In the end, wins for Day-Lewis—an unprecedented third Oscar for a lead actor—and production designer Rick Carter have to suffice for *Lincoln*.

When Affleck won the predictive Directors Guild award, *Argo* became the front-runner, and Spielberg was competing in the Oscar director race with Ang Lee, who is respected, even beloved, for his enormous range and depth (with one Oscar win to Spielberg's two). Emotionally uplifting, *Pi* scores four Oscars, including Director, Visual Effects (from Rhythm & Hues, on the verge of bankruptcy), Cinematography, and Score. It's the second time Lee has won directing without taking Best Picture (in 2006, Academy steak-eaters voted for *Crash* over *Brokeback Mountain*).

In the competitive year 2012, the awards are spread out among eight of the nine Best Picture contenders (only indie *Beasts of the Southern Wild* goes home empty-handed). In fact, the six top awards go to six different movies for the first time since the *Crash* year of 2006, which was also the last time a Best Picture winner won only three Oscars.

Britain's Working Title has a good night as *Les Misérables* nabs three awards, the same number it won at the Golden Globes, this time for Hathaway, Sound Mixing, and Makeup and Hairstyling; meanwhile, *Anna Karenina* earns a well-deserved Costume Design statuette. And the Oscar show's rousing, neck-chilling *Les Mis* number—featuring the key cast and some sixty total people on the Dolby stage—doesn't hurt to boost DVD sales around the world. (Hugh Jackman agreed to do it first and then wrangled Russell Crowe into participating.)

While some are shocked by the win for Ang Lee, the biggest surprise of the evening is the two wins for the Weinstein Company's *Django Unchained*, which repeats its wins from the Golden Globes. At the start of the night, Christoph Waltz wins Best Supporting Actor—in this case, demonstrating that a BAFTA win can be more predictive than the SAG, which was won by wily *Lincoln* scene-stealer Tommy Lee Jones. (Later, Waltz tells me that while he's lost awards in Austria, he wins when he works with Quentin Tarantino. Let them both continue!)

And Tarantino accepts the win for Best Original Screenplay, beating Michael Haneke, who takes home just one Oscar for *Amour*, for Best Foreign Language Film. Tarantino is well liked by the Academy. He dedicated his win to his fellow writers and to the actors who brought his words to life. "It's the writers' year at the Oscars," he declares.

Zero Dark Thirty has to settle for a tie with *Skyfall* in the Sound Editing race. Ties are a rare occurrence, happening only five other times in Academy history, and that accounts for the show going five minutes over its planned three-and-a-half-hour running time.

Even though Riva, the oldest Best Actress nominee ever, makes the trek to Los Angeles to celebrate her eighty-sixth birthday after her back-to-back BAFTA and César wins for *Amour*, she loses to twenty-two-year-old ingenue Lawrence, who represents the one win for *Silver Linings Playbook*. Lawrence is now a major movie star who has banked both a franchise (*Hunger Games*) and an Oscar win. *Beasts of the Southern Wild*'s youngest-ever Best Actress nominee Wallis also emerges from the Oscar season a star, set to topline musical *Annie*.

Silver Linings Playbook has to settle for its wins the Saturday before the Sunday Oscars at the sunny 28th Independent Spirit Awards, the younger and hipper indie awards show mounted by Film Independent inside a white beach tent in a breezy parking lot in Santa Monica. Going in, it was Fox Searchlight's scrappy *Beasts of the Southern Wild* vs. the Weinstein Company's *Silver Linings Playbook*, which in the end prevails with four awards: Best Feature, Actress (Lawrence), Director, and Screenplay (Russell). *Beasts* has to settle for the same prize it won back at Sundance, Cinematography (Ben Richardson).

And *The Sessions* takes home two Spirit awards, for Supporting Actress Helen Hunt, and for Best Actor John Hawkes—not nominated for an Oscar—in a surprise win over *Silver Linings* star and Oscar nominee Bradley Cooper. At the Spirits, the Oscar nominee often wins; in this case, a dramatic performance beat out the comedic one. Hunt, who was not expected to win at the Oscars, says she is thrilled that writer-director Ben Lewin "made a movie about healthy sexuality . . . A miracle."

Finally, the constant spinning about the movie being about mental illness cannot change the fact that *Silver Linings* is a delightful talking heads romantic comedy. Serious drama also trumps comedy at the Oscars, almost every time. *Silver Linings* lucks out by riding Harvey Weinstein's conservative long-slow distribution plan all the way to bank. What starts as risky and indecisive pockets winds up looking like genius. With *Silver Linings* and *Django Unchained*, the Weinsteins finally climbed out of the red and are collecting cash profits again. But this is not to be a repeat of the Weinsteins' upset Best Picture win against Spielberg's *Saving Private Ryan* with *Shakespeare in Love,* which had more period scale and scope. This is an actors' film, and so Lawrence marks its big win.

The Weinstein Company's critics' favorite *The Master,* on the other hand, which scored three acting nominations for Oscar perennials Joaquin Phoenix, Amy Adams, and Philip Seymour Hoffman, but no writing or directing nods for Paul Thomas Anderson, proves to be too opaque and complex a movie for the Academy at large. All the money that goes into obtaining those nominations, while it boosts the reps of the actors, doesn't necessarily improve the movie's bottom line. Annapurna's Megan Ellison and

Harvey Weinstein clash over releasing the film; he reportedly brings her to tears more than once. Weinstein later blames himself for not finding the right way to bring it to audiences. The picture tops out at $16 million domestic.

THE DAY AFTER THE SPIRIT Awards, Harvey Weinstein's contribution to the Oscar telecast is known: he made the connection between the Oscar producers and First Lady Michelle Obama, who agrees to present the Best Picture award live from the White House. Like Bill Clinton's introduction of *Lincoln* at the Golden Globes, some people look askance at this intrusion of Washington into show business. But Obama is a warm, beaming presence on Oscar night. She pulls it off.

Being set in the past is a boon for *Argo*, which wins its three awards (Picture, Adapted Screenplay, and Editing) without courting commentary from Washington, although the filmmakers do quickly change a title card to placate the Canadians and give them more credit. Ripped from the headlines, contemporary Middle East CIA drama *Zero Dark Thirty*, on the other hand, is hit hard by Washington's politically motivated campaign against it. But crucially, *Zero Dark Thirty* is too smart and unconventional for the Oscar arena. Director Bigelow, writer-producer Boal, and gifted lead Chastain deliver a memorably tough real-world feminist hero. But the steak-eaters in the Academy aren't quite ready to go there.

In the Animated Feature category, the fierce battle between two Disney releases, Pixar's *Brave* (which won the Visual Effects Society, Editing, Sound Mixing, and BAFTA awards) and box-office juggernaut *Wreck-It Ralph* (which won the PGA, Critics' Choice, and five Annie awards) yields a win for *Brave* directors Chapman and Andrews. In the end, the Academy goes for *Brave* as the classier, more beautiful film over the scruffy video-game-themed *Wreck-It Ralph*.

Sony Pictures Classics' Michael Barker and Tom Bernard do

well that weekend. *Amour* wins Best International Film at Saturday's Spirit Awards, where white-haired Michael Haneke thanks them and his actors Emmanuelle Riva and Jean-Louis Trintignant, who had both won at the French Césars the night before, and says, "I'm the oldest man in the whole room!"

Barker and Bernard's *Amour* wins the Best Foreign Language Film Oscar, and their *Searching for Sugar Man* wins for Best Documentary, which gains an advantage from the category having, for the first time, the entire Academy membership voting in it. Whether everyone eligible to vote saw all five of the nominated documentaries as they are honor-bound to do before casting their vote is another question.

(In 2013, for the first time, members will get all five foreign DVDs, too. But the unwieldy and hidebound foreign nominations process remains tangled in arcane committees. Many Academy members clamor to reform it.)

February 24:
THE NIGHT OF THE OSCARS

To host an entertaining musical Oscar night, producers Craig Zadan and Neil Meron pick as their host song and dance man and TV writer Seth MacFarlane (*Family Guy*), who has recently earned his stripes as a movie biz insider by writing, directing, and voicing the stuffed bear in the sleeper comedy summer hit *Ted*. MacFarlane has proved himself as a witty host of the Writers Guild Awards. In the run-up to the Oscars, the Oscar show producers collaborate closely with him and his handpicked writing team every day in an attempt to liven up the show, always fighting against going into overtime.

Predictably, the spanking-new host, who is crudely flat as an entertainer—not nearly as spot-on with his inside industry jokes as the Golden Globes' team of Tina Fey and Amy Poehler—boosts the show with young viewers, although its mainstream popularity is as usual mainly due to the films in contention, six of which have passed the $100 million domestic mark.

I have a blast attending the Oscars as a guest, as opposed to standing for four hours in high heels doing red carpet interviews, or backstage in the pressroom trying to simultaneously track the live show and winners' interviews, as I've done for too many years to count. It has been a few years since I've covered the Oscar show for *Premiere* and *Entertainment Weekly*—back at the Shrine and the Dorothy Chandler Pavilion.

My *Indiewire* colleague and Oscar virgin Peter Knegt, wearing a new tuxedo, and I opt to walk from his Sunset Strip hotel instead of driving. This requires, it turns out, that we be accompanied by a police escort as we walk up Highland from Sunset to the red-carpet entrance on Hollywood Boulevard. Sparkling big-haired Adele, whom the producers have lined up far in advance, figuring her *Sky-fall* theme would be an easy nomination, is in the queue behind us, while wraithlike Anne Hathaway is just ahead filing through security.

The Oscar red carpet at Hollywood and Highland is like a river with strong currents—and pesky security guards—pushing you forward on the outside past the *inside* red carpet, where celebrities such as Best Actress nominee Quvenzhané Wallis, presenter Octavia Spencer, Michael Haneke, and MPAA chief Christopher Dodd are walking the press gauntlet.

On the outside, rubber-necking, nonpress carpet, we run into writer-director Alexander Payne (*The Descendants*), who likes to go every few years just for fun (he may be back in the game with his 2013 *Nebraska,* starring Cannes Best Actor winner Bruce Dern) and Fox Searchlight chief Nancy Utley, who is rooting for *Beasts of the Southern Wild* and *The Sessions*' Indie Spirit winner Helen Hunt.

While many security people warn me not to take pictures, I keep moving and ignore them, even trying to shoot with my iPhone Academy CEO Dawn Hudson, who shies away. I do get affable Universal chairman Ron Meyer and his wife, Kelly, to pose. Moving through the giddy throng is grinning Chastain, all curves in her formfitting nude-gold Armani Privé couture gown. "It's a very 'Happy Birthday, Mr. President' kind of dress," she says on the red carpet, in the company of her grandmother. After the Oscars she plans to attend Fashion Week with her handsome boyfriend, Italian fashion executive Gian Luca Passi de Preposulo, as well as visit fashion capital Milan, before starting the title role in Liv Ullmann's *Miss Julie*. Also passing by are Joseph Gordon-Levitt, Jennifer Aniston, Amanda Seyfried, and Olivia Munn, who takes my stepping on her train with good grace: it held firm, thankfully.

Inside the Dolby Theatre, Peter and I arrive too late for the champagne; the mezzanine is cordoned off due to a women's room flood soaking the carpet. Hungry, *A Royal Affair* star Mads Mikkelsen asks a waiter for a mini-burger. When Eddie Redmayne brushes past me heading for the men's room, I spill some caviar on my iPhone. Nice problem to have.

The Academy Awards brings out the top moguls: I spot not only usual suspects Tom Bernard of Sony Pictures Classics and Working Title's Tim Bevan, who produced *Les Misérables* and *Anna Karenina,* but also Tim Burton, Lionsgate's Friedman, Paramount chairman Brad Grey, Disney CEO Robert Iger, Time Warner CEO Jeff Bewkes, and recent Fox chairman Tom Rothman and his ex-boss, News Corp's Rupert Murdoch, who are both rooting for *Life of Pi.*

The Dolby Theatre boasts a vertiginous balcony, which also houses fellow journalists Manohla Dargis of the *New York Times* and *The Wrap* editor Sharon Waxman. I inch in high heels across a pitch-dark narrow ledge to my seat, afraid of slipping. This means that I'm trapped in the middle of a long row for the entire evening—Peter does skip down to the lobby bar for a bit to check out the losers getting drunk.

Producers Zadan and Meron come onstage before the show to humbly request that the winners keep their speeches "lively but succinct," knowing that they are courting length records with all their musical numbers. Clearly, the producers have an enormous show to mount with many moving parts: the sets moved in and out during the commercial breaks.

The Bond fiftieth anniversary celebration brings the magnificent seventy-six-year-old Dame Shirley Bassey, who earns a standing ovation when she hits that high note at the end of "Goldfinger." It's too bad Adele can't follow with her Oscar-winning "Skyfall," but they go straight to a commercial. The planned reunion of the Bonds doesn't happen because both Roger Moore and Sean Connery weren't up for the trip, Bond George Lazenby told me as we sipped champagne at the BAFTA nominee celebration two days before in the British Consul's garden in Hancock Park.

The 2012 Oscars sees plenty of song-belting, from Bassey to Streisand; some charmingly old-school dance numbers; and moving speeches from award recipients. Sure enough, we enjoy Oscars: The Musical, even though the sound is a little strange—is it because the orchestra is piped in for the first time from the Capitol Records building? The music plays better than host MacFarlane, who earns many audible groans and fails to engage with this audience, at least. The Academy insists on continuing to chase the young male demographic while alienating the core older audience that goes to see the actual nominees in theaters. The Academy will consider Mac-Farlane a success by virtue of a slight uptick in ratings. But while he has presumably improved his audience familiarity TV Q rating, MacFarlane later states that he has no intention of repeating the gig, and his foul press seals his fate.

In terms of ratings, ABC reports a 2 percent gain in show viewership, which makes the 2013 telecast the best since 2010. The show averages a 26.6 rating, or an average of 40.3 million viewers. It also scores on social media, with 13.3 million interactions on February 24. Love or hate host MacFarlane, he does help to pull in that cherished eighteen-to-forty-nine demographic, with an 11 percent ratings boost in that group.

We follow the stream over to the sumptuously decorated Governor's Ball, where the winners have to make an appearance if only to get their Oscars engraved before heading out into the night to Vanity Fair and private parties dotting the hills. As Michael Feinstein croons standards on the bandstand, I sip champagne and line up behind William Shatner, with cane, for lobster and shrimp on ice. Steering away from the river of molten chocolate, strawberries, and desserts, I check out the Weinstein Company tables as Jennifer Lawrence leans over the balustrade to thank Harvey, hanging onto her Oscar. When I ask her why she fell on her way up the stairs to the stage, she gestures at her voluminous gown: "Look at this dress!" Quentin Tarantino forgives me for not picking him to win by planting a big wet one on the lips.

Engraved Oscar in hand, happy producer Clooney, sporting one of many beards on display that night (for a role in his next directing gig, *The Monuments Men,* which is to start shooting in a few days in Europe), with leggy then girlfriend Stacy Keibler, slips out a back door exit toward their waiting limo. He goes to meet up with Affleck and their buds at Craig's, a grill on Robertson Boulevard that they've reserved for the evening. Affleck goes into the men's room and shaves off the beard he wore, superstitiously, throughout the season. He doesn't need it anymore.

At night's end Peter and I wind up at Fox's celebration at Lure, where the *Beasts* contingent is dancing up a storm alongside all the *Life of Pi* winners. I hoist an Oscar and remember how heavy they are. Fox 2000's Elizabeth Gabler is bone-weary after her decade-long fight to get *Life of Pi* made and turn it into a worldwide hit heading for a total $609 million. On our way out, Ang Lee finally arrives. He's smiling.

Thing is, none of the nine movies that wound up vying for Best Picture—among the best selection ever, many observers agreed—would have gotten made if they hadn't been passion projects that their makers were compelled to push through. None were easy, all were tough. And the indies aside, the studio projects were also hugely commercial year-end broad entertainments—six grossed over $100 million, which is not the usual—and *Zero Dark Thirty* topped out at $95 million domestically.

In each case the studios agreed to support—with outside investors taking some of the risk—movies that with an experienced Oscar-winning director behind them could play commercially. Oscars were the icing on an already sweet cake.

AFTERWORD

The best movies get made because filmmakers, financiers, champions, and a great many gifted creative people stubbornly ignore the obstacles. The question going forward is how adaptive all these people are. How long will they struggle before they give up on the film business and take their talents elsewhere? And how flexible is the industry itself?

As AMC's TV drama *Breaking Bad* took over the water-cooler conversation in 2013, and television critics dominated Twitter in a way that no movie debaters did, it served to reinforce the fact that film's glory days are over. In today's omnivorous world, it's no longer about seeing the new movie opening on Friday or waiting eagerly for the next *New Yorker* review. Cinephiles go to film festivals for their fix, or to SnagFilms, Criterion, Indieflix, Fandor, Mubi, or Turner Classic Movies. Why schlep out to the new *Dumb and Dumber* sequel when the glories of Hollywood's Golden Age are easily Netflixed? (As of this writing, Netflix boasts "38 million members in 40 countries enjoying more than one billion hours of TV shows and movies per month, including original series" even partnering with

Marvel on four new live-action MTV series) Even the *New York Times* film critic A. O. Scott admitted that he was according many of his weekly viewing hours to television—just like everyone else.

There was a time during the golden age of the studio system when Hollywood churned out hundreds of quality films for grownups. In many ways 2012 boasted the best crop of films since the banner year of 1939 that yielded *Gone with the Wind, Mr. Smith Goes to Washington, Wuthering Heights, Stagecoach, The Wizard of Oz, Ninotchka,* and *Dark Victory.*

Six of the nine 2012 Best Picture Oscar nominees passed the $100 million mark—the biggest numbers, even with ticket-price adjustments, in recent box-office history. All six were released in the later part of the year. So why don't the studios finance even more quality "prestige" films—by proven directors, at high budget levels—and aggressively back them, aiming for mass audiences all year long?

Admittedly, this is hard to do. It demands confidence and risk-taking. In late 2012, the studios released a group of films that were made by directors who had won Best Picture and/or Best Director (Steven Spielberg's *Lincoln,* Sam Mendes's *Skyfall,* Ang Lee's *Life of Pi,* Robert Zemeckis's *Flight,* Kathryn Bigelow's *Zero Dark Thirty,* Peter Jackson's *The Hobbit,* Tom Hooper's *Les Misérables*), and all but one of those films were released initially in over 2,000 theaters, rather than platformed like the majority of top Oscar contenders in most other years—which is the usual sign of high awards expectations. And they all not only earned consensus rave reviews but made a healthy profit. (Specialty Oscar nominees *Amour* and *Beasts of the Southern Wild* took the usual slow-release route.)

But despite 2012's bountiful harvest of strong, substantive films and action and animated blockbusters that scored record global box office, from *Brave* to *The Hunger Games,* there's precious little optimism about the future of movies. The Best Picture Oscar nominees (whether in 2012 or 2013) are always exceptions that prove the rule, from outsiders jumping over the wall at Sundance (*Beasts of the Southern Wild*) to insiders willfully refusing to play by the rules (*12 Years a Slave*). Sure, the studios will permit a few top-of-the-line filmmakers to chase adults in the fourth quarter, but no wholesale changes are in store.

No wonder Spielberg was pissed off. He saw a crowd pleaser in *Lincoln*. And he was right. It was the top-grossing Oscar contender ($182 million), the eleventh most successful domestic performer of 2012. Why was it so difficult to get traditional studio financing? Like many independents these days, Reliance-backed DreamWorks cobbled together presales on territories overseas (via Twentieth Century Fox, which also took home-video rights) and brought in an outside investor (Participant Media) to fund the movie, which was released by DreamWorks distributor Disney.

The old days of studio largesse are over—even for Spielberg, arguably the most powerful and versatile filmmaker in Hollywood. And if he has to hustle, what about the hordes of less prepossessing talent who find themselves frozen out by the studios? They're heading where the money is: foreign financing, television, cable, HBO, or Netflix.

While the studios could build on these year-end successes and try to make more of them, they won't. While they could try to diversify and make movies for underserved constituencies like Hispanics, African Americans, adults, and women, they won't. They'd rather stick to what they know: cookie-cutter movies for families and young men, and throwing millions of dollars at building a bigger mousetrap. Truth is, the more expensive a movie, the tougher it is for it to have any noticeable personality: all the edges get shaved off. By default the picture has to appeal to the widest number of people—all over the globe. That's how genre formula, nonstop action, and eye-popping pixel effects keep trumping witty dialogue and old-fashioned storytelling.

To the winners go the spoils. But 2013 revealed the hazards of the tentpole, all-or-nothing approach. Just as Spielberg predicted in his June 12, 2013, panel at USC, six costly would-be summer block-busters tanked domestically, although a few were barely bailed out by their international grosses. 2013 proved the cyclical theory held by the late A. D. Murphy, a *Variety* box-office analyst and professor at USC's Peter Stark program. He declared that it's perilous to follow the trends of what works at the box office, because when the studios throw imitations of recent hits at moviegoers, moviegoers inevitably get bored. Tom Rothman, an eighteen-year Fox veteran and Fox chairman and CEO until January 2013, who during his tenure backed such risky films as Peter Weir's *Master and Commander* and Ang Lee's *Life of Pi*, concurs: "Movies struggled this summer because they were, essentially, all the same and the audience was bored. No longer can an audience be pounded into attendance by dint of spending. Now, exactly because of how much great work there is on television, films have to raise the bar, to be more original, more complex, more imaginative, more daring. That is hard because of the huge cost/risk involved, and cost often has an inverse relationship with creativity. But I am fervently optimistic. We can make the films for less, sell them for less, and push creative boundaries more. And when we do, the audience will set the DVR, go out of the house, and come to the theaters. As long as we don't underestimate them, they will reward us."

In Hollywood you have to keep moving and stay ahead of the trends. And being able to adapt to digital is key, as is the recognition that consumers' viewing habits have irrevocably changed.

From the point of view of the seven major studios, the migration of film talent to television isn't an issue, because their corporations are not losing income; they own pieces of that business too. If HBO makes money, that's good for Warner Bros. Viacom and Paramount want MTV, VH1, and CBS to succeed. Comcast owns Universal and NBC; Disney owns ABC and ESPN; Sony produces *Breaking Bad*, *Jeopardy*, and *Wheel of Fortune*; and Lionsgate roots for its own shows on AMC Networks.

Tellingly, three studios (Disney/ABC, Twenty First Century Fox, and NBC Universal) decided to hang on to their online streaming service, Hulu, instead of selling it. Finally, they recognized its value—and didn't want anyone else to get it. Hulu has conducted valuable experiments in what audiences want, even if it's mostly TV shows. But challenging the studios' dominance in entertainment are digital powerhouses Google, Apple, Amazon, and Netflix. They are encroaching more and more on the studios' territory—as Apple did in the music business. Mobiles are the new window into viewing content, and everyone knows it.

Netflix and Amazon are all about giving their customers what they want by constantly tweaking complex algorithms to determine how to anticipate consumer desires. That's how Netflix knew their subscribers would love a remake of *House of Cards*, directed by David Fincher and starring Kevin Spacey, and banked $100 million launching their own content division. They probably won't spend that much again, but they were right. Their high-stakes gamble paid off and made them a potentially strong competitor to HBO, Showtime, FX, and AMC.

While the studios are trying to hang on to their market-share dominance, they are keenly aware that smaller, more nimble companies with less to lose have more freedom to experiment. They saw the music industry's rapid decline, reinvention, and ascension. The indies can take advantage of new funding sources like Kickstarter and IndieGoGo, produce microbudget films that can make back their money by reaching out to burgeoning online fanbases, and figure out the video-on-demand paradigm as the old windows model eventually falls away. The new indie entrepreneurs are getting their scripts rated on Spec Scout or The Black List. They are connecting with potential investors and sales agents through Slated. They're going to Seed & Spark for marketing expertise, hiring the best marketing and distribution experts, and using on-demand theater-booking service Tugg to predetermine audience interest in seeing their film in specific markets before making a booking as they control their medium and message.

Digital is winning, even inside the studios. Kevin Tsujihara grabbed the reins at the Warner Bros. studio, knocking out his rivals from TV and motion pictures. Comcast's Steve Burke let go the movie-bred chairman of Universal, Adam Fogelson—even after what looked like a successful year in 2012—in favor of cable guy Jeff Shell. After a rocky box office in 2013, Sony replaced their marketing chief with their digital marketing pro. And innovative digital-marketing guru Amy Powell—who pioneered Paramount's on-demand booking of movies—continues to rise in the executive ranks at that studio.

The motion picture CEOs aren't stupid. While they may be hanging on tight to the old ways so that they can grab as much short-term cash as possible via top-down models that manipulate consumers by telling them what to buy, they know the ground under their feet is unstable. In order to survive they will have to learn to listen to their customers, find out what they want and how to best serve them. The old strategies in the movie business are disintegrating, as the ownership model gives way to one that is all about access. Adapt or die.

—Anne Thompson, October 2013

ACKNOWLEDGMENTS

Writing a book while churning out a daily blog is not for the faint of heart. There were many moments along the way when I thought I couldn't manage it.

Many people helped to make it happen. Radio journalist Gail Eichenthal saved the day as reporter, editor, legman, and cheering section. Aljean Harmetz, for twelve years the Hollywood correspondent for the *New York Times* and the author of several Hollywood book classics, saw a kindred spirit when I arrived in Hollywood in 1982 and has been a generous and loving friend ever since. Without her astute contributions to the original proposal fifteen years ago, this book would not have been possible. My agent Eric Myers, who I've known since my early days in New York, also offered invaluable support, along with two chums, former *New York* magazine editor Mark Horowitz and film author and scholar Cari Beauchamp. *Thompson On Hollywood* box-office mavens, Anthony D'Alessandro and Tom Brueggemann, supplied valuable research. I can't thank all of them enough. I couldn't have finished this book without them.

ACKNOWLEDGMENTS

My earliest influences were my brainy parents, who met at Cornell University and are sadly no longer with us: writer-photographer Charles Thompson, who sat at our dining room table tapping at his Royal typewriter most nights and used the Thalia and New Yorker theaters as babysitters, and Eleanor Callahan DeKins, the first female reporter at the *Cornell Sun* who went on to teach English in Cambodia, Thailand, the Belgian Congo, and, finally, St. Louis, Missouri. Both set a high standard for erudition, as does my close friend, New York writer Rebecca Morris, whose best advice was "hit those keys!"

Thanks as well go to my teachers and mentors: NYU Cinema Studies professors Bill Simon and Bill Rothman; WNYU FM newshounds Ray Suarez and Richard Roth; the *New York Times* At the Movies columnist Guy Flatley who taught me how to take written notes during interviews; my Holt, Rinehart & Winston boss Phil Monger, who introduced me to market research; and my tough New York publicity bosses, from United Artist's John Dartigue to PMK's Pat Kingsley, the late Michael Maslansky, and Neil Koenigsberg.

Several mentors taught me how to write: *Time*'s Richard Corliss, who took me away from publicity to join *Film Comment* magazine, first as associate, then as West Coast Editor; the late writer and publicist Lee Beaupre; my long-suffering husband and best friend, David Chute, who is cooler than I'll ever be and has talked me off the ledge more than once; and the late *Village Voice* writers Andrew Sarris, Tom Allen, and Stuart Byron, who launched the Risky Business column with me at the *LA Weekly* and always admired the method that William Goldman used to write about Broadway in his book *The Season*. He thought it could be applied to writing a book about the movie business, and when he passed the challenge on to me years ago, I never let go of it.

Thanks also to the editors who believed in me and made me look good: Andy Olstein at *California Magazine*; *The L.A. Weekly*'s Jay Levin, Kit Rachlis, Eric Mankin, John Powers, Ella Taylor, Michael Kurcfeld, and Ron Bernstein; Jim Seymore, Barbara Odair, Mark Harris and Maggie Murphy at *Entertainment Weekly*; James B. Meigs at *Premiere* magazine (now editor-in-chief at *Popular Mechanics*), as well as Kathy Heintzelman (now with Murphy at *Parade*); *Filmmaker Magazine*'s Scott Macaulay; the *London Observer*'s Akin Ojumu; the *New York Times*'s Lorne Manley; the *Washington Post*'s John Pancake; the *Daily Beast*'s Michael Solomon; the *Hollywood Reporter*'s Gregg Kilday and Gina McIntyre (now at the *Los Angeles Times*); *Variety*'s Cynthia Littleton, Brian Cochrane, and Peter Bart, who defines the Hollywood insider journalist; and the Film Society of Lincoln Center's Eugene Hernandez, who brought me to *Indiewire*, my current home.

Heartfelt thanks to all my collaborators at *TOH*, who kept the blog rolling through thick and thin. I got stalwart support from staff writers Sophia Savage and Beth Hanna, as well as from contributors Bill Desowitz, Ryan Lattanzio, John Anderson, Maggie Lange, Jacob Combs, Meredith Brody, Matt Brennan, Matt Mueller, Terry Curtis Fox, and Amy Dawes. My partners at *Indiewire* also kept me going, from SnagFilms CEO Rick Allen and *Indiewire* editor-in-chief Dana Harris to staffers Eric Kohn, Peter Knegt, Nigel Smith, and Joel Withrow.

HarperCollins supported me all the way, from assistant editor Bethany Larson and book and cover designers Shannon Plunkett and Amanda Kain, to book production experts Cathy Felgar, Rachel Meyers, and Karen Lumley and copyeditor Danny Mulligan, to ace marketers and publicists Kevin Callahan, Michael Barrs, Shannon Donnelly, and Cayla Cocanour, publisher Lynn Grady, and most of important of all, my patient and brilliant editor Esther Margolis, who willed this book into being. No one has ever handled me or shaped my copy better.

I am deeply grateful to you—as well as to all my dear friends and family (forgive me, Nora) who put up with and sustain me every day.

BOX-OFFICE CHARTS

The following charts are updated versions of box-office analyst Tom Brueg-gemann's year-end wraps for *Thompson On Hollywood*. They break down movies into categories reflecting box-office results, adding estimated production budgets to provide a look at the films' costs vs. returns.

Also in the equation are marketing costs. In the United States an average movie campaign costs about $25 million, while a studio-backed wide release covered by TV and other media over several weeks can reach $50 million or more in "prints" (now digital) and ads.

Most media report opening-weekend ticket sales, or lists of seasonal hits and top-ten grossers. Few reveal how movies perform over the global long haul.

Many people don't know that U.S. distributors collect an average of 50 percent of revenue that comes into theaters. The biggest hits often take in more, while smaller releases collect much less.

If the cash returned to studios is less than what it costs to make, market, and release the movie, it's a flop—unless they recoup via DVDs, cable, TV, VOD, or other ancillary revenues. (Many indie films are acquired by studios for U.S. distribution but are released by various other distributors in foreign territories.)

NA means that numbers are not available. Total grosses on titles are through the end of their 2013 runs.

For 2012, Box Office Mojo, which supplies numbers based on data that distributors give to the media, counts 663 movies released for a total of $10,957,460,255, which, rounded up, provided me with the title of this book. Other sources for box-office revenues include Exhibitor Relations Co., Rentrak, and the Numbers.

BLOCKBUSTERS (Over $500 million worldwide, major profit)	U.S. Distributor	Total Gross ($ millions)	Production Budget (estimated)
The Avengers	Buena Vista	1.519	220
The Dark Knight Rises	Warner Bros.	1.084	250
The Hunger Games	Lionsgate	691	78
Skyfall	Sony	1.109	200
The Hobbit: An Unexpected Journey	Warner Bros.	1.017	150
The Twilight Saga: Breaking Dawn—Part 2	Lionsgate	830	120
Ted	Universal	549	50
Madagascar 3: Europe's Most Wanted	Paramount	747	145
Ice Age: Continental Drift	20th Century Fox	877	95
Life of Pi	20th Century Fox	606	106

SMASHES (Over $125 million worldwide, significant profit)	U.S. Distributor	Total Gross ($ millions)	Production Budget (estimated)
The Amazing Spider-Man	Sony	752	230
The Lorax	Universal	349	70
Lincoln	Buena Vista	275	65
Django Unchained	Weinstein	425	100
Les Misérables	Universal	442	61
Hotel Transylvania	Sony	357	85
Taken 2	20th Century Fox	376	45
Argo	Warner Bros.	232	45
The Silver Linings Playbook	Weinstein	236	21
The Vow	Sony	196	30
Magic Mike	Warner Bros.	167	7
Flight	Paramount	152	31
American Reunion	Universal	235	50
Paranormal Activity 4	Paramount	143	5
The Best Exotic Marigold Hotel	Fox Searchlight	137	10
The Impossible	Lionsgate	180	45
Intouchables	Weinstein	427	12

HITS (Over $90 million worldwide, some profit)	U.S. Distributor	Total Gross ($ millions)	Production Budget (estimated)
Brave	Buena Vista	539	185
Wreck-It Ralph	Buena Vista	471	165
Men in Black 3	Sony	624	225
Snow White and the Huntsman	Universal	397	170
21 Jump Street	Sony	201	42
Journey 2: The Mysterious Island	Warner Bros.	335	102
The Expendables 2	Lionsgate	310	100
Jack Reacher	Paramount	218	60
Looper	Sony	176	30
Chronicle	20th Century Fox	127	12
Hope Springs	Sony	114	30
The Woman in Black	CBS	127	15
The Devil Inside	Paramount	101	1
Resident Evil: Retribution	Sony	240	65
Step Up Revolution	Lionsgate	135	33

LOW-BUDGET HITS (Under $125 million worldwide, some to major profit)	U.S. Distributor	Total Gross ($ millions)	Production Budget (estimated)
Think Like a Man	Sony	96	12
Act of Valor	Relativity	83	12
Contraband	Universal	96	25
Madea's Witness Protection	Lionsgate	66	20
Pitch Perfect	Universal	113	16
The Lucky One	Warner Bros.	99	25
Project X	Warner Bros.	103	12
The Grey	Open Road	79	25
The Possession	Lionsgate	85	14
Sinister	Lionsgate	78	3
Moonrise Kingdom	Focus	68	16

Chart continued on following page

LOW-BUDGET HITS (Under $125 million worldwide, some to major profit)	U.S. Distributor	Total Gross ($ millions)	Production Budget (estimated)
End of Watch	Open Road	48	7
2016: Obama's America	Rocky Mountain	33	3
To Rome With Love	Sony Classics	73	25
Beasts of the Southern Wild	Fox Searchlight	13	2

UNDER-PERFORMERS (Grossed well, but less than expected for cost)	U.S. Distributor	Total Gross ($ millions)	Production Budget (estimated)
Safe House	Universal	208	85
Prometheus	20th Century Fox	402	130
The Bourne Legacy	Universal	275	125
The Campaign	Warner Bros.	105	50
Underworld Awakening	Sony	160	70
The Dictator	Paramount	179	65
This Means War	20th Century Fox	157	65
Ghost Rider: Spirit of Vengeance	Sony	133	57

3-D REISSUES	U.S. Distributor	Total Gross ($ millions)	Production Budget (estimated)
Titanic 3-D	Paramount	345	(reissue)
Beauty and the Beast 3-D	Buena Vista	110	(reissue)
The Phantom Menace 3-D	20th Century Fox	102	(reissue)
Finding Nemo 3-D	Buena Vista	72	(reissue)
Monsters Inc 3-D	Buena Vista	37	(reissue)

RECOUPERS (Varying budgets, should break even or close)	U.S. Distributor	Total Gross ($ millions)	Production Budget (estimated)
Zero Dark Thirty	Sony	108	53
Wrath of the Titans	Warner Bros.	305	150
Parental Guidance	20th Century Fox	120	25
Mirror Mirror	Relativity	166	85
ParaNorman	Focus	107	60
The Odd Life of Timothy Green	Buena Vista	52	25
Diary of a Wimpy Kid: Dog Days	20th Century Fox	77	22
The Cabin in the Woods	Lionsgate	66	30
The Lawless	Weinstein	53	12
Good Deeds	Lionsgate	35	14
House at the End of the Street	Relativity	39	10
The Pirates! Band of Misfits	Sony	123	55
Chimpanzee	Buena Vista	35	12
Katy Perry: Part of Me	Paramount	33	12
Secret World of Arrietty	Buena Vista	143	23
Perks of Being a Wallflower	Lionsgate	33	13
The Chernobyl Diaries	Warner Bros.	37	1
Silent Hill: Revelation	Open Road	52	20
Killing Them Softly	Weinstein	38	15
Seven Psychopaths	CBS	19	15
Hit and Run	Open Road	15	2
Anna Karenina	Focus	69	45
Cirque du Soleil: Worlds Away	Paramount	34	25
Silent House	Open Road	14	2
The Words	CBS	13	6
Salmon Fishing in the Yukon	CBS	35	15

FLOPS (Lost money)	U.S. Distributor	Total Gross ($ millions)	Production Budget (estimated)
Rise of the Guardians	Paramount	307	145
Dark Shadows	Warner Bros.	246	150
John Carter	Buena Vista	284	250
This Is Forty	Universal	88	35
Battleship	Universal	303	209
Total Recall	Sony	199	125
Red Tails	20th Century Fox	50	58
Savages	Universal	83	45
Here Comes the Boom	Sony	73	73
Red Dawn	FilmDistrict	45	65
The Three Stooges	20th Century Fox	55	30
What to Expect When You're Expecting	Lionsgate	84	40
Rock of Ages	Warner Bros.	59	75
Abraham Lincoln: Vampire Hunter	20th Century Fox	116	69
That's My Boy	Sony	58	70
Guilt Trip	Paramount	42	40
Trouble with the Curve	Warner Bros.	49	60
The Watch	20th Century Fox	68	68
Frankenweenie	Buena Vista	81	39
Joyful Noise	Warner Bros.	31	28
The Five-Year Engagement	Universal	54	30
Cloud Atlas	Warner Bros.	130	100
One for the Money	Lionsgate	36	40
Alex Cross	Lionsgate	30	35
Sparkle	Sony	24	14
Premium Rush	Sony	33	35
Big Miracle	Universal	25	40
Haywire	Relativity	33	23
Man on a Ledge	Lionsgate	45	42
A Thousand Words	Paramount	22	40
Safe	Lionsgate	40	30
Wanderlust	Universal	22	35

FLOPS (Lost money)	U.S. Distributor	Total Gross ($ millions)	Production Budget (estimated)
The Raven	Relativity	30	26
The Man With the Iron Fists	Universal	20	15
The Master	Weinstein	28	30
Lockout	FilmDistrict	32	20
Dredd	Lionsgate	35	50
Playing for Keeps	FilmDistrict	13	35
People Like Us	Buena Vista	12	16
Gone	Lionsgate	18	NA
Fun Size	Paramount	11	14
Promised Land	Focus	9	15
Chasing Mavericks	20th Century Fox	6	20
The Apparition	Warner Bros.	10	17
Won't Back Down	20th Century Fox	5	25
The Cold Light of Day	LG	17	20

GLOSSARY

actioner
A B-movie in the action genre, violent, with a fast-moving plot targeted toward the global male demographic. Examples, the *Lethal Weapon*, *G.I. Joe*, and *Die Hard* series.

ancillary markets
Any market other than the primary domestic theatrical market for feature films, including foreign markets. Home video (DVD and Blu-ray), cable, pay-per-view, hotels, airplanes, and television are ancillary windows. VOD and streaming services are starting to compensate for declining DVD revenues in the home-entertainment realm.

animatics
Rough animation assemblages developed during preproduction and production, often in the form of storyboard pictures synchronized with a soundtrack or, for animated films, voice-overs.

arthouse
Theaters that play high-brow independent, foreign, and specialty films catering largely to an older audience, although some theaters attract a younger clientele. (My variation on this well-known industry term is "smarthouse.")

biopic

Biographical picture about a real person, either slice-of-life or cradle-to-grave. A subset is the biodoc, or biographical documentary.

blockbuster

A movie that is a huge box-office success. The term applies to films with a domestic box-office gross that far exceeds their production budget and marketing costs—over $100 million in North America. *The Avengers, The Hobbit,* and *The Hunger Games* were among 2012's blockbusters, all passing $400 million domestic.

CGI

More and more animation companies have abandoned 2-D hand-drawn animation in favor of 3-D computer-graphic imagery, which has become more complex over time. CGI can be used in the live-action realm for environments, costumes, fixes, visual effects, and fully animated characters, from Gollum to King Kong.

dating

Distributors often set a release date for a film years in advance in order to plant their flag on a key date like the Fourth of July weekend. They try to pick a date that will maximize the film's box-office potential.

day-and-date release

When a film opens in theaters and becomes available on video on demand on the same day.

Digital Cinema Package (DCP)

A Digital Cinema Package is a set of files used to store a film's images and sound; it's essentially the high-definition digital replacement for a 35-millimeter film print, usually opened with a computer key provided by the distributor.

fanboys

Usually male and often the target demographic of genre films—sci-fi, comic-book adaptations, and actioners—these enthusiastic audiences will often follow a film or film series to the point of obsession. San Diego's annual

Comic-Con is the Valhalla where fanboys worship as studios promote their summer tentpoles.

four-wall
When a distributor or filmmaker rents a movie theater for a period of time at a fixed rate and collects all the box-office revenue, as Roadside Attractions did with day-and-date sleeper hits *Arbitrage* and *Margin Call.*

franchise
A series of related films, often in the form of sequels and prequels, and frequently based on a preestablished and known piece of intellectual property. James Bond, Bourne, *Star Wars, Star Trek,* and *Mission: Impossible* are all active franchises.

granola film
A well-intentioned, earnest film that is educational and/or "good" for you.

gross
The total amount of tickets sold during a movie's run at the box office. Approximately half of that is returned by theaters to the distributor. That final sum is known, confusingly, as the film's "rental."

hit
A hit is a film that takes off with audiences (often backed by critics), exceeds expectations by connecting with viewers, and has a profitable box-office payoff. There are blockbusters, like *The Avengers* and *The Hunger Games,* but also surprise word-of-mouth hits, like *Beasts of the Southern Wild* and *Lincoln.*

intellectual property (IP)
The new Holy Grail in Hollywood is owning a well-known preestablished brand that will yield multiple iterations—that is, a franchise like *Star Wars* or *Star Trek* or characters from Tom Clancy's Jack Ryan to Ian Fleming's James Bond.

juttering
A jittery characteristic of the 24-frames-per-second motion picture camera that James Cameron and Peter Jackson are trying to avoid with faster 48 frames per second.

keyframe animation

A single still in an animated sequence—often picked up and built upon by computers.

majors

The deep-pocketed motion picture and television studios that have reigned over Hollywood since the twentieth century, with a significant breadth of films annually and big stakes at the box office. As originally defined, a major studio was housed on a lot with soundstages and post-production facilities and owned theaters: Metro-Goldwyn-Mayer (MGM), Twentieth Century Fox, Warner Bros., and Paramount Pictures.

Before the studios were divested of their theaters in 1948, the distributors that did not own theaters were known as the minors: Universal Pictures, Columbia Pictures, and Walt Disney Studio.

In today's entertainment industry, the six majors are defined as MPAA signatories: News Corp–owned Fox, Sony (which acquired Columbia, as well as the old MGM lot in Culver City), Warner Bros. (which owns HBO), Viacom-owned Paramount (which owns CBS and Nickelodeon), Comcast-owned NBCUniversal (which owns USA and the Sci-Fi Channel), and Disney (which owns ABC and ESPN). Non-MPAA member Lionsgate, once considered a mini-major along with New Line Cinema (which was acquired by Warner Bros.), is now considered a seventh major studio, while the mini-majors are such companies as MGM, which is now largely a library and film and TV production company that partners with major film distributors, and independent The Weinstein Company. One-time mini-major DreamWorks now releases its films through distributor Disney's Touchstone label. And sadly, the late great United Artists, while technically a label at MGM, is now defunct.

microindie

An independent film produced on a microbudget of less than six figures.

motion capture

A visual-effects technique, also called performance capture, in which an actor like Andy Serkis, who played Gollum in Peter Jackson's *The Lord of the Rings* and the title role in his *King Kong*, is covered with dots and shot with digital cameras that can track his motions, which animators then plug into a complex computer algorithm for that character.

Motion Picture Association of America (MPAA)

A Washington, D.C.–based lobbying group for the six major studios, which comprise a diverse set of global needs.

mumblecore

Coined by Andrew Bujalski's sound editor Eric Masunaga in 2005, the term has now been applied both to a generation of young independent filmmakers and the microbudget relationship films they shoot with a low-key naturalistic aesthetic. Key filmmakers of the movement include Bujalski (seminal mumblecore film *Funny Ha Ha*), Joe Swanberg (*Drinking Buddies*), Lynn Shelton (*Your Sister's Sister*) and the Duplass brothers (*The Puffy Chair*).

negative pickup

An independently financed movie acquired for release in certain territories by a distributor.

prints and advertising (P & A)

The budget accorded to pay for marketing, delivering 35-millimeter prints or DCPS to theaters, and releasing a movie.

platform release

A platform or limited release is the way distributors roll out films on a piecemeal basis, tuned in to audience demand, and gauge the appeal of specialty films. Major studios typically stage a limited release in New York and LA in the fall and winter to qualify for Academy consideration, with a wide release to follow in January. Video on demand (VOD) is now a significant piece of the limited-release equation, as distributors such as IFC Films or Sundance Selects coordinate their theatrical play with a film's wider availability via digital downloads and cable VOD rentals.

rotoscoping

An animation technique by which animators trace over live-action movements frame by frame. Though its origins date back to early Disney and Warner Bros. cartoons, in 2001 director Richard Linklater created the first full-length rotoscoped feature, *Waking Life*.

run and gun
A fast-paced verité-style of guerilla filmmaking on location with a small crew and hand-held cameras.

screener
An advanced copy of a film sent to critics, awards voters, and industry professionals as a DVD, Blu-ray, or digital file, often without color correction or post-processing. Particularly during awards season, DVD screeners have been a source of Internet piracy, leading to much debate in the MPAA as to whether they should be eliminated entirely. More and more publicists are providing Vimeo links to films so they can be viewed on a computer.

sleeper
An unexpected hit that connects with audiences without the aid of huge marquee stars or a massive marketing campaign. Examples: *The Best Exotic Marigold Hotel, 21 Jump Street, Magic Mike, Chronicle, The Grey.*

split rights
A split-rights deal is a film finance and distribution method whereby a producer presells some rights (international or VOD rights, for example) to a distributor but retains others (such as domestic theatrical or television).

Steadicam
A portable camera rig worn by a cameraman so that he can follow the action on foot. John Carpenter's *Halloween* (1978) was one of the first films to use a Steadicam to move fluidly with the action.

studio
A major entertainment company and MPAA signatory that produces, finances, and releases films and television domestically and overseas.

tentpole
A costly wide-release movie expected to hold up and balance out the financial performance of a studio. When they hit, a tentpole pays for a studio's overhead. The flop of *John Carter* ignited a major shift in how the industry views such films.

turnaround

A studio often decides not to pursue a given project and allows the rights to become available to another buyer; they are often sold to a rival studio for cost plus interest, but studios will occasionally help out a favored producer, filmmaker, or star who wants to take over a project.

video on demand (VOD)

Video on demand allows users to view content when and how they want, whether streaming on a set-top box such as Roku or TiVo, on computers or television via Netflix or Hulu, on smartphones or tablets via iTunes or Amazon, or through cable providers.

VFX

Visual effects describe myriad and increasingly complex digital enhancements to live-action images that are manipulated to add computer-generated environments and characters. With its ambitious visual environment, the Oscar winner *Life of Pi* is a gold standard in VFX imagery, and revealing the economic weakness of the field, the film's VFX house, Rhythm & Hues, declared bankruptcy after winning the Oscar.

wet print

A 35-millimeter film that is fresh from the lab, still dripping wet from bathing in chemicals. Industryites still apply the term to a brand-new DCP "print."

wicket

Theater box office where tickets are sold.

INDEX

INDEX

ABOUT THE AUTHOR

Anne Thompson, who launched *Indiewire*'s daily film blog *Thompson On Hollywood* for *Variety* in 2007, has covered the Hollywood beat for more than twenty-five years, writing for monthly, weekly, bi-weekly, and daily publications. For seven years she wrote the Risky Business column for the *LA Weekly* (and the *Los Angeles Times* Syndicate), followed by *Filmmaker* magazine and *The Hollywood Reporter*, where she also founded their first blog, *Riskybiz*, in 2005. Before that, she was West Coast Editor for *Premiere, Empire*, and *Film Comment*, and Senior Writer at *Entertainment Weekly*. She has also reported on film for the magazines *Vanity Fair, More, Wired, Sight and Sound, Filmmaker*, and *New York*, as well as for the newspapers the *New York Times*, the *Chicago Tribune*, the *London Observer*, and the *Washington Post*. Thompson currently hosts Sneak Previews at UCLA Extension, moderates and participates on industry panels, and does media interviews, especially at Oscar time, for such networks as MSNBC, ABC, CBS, and CNN. Born and raised in Manhattan, she now lives in Los Angeles. *The $11 Billion Year* is her first book.

blogs.indiewire.com/thompsononhollywood/